FREEDOM OF INFORMATION
AND THE
RIGHT TO KNOW

FREEDOM OF INFORMATION
AND THE
RIGHT TO KNOW

The Origins and Applications
of the Freedom of Information Act

Herbert N. Foerstel

Greenwood Press
Westport, Connecticut • London

Library of Congress Cataloging-in-Publication Data

Foerstel, Herbert N.
    Freedom of information and the right to know : the origins and
applications of the Freedom of Information Act / Herbert N. Foerstel.
        p.   cm.
    Includes bibliographical references and index.
    ISBN 0–313–28546–2 (alk. paper)
    1. Government information—United States.   2. Public records—Law
and legislation—United States.   3. Freedom of information—United
States.   4. United States.   Freedom of Information Act.   I. Title.
    KF5753.F64   1999
    342.73'0662—dc21   99–17951

British Library Cataloguing in Publication Data is available.

Library of Congress Catalog Card Number: 99–17951
ISBN: 0–313–28546–2

First published in 1999

Greenwood Press, 88 Post Road West, Westport, CT 06881
An imprint of Greenwood Publishing Group, Inc.
www.greenwood.com

Printed in the United States of America

The paper used in this book complies with the
Permanent Paper Standard issued by the National
Information Standards Organization (Z39.48–1984).

10 9 8 7 6 5 4 3 2 1

Copyright Acknowledgments

The author and the publisher gratefully acknowledge permission for use of the following
material:

Excerpts from interviews conducted by Herbert N. Foerstel with Tom Blanton, Ross
Cirrincione, Ramsey Clark, Carl Coleman, Rebecca Daugherty, James X. Dempsey, Will Fer-
roggiaro, Morton Halperin, Anthony Lake, Duncan Levin, James MacKenzie, Kate Martin,
Elliot Mincberg, Patsy Mink, Ralph Nader, Ellen Ray, Russell Roberts, William Schaap, Arthur
Spitzer, Thomas M. Susman, John P. Swann, Charles Talbott, Mike Tankersley, Charlene
Thomas, David Vladeck, and Les Weinstein. Used by permission.

Contents

Contents

CHAPTER 1

The Right to Know

COLONIAL AND CONSTITUTIONAL HISTORY

The American origins of a citizen's "right to know" derive from seventeenth- and eighteenth-century England, where a dauntless press struggled to circumvent the official prohibition on reporting the actions of the House of Commons and the House of Lords. Members of the British press who violated this ban were fined and many were imprisoned, to be released only after they swore to cease and desist from such radical activities.

In the American colonies, the campaigns for the people's right to know about the workings of their government paralleled those waged in England and were a natural corollary of the demand for free expression. The British associated an informed citizenry with an elite class; however, the American colonists developed a more expansive notion of a simple freeholder or taxpayer citizenship and a more broadly based political participation. Nonetheless, colonial governments showed the same hostility toward the notion of the common citizen's right to know as did the English Parliament.

In 1671, in correspondence to his lords and commissioneers, Governor Berkeley of Virginia expressed the common attitude of colonial officials: "I thank God, we have no free schools nor printing; and I hope we shall not have these hundred years; for learning has brought disobedience and heresy and sects into the world; and printing has divulged them, and libels against the government. God keep us from both."[1]

The American colonists chafed under such strictures. In 1689 John Coode led a protest against Lord Baltimore's Maryland government because of a law punishing "all speeches, practices, and attempts relating to his lordship and government, that shall be thought mutinous and seditious." Among the punishments for violation of that law were whipping, branding, boring through the tongue, fines, imprisonment, banishment or death.[2]

In 1695 Thomas Maule, a Quaker merchant, criticized Massachusetts civil and ecclesiastical authorities in his book *Truth Held Forth and Maintained*. He was arrested, whipped, and imprisoned under a high bail. He was not tried until the following year, when he won acquittal by appealing to a jury that his actions were a matter of conscience.

In 1722 the governor of Pennsylvania ordered author Andrew Bradford "that he must not for the future presume to publish anything relating to or concerning the affairs of this Government, or the government of any of the other of His Majesty's Colonies, without the permission of the Governor or Secretary of this province." During that same year, James Franklin, publisher of the *New England Courant*, was jailed for making fun of the colonial government's attempts to catch pirates. The Boston General Court subsequently ordered that Franklin "be strictly forbidden to print or publish the *New England Courant* or any pamphlet or paper of the like Nature. Except that it be first supervised, by the Secretary of this Province."[3]

In 1723 two citizens of Pennsylvania were arrested for making derogatory comments about the royal house of the English Hanoverian king. One of the men was fined and sentenced to two hours in the pillory. The other spent two days and two hours in the pillory, was dragged through the streets by a cart, and was given forty-one lashes of the whip before being imprisoned.

In 1725 William Bradford founded New York's first newspaper, the *Gazette*, and within months he was jailed for wicked and seditious libel.

In 1727 Virginia's governor Alexander Spotswood threatened execution or loss of an arm or leg for disseminators of seditious principles or other insinuations tending to disturb the peace.

In 1753 Daniel Fowle was arrested by order of the Massachusetts General Assembly on suspicion of having printed a pamphlet, *Monster of Monsters*, which reflected upon some of the assembly's members. He was interrogated and jailed but subsequently released. Also in 1753, the New York Assembly punished Hugh Gaine for publishing the proceedings of the assembly in his *New York Mercury*. Gaine was censored, fined, and jailed.[4]

In 1758 Samuel Townsend was found guilty of a high misdemeanor by the New York Assembly for sending to the assembly a letter requesting relief for refugees on Long Island. He was imprisoned, and only after an abject apology was he released with a reprimand.

This official desire to maintain an ignorant public and a shackled press was bound to fail. Between 1763 and 1775, British attempts to reform imperial tax law and administration mobilized colonial sentiments around the idea of an informed citizenry. In 1765 the young John Adams published an unsigned essay in the *Boston Gazette* describing a knowledgeable citizenry as the most effective opposition to British rule. Adams declared that "whenever a general Knowledge and sensibility have prevailed among the People, Arbitrary Government and every kind of oppression have lessened and disappeared in Proportion."[5]

Adams emphasized that it was essential that the people acquire knowledge in order to participate in politics. "The people have a right, an indisputable, inalienable, indefeasible divine right to that most dreaded and envied kind of knowledge, I mean of the characters and conduct of their rulers," stated Adams. "The preservation of the means of knowledge among the lowest ranks, is of more importance than all the property of all the rich men in the country."

Adams regarded the press as the natural instrument for informing the citizenry about their government. "None of the means of information is more sacred, or have been cherished with more tenderness and care than the Press," he declared, and he urged his countrymen not to be "intimidated from . . . publishing with the utmost freedom, whatever can be warranted by the laws of your country; nor suffer yourself to be wheedled out of your liberty, by any pretences of politeness, delicacy or decency."[6]

Adams's writings were accompanied by increased popular participation in colonial politics. In November 1764, Virginia's House of Burgesses voted to erect a public gallery in their legislative chamber to permit newspaper reporters and the public to follow their debates. In May 1766, the Boston town meeting instructed its representatives to make the debates in the house of representatives public, and in June the legislature added a public gallery.

In 1774 the Continental Congress passed the Quebec Declaration, stating that freedom of the press was essential for "its diffusion of liberal sentiments on the administration of government, its ready communication of thoughts between subjects, and its consequential promotion of union among them, whereby oppressive officials are shamed or intimated into more honorable and just modes of conducting affairs."[7] For the first time in America, a group of public officials declared that freedom of the press was a natural right and a fundamental trust of civil liberty.

In January 1776, Thomas Paine's unsigned pamphlet *Common Sense* exploded on the colonial scene. It was reprinted up and down the coast, and by the end of the year it had gone through nineteen American editions. The truly revolutionary *Common Sense* rejected the entire British political system and its vaunted constitution. Soon, revolutionary advocacy throughout the colonies prescribed an independent state in which the channels of information would be liberated by the right to free speech, a free press, freedom of assembly and petition, and freedom of religion.

In his book, *The Strength of a People*, Richard D. Brown explains, "The opposition to imperial policy and the independence movement it spawned changed the situation decisively in the 1760s and 1770s, propelling the idea of an informed citizenry onto the center stage of public discourse. Now, suddenly, it mattered greatly whether colonists knew their political rights and understood the ways in which Parliament and the king were infringing upon them. When the Continental Congress declared independence in 1776, and thus transformed the thirteen colonies into functioning, de jure republics, the idea of an informed citizenry took on new meanings and added significance."[8]

The framers of America's Declaration of Independence and drafters of the Constitution considered certain individual rights to be natural and inalienable, not dependent on the largess of the state. For this reason, many of our nation's founders were opposed to the attachment of a bill of rights to the Constitution. Alexander Hamilton argued that a bill of rights would be "not only unnecessary . . . but would even be dangerous." Hamilton said that the Constitution itself was a bill of rights that granted limited power to the government and left all other power to the people.[9]

Libertarians like James Madison and Thomas Jefferson spoke in favor of a bill of rights; Jefferson argued that its passage would place a legal check in the hands of an independent judiciary, in which he had great confidence. In 1789 the Bill of Rights was passed, but clearly both sides in the debate assumed that the ten amendments that formed it were a clarification of important aspects of the people's inherent rights, not a limiting grant of power by the state.

According to journalist Alan Barth, "The men who established the American Republic sought censorship of government by the press rather than censorship of the press by the government. This concept of the press was expressed by Americans even before they became a nation."[10]

SEDITIOUS SPEECH

James Madison recognized that if the press were to assume responsibility for informing the people about their government, it would first have to overcome the stifling effects of federal power. Prominent among the government's weapons was the common law crime of "seditious libel," which punished the press or individual citizens for criticizing the government. Madison regarded laws against seditious speech as a threat, not just to a free press, but to American democracy. In 1798 he spoke forcefully against the Alien and Sedition Acts:

Had "Sedition Acts," forbidding every publication that might bring the constituted agents into contempt or disrepute, or that might excite the hatred of the people against the authors of unjust or pernicious measures, been uniformly enforced against the press, might not the United States have been languishing at this day under the infirmities of a sickly Confederation? Might they not, possibly, be miserable colonies, groaning under a foreign yoke.[11]

The seditious speech laws under which the American colonies and early Republic labored originated in thirteenth-century England. The earliest English law on seditious speech, enacted in 1275 during the reign of Edward I, was *de Scandalis Magnatum*. Rather than redressing private wrongs, it was designed to censor speech and press in order to preserve the public realm. The statute directed that "henceforth none be so hardy to cite or publish any false news or tales whereby discord or occasion of discord or slander may grow between the king and his people or the great men of the realm."[12] By the 1530s, seditious speech laws had been extended to cover criticism of royal advisers and the ruling, class generally.

A 1555 law made the penalty for "speaking seditious and slanderous words of the king and queen" the loss of both ears or a fine of £100, plus three months in prison. Writing such words, considered worse than speaking them, cost the offender one hand.[13] The royal fear of the written word was seen in 1558 when Elizabeth I pushed a separate law making it treason to assert—in writing or printing or by overt act—that she was not the rightful queen. A number of Englishmen were executed under this act. The rise of the printing press encouraged the dissemination of political criticism, but as of 1580, writing seditious words was still punished as a felony, though speaking them was only a misdemeanor.

The worst was yet to come. When the most important statutes against seditious speech expired upon Elizabeth's death and were not reenacted by Parliament, James I turned to the King's Council, which administered the *Scandalis Magnatum* from its "starred chambre" at Westminster. In 1606 the infamous Star Chamber initiated a libel case, *de Libellis Famosis*, which defined and extended the crime of seditious libel.

In that case, Lewis Pickering was called before the Star Chamber and charged with writing a rhyme that defamed Elizabeth I and Archbishop Whitgift. Chief Justice Coke went on to distinguish simple slander from defamation of great men and officials. "[I]f it [libel] be against a magistrate or other public person, it is a greater offense," said Coke, "for it concerns not only the breach of the peace, but also the scandal of government; for what greater scandal of government can there be than to have corrupt or wicked magistrates to be appointed and constituted by the King to govern his subjects under him?"[14]

Coke's opinion also established the unfortunate precedent that the truth of a criticism of government was no defense: the negative effect of the words on government was the court's only concern.

With its *de Libellis Famosis* ruling, the Star Chamber created the basic structure of the law of seditious libel on the eve of American colonization, and the colonists brought this understanding with them to the New World. In the American colonies, laws against seditious libel covered any speech that criticized the government, its officials, or its general authority. For example, a typical 1637 law in Massachusetts specified fines, imprisonment, disenfranchisement, or banishment for anyone who "openly or willingly defame[d] any court of justice, or the sentences or proceedings of the same, or any of the magistrates or other judges of any such court."[15]

In 1647 the Rhode Island Assembly declared it a crime "for any man to use words of contempt against a chief officer, especially in the execution of his office." In 1677 the Virginia Council reaffirmed that anyone who "shall maliciously express, publish or declare any words to incite and stir up the people to hatred and dislike of his Majesty or the established government" would suffer the punishment of common or statute law, as well as being "disabled to enjoy any place, office or promotion either civil or military." Three years later, the law's penalties were increased for anyone who would "asperse the government and defame the Governor and chief magistrates, which cannot but tend to the future disturbance of the peace and welfare if not timely prevented."[16]

Despite the presence of such statutes throughout the colonies, by the end of the seventeenth century, colonial authorities were increasingly tolerant of criticism that did not immediately threaten the government. At the same time, a growing number of defendants in seditious libel trials turned to juries to decide their cases, and though it was contrary to law, some magistrates allowed the resulting acquittals to stand.

The defendants in such trials were all individuals. The more subversive right of the press to criticize government had never been tested. Indeed, the first newspaper in the colonies, the *New York Weekly Gazette*, which was not established until 1725, served as a mouthpiece for the administration in power. Only when a competing newspaper, the *New York Weekly Journal*, was founded nine years later did problems arise for the government. The result was the most prominent free speech trial in American colonial history—the case of John Peter Zenger, the publisher of the *Weekly Journal*.

Zenger was prosecuted in 1735 for printing criticism of the British colonial governor, William Cosbie, who charged that the *Weekly Journal*, with the support of his political opponents, was seeking to lead the public into tumult, sedition, and disturbance of the peace. Cosbie complained of false and scandalous libels printed in Zenger's *Journal*.[17]

The *Journal* had printed a manifesto on freedom of the press which claimed that a critical press was necessary to protect the citizenry from the arbitrary power of corrupt officials who were beyond the reach of the law. In colonial New York, the law of seditious libel said that any published statement, whether true or false, that contained written criticism of public men for their conduct or of the laws or institutions of the country, was liable to prosecution. Indeed, the law of seditious libel was governed by the maxim, "The greater the truth, the greater the libel."[18]

Common law courts had jurisdiction over such prosecutions, and the judges reserved to themselves the power to decide whether words were libelous. The only function of juries, according to the law, was to establish whether the words actually referred to the people or institutions as charged.

Zenger had been publishing the *Journal* for only two months when Cosbie took action to silence it. On November 2, 1734, the New York Council declared that four issues of the *Journal* were seditious, that they should be burned, and that Zenger, the printer, should be imprisoned. Zenger's lawyers, James Alexander and William Smith, requested moderate bail, but Chief Justice DeLancey set bail at £400, an unprecedented amount. Unable to raise bail, Zenger remained in jail until the end of his trial eight months later.

In an attempt to improve the defense team, Andrew Hamilton of Philadelphia, reputedly the best lawyer in America, was hired. It has been said that Hamilton conducted his defense according to "the law of the future," since the law of 1735 was clearly against him. Disregarding contemporary English practice, he argued that the court's law was out of date, that truth was a defense against the charge of libel, and that the jury had a right to render a verdict where law and fact were intertwined.

The basis for Hamilton's defense of Zenger was his claim that citizens had a right to criticize their rulers. He declared that when political power threatens individual rights, citizens need not obey their magistrates. In arguing that public criticism is the best safeguard against the misuse of political power, Hamilton asserted that all free men had a right to speak publicly against official abuses of power.

The attorney general argued that since Zenger had admitted printing and publishing the offending articles, "the Jury must find a Verdict for the King; for supposing they were true, the Law says that they are not the less libelous for that; nay indeed the Law says, their being true is an Aggravation of the Crime."[19]

When the chief justice declared that the truth of a libel could not be entered into evidence, Hamilton not only ignored his ruling on the matter, but questioned his authority to judge guilt or innocence in the case, something well established under current law. Instead, Hamilton boldly asked the jury to find Zenger innocent.

The jury did just as Hamilton had asked. At the end of a single day of arguments, it took the jury only a few minutes to return a verdict of not guilty. When the acquittal was announced by the jury foreman, the small courtroom erupted in cheers. Though the Zenger verdict was not regarded as formal legal precedent, it rendered prosecutions for seditious libel uncertain at best. Throughout the colonies, the people regarded the verdict as a great victory for freedom of the press and the right of the people to confront arbitrary political power, preparing the way for the revolutionary concepts of popular sovereignty and the people's right to know, which were eventually embodied in the American Constitution.

The ideal represented by Zenger's stirring victory was not easily transformed into legal and practical reality. The passage of the Alien and Sedition Acts in 1798 was followed by official actions against the press that provoked only a limited examination of First Amendment protections. The first indictment of an editor by the fledgling American government came on June 26, 1798, when Benjamin Franklin Bache, a grandson of Benjamin Franklin and the editor of the Philadelphia *Aurora*, was arrested under a common law indictment for seditious libel against the president. Bache had printed the complete text of a treaty that the Senate was still considering in secret.

Bache died before he could be tried, but within a month, thirteen new indictments were brought against Republican newspapers critical of the Federalist government. Each journalist convicted under the Sedition Law was fined and imprisoned for political expression critical of the administration in power. Much of the action against newspapers was in anticipation of the 1800 presidential campaign between Jefferson and Adams.

In *People v. Croswell* (1803), the Republican administration prosecuted a Federalist newspaper editor for seditious libel against the new president, Thomas Jefferson. In *United States v. Hudson and Goodwin* (1812), another libel action against the president, the U.S. Supreme Court ruled that there was no federal common law of crimes, including the crime of seditious libel, but the absence of a decision on the constitutionality of the Sedition Acts left matters ambiguous. Indeed, no other federal legislation raised major First Amendment questions for well over a century, during which the views of the framers were not fully explicated in Congress, the courts, or legal treatises.

The next significant application of the law of seditious libel would not come until 1908, when President Theodore Roosevelt threatened to prosecute the *Indianapolis News* and *New York World* for their attacks on the administration's handling of the Panama Canal Zone purchase. Roosevelt chose to open his case in a special message to Congress in which he threatened the *World*'s Joseph Pulitzer by name. Federal indictments against both papers were returned in the District of Columbia. The newspapers challenged the authority of the government to bring them before a federal court, and the U.S. Supreme Court eventually ruled that the president could initiate suits only in state courts.

The xenophobia surrounding World War I, which revived the legacy of seditious libel, produced a trio of disturbing Supreme Court cases. *Frohwerk v. United States* (1919) involved a small German-language newspaper in Missouri that printed a series of articles criticizing the war effort and opposing the use of American troops in Europe. For writing these articles, Frohwerk was convicted under the Espionage Act, fined, and sentenced to ten years in prison. The Supreme Court upheld the conviction, with Justice Oliver Wendell Holmes writing for a unanimous Court.

Just a few months later, in *Abrams v. United States* (1919), the Court upheld the use of the Espionage Act to impose a twenty-year jail sentence for the printing and distribution of a leaflet urging a strike. The third case in the trio, *Schenck v. United States* (1919), involved the prosecution of Charles Schenck for producing leaflets characterizing World War I as a capitalist conspiracy engineered by Wall Street. Justice Holmes, again speaking for the Court, admitted that in ordinary times Schenck's pamphlets would be protected by the First Amendment, but in time of war Schenck's words could create "a clear and present danger" that Congress had a right to prevent.

After World War I, bolshevism came to be regarded as a major threat to entrenched political and financial interests in the United States, and the courts were inclined to uphold the suppression of any leftist political expression. In *Gitlow v. New York* (1925), the Supreme Court upheld the prosecution of an individual for disseminating a left-wing leaflet. Despite its acceptance of such federal suppression of freedom of the press, the Court in *Gitlow* recognized that the First Amendment was applicable to the states through the "liberty" provision of the Fourteenth Amendment's due process clause. This judgment resulted in an extensive judicial examination of state restrictions on free expression and a rejection of common law principles to construe the First Amendment. The Court would henceforth look to currently applicable goals and principles underlying the Constitution, rather than the intentions of the founders, to interpret the First Amendment. It was in this context that support for the right to know grew in strength.

The landmark case of *Near v. Minnesota* (1931) established the right of newspapers to criticize public officials aggressively without fear of government retribution. In the process, *Near* used the liberty clause of the Fourteenth Amendment to protect the press from impingement by state law. Chief Justice Charles Evans Hughes stated that the American conception of a free press "had broadened with the exigencies of the colonial

period and with the efforts to secure freedom from oppressive administration." Hughes quoted approvingly Madison's judgment that "the press
has exerted a freedom in canvassing the merits and measures of public
men of every description which has not been confined to the strict limits
of the common law. On this footing the freedom of the press has stood;
on this footing it yet stands. . . . And can the wisdom of this policy be
doubted by any who reflect that to the press alone, chequered as it is
with abuses, the world is indebted for all the triumphs which have been
gained by reason and humanity over error and oppression."[20]

In ruling that the First Amendment applied to the states through the
guarantee of due process, Chief Justice Hughes recognized a broad view
of press freedom that was subsequently amplified in *Grosjean v. American Press Co.* (1936). Here Justice George Sutherland declared, "It is
impossible to concede that by the words 'freedom of the press' the framers of the amendment intended to adopt merely the narrow view then
reflected by the law of England that such freedom consisted only in immunity from previous censorship." The Court asserted that the predominant purpose of the free speech and press clauses was "to preserve an
untrammeled press as a vital source of public information," and it concluded that "since informed public opinion is the most potent of all
restraints upon misgovernment, the suppression or abridgement of the
publicity afforded by a free press cannot be regarded otherwise than with
grave concern."[21]

THE CASE FOR A CONSTITUTIONAL RIGHT TO KNOW

Even before the *Grosjean* decision, Justice Louis Brandeis had emphasized the need for an informed citizenry in *Whitney v. California* (1927):
"Those who won our independence believed that the final end of the
State was to make men free to develop their faculties. . . . They believed
that freedom to think as you will and to speak as you think are means
indispensable to the discovery and spread of political truth; that without
free speech and assembly discussion would be futile; that with them,
discussion affords ordinarily adequate protection against the dissemination of noxious doctrine; that the greatest menace to freedom is an inert
people; that public discussion is a political duty; and that this should be
a fundamental principle of the American government."[22]

With *Grosjean*, the press seemed at last to have been freed from the
oppressive federal power to punish critical or embarrassing coverage of
the government and its workings. But had the press or public gained the
right of *access* to information about the government? *Grosjean* had much
to say on this matter as well. In describing the scope of First Amendment
protections, the Court referred to the century-long struggle of the English
people "to establish and preserve the right . . . to full information in re-

spect of the doings or misdoings of their government," and concluded that it was this experience that brought about the adoption of the First Amendment to the U.S. Constitution.[23]

The existence of such a constitutional right to know about the doings of government has long been in dispute. There is no phrase in the Constitution that explicitly grants the public a "right to know." The language of the First Amendment comes closest through its statement: "Congress shall make no law . . . abridging the freedom of speech, or of the press, or of the right of the people peaceably to assemble, and to petition the government for a redress of grievances."

Shortly after the passage of the First Amendment, James Madison summarized its most fundamental purpose: "[T]he right of freely examining public characters and measures, and of free communication thereon, is the only effective guardian of every other right."[24] Madison later wrote, "A popular Government, without popular information or the means of acquiring it, is but a Prologue to a Farce or a Tragedy; or, perhaps, both. Knowledge will forever govern ignorance: And a people who mean to be their own Governors, must arm themselves with the power which knowledge gives."[25]

Perhaps the most powerful twentieth-century argument for a constitutional right to know has come from First Amendment scholar Alexander Meiklejohn, who believed that right to be the principal, perhaps the sole, basis for all First Amendment protections. Meiklejohn took the position that the sovereign right of the citizen to receive and obtain information was the exclusive justification for according freedom of speech and other First Amendment rights to the citizenry. "The First Amendment does not protect a 'freedom to speak,' " wrote Meiklejohn. "It protects the freedom of those activities of thought and communication by which we 'govern.' "[26]

During the 1950s, Wallace Parks, a legal scholar and staff attorney for the House Government Affairs Committee, interpreted Meiklejohn's ideas as follows: "It is clear that the primary purpose of the freedom-of-speech and press clause of the First Amendment was to protect the government from interfering with the communication of facts and views about governmental affairs, in order that all could properly exercise the rights and responsibilities of citizenship in a free society. This clause was intended as one of the guarantees of the people's right to know. It is certainly reasonable to conclude that freedom of the press and speech under contemporary conditions includes the right to gather information from government agencies and stands as a constitutional prohibition against all forms of withholding information beyond that reasonably required for the exercise of delegated power or the protection of other rights."[27]

A similar theory was articulated by constitutional scholar Thomas I. Emerson: "It is clear that the right to know fits readily into the first amendment and the whole system of freedom of expression. Reduced to its simplest terms the concept includes two closely related features: First, the right to read, to listen, to see, and to otherwise receive communications; and second, the right to obtain information as a basis for transmitting ideas or facts to others. Together these constitute the reverse side of the coin from the right to communicate. But the coin is one piece, namely the system of freedom of information."

Emerson concluded that the right to know was an emerging constitutional right. "The old doctrines remain important," he asserted, "when one is considering the right of the government to impose direct sanctions upon the right to read, listen, or observe. But the role of the right to know in formulating government controls to allocate scarce facilities, to provide mandatory access to the means of communication, or to compel disclosure, calls for the development of new doctrine."[28]

The press has been foremost in propagating that new doctrine. According to prominent newspaper attorney Harold L. Cross, "The language of the [First] Amendment is broad enough to embrace, if indeed it does not require, the inclusion of a right of access to information of government without which the freedom to print could be fettered into futility. The history of the struggle for freedom of speech and of the press bars any notion that the men of 1791 intended to provide for freedom to disseminate such information but to deny freedom to acquire it."[29]

Cross may be correct in declaring that the First Amendment embraces the inclusion of a right to know. The wording of the First Amendment was general, and at the time of its creation there existed competing philosophies that placed different interpretations upon the broad concept of freedom of speech, press, assembly, and petition. There was, however, a consensus among the founders on the purpose of the First Amendment. It was assumed that free expression was necessary for citizens to reach the best social decisions and to promote the democratic process.

Despite ample evidence that the founders regarded the right to know as essential to the budding American democracy, the legal authority to enforce that right remains problematical. The right to know is often cited by the courts, including the Supreme Court, but such commentary is usually found in dicta rather than in judgments forming legal precedent. Because of the unsettled nature of the right to know, we may conclude that it has influenced judges' decisions, though it is not as yet a legal principle upon which cases may be decided. In this limited sense, the courts have long acknowledged a citizen's right to know.

In *Martin v. City of Struthers* (1943), the Supreme Court gave the first explicit recognition of the right to *receive* information. In describing the constitutional right to free speech and press, Justice Hugo Black wrote, "This freedom embraces the right to distribute literature, and necessarily protects the right to receive it." In Black's view, the right to receive information was "vital to the preservation of a free society."[30]

In *Lamont v. Postmaster General* (1965), the Court again affirmed a citizen's right to receive information in a case concerning postal restrictions on the delivery of Communist propaganda. The Court held that the postal statute violated the addressee's right of free speech. Justice William Brennan's concurring opinion stated, "I think the right to receive publications is . . . a fundamental right. The dissemination of ideas can accomplish nothing if otherwise willing addressees are not free to receive and consider them. It would be a barren marketplace of ideas that had only sellers and no buyers."[31]

Also in 1965, the Court declared, in *Griswold v. Connecticut*, "The right of freedom of speech and press includes not only the right to utter or to print, but . . . the right to receive, the right to read . . . and freedom of inquiry [and] freedom of thought."[32] Just a few years later, in *Stanley v. Georgia* (1969), the Court declared, "It is now well established that the Constitution protects the right to receive information and ideas."[33]

In *Red Lion Broadcasting Co. v. FCC* (1974), the Court upheld the constitutionality of the personal attack rules and Fairness Doctrine that applied to broadcasters. Here, the Court asserted that the public has the right to "receive suitable access to social, political, esthetic, moral and other ideas and experiences." Indeed, the Court declared that it was the "right of the viewers and the listeners, not the right of the broadcasters, which is paramount." Thus, a statute requiring broadcasters to air both sides of controversial issues was upheld because the public has a right to hear such views, and broadcasters have an obligation to fulfill that right.[34]

This seemingly strong affirmation of the right to know was weakened by the Court in *Miami Herald v. Tornillo* (1974) when a Florida right-of-reply statute was declared unconstitutional. The statute required newspapers to allow candidates for public office to publish replies when their official record or personal character was attacked. A similar judgment was rendered in *CBS v. Democratic National Committee* (1973), in which the Court upheld the right of broadcasters to refuse to sell time for advertising dealing with political campaigns or controversial issues. In *CBS v. Federal Communications Commission* (1981), however, the Court ruled that broadcasters must sell time to "legally qualified candidates for federally elective office" once a campaign has begun. The Court stated that giving federal candidates a right of access to broadcast stations "makes a significant contribution to freedom of expression by enhancing the ability of candidates to present, and the public to receive, information necessary for the effective operation of the democratic process."[35]

The Court's opinion in *Virginia State Board of Pharmacy v. Virginia*

Citizens Consumer Council (1976) has become a cornerstone for the arguments supporting the right to receive information. In ruling that a statute prohibiting pharmacists from advertising prescription drugs was unconstitutional, the Court declared: "Freedom of speech presupposes a willing speaker. But where a speaker exists as in the case here, the protection afforded is to the communication, to its source and to its recipients both."[36]

In *Board of Education, Island Trees Union Free School District No. 26 v. Pico* (1982), a plurality of the Supreme Court attempted to establish that the Constitution protects the right to receive information, but opinions within both the majority and dissenting justices specifically denied such a right. The plurality nonetheless proclaimed that "a right to receive ideas follows ineluctably from the *sender's* First Amendment right to send them" and "the right to receive ideas is a necessary predicate to the *recipient's* meaningful exercise of his own rights of speech, press, and political freedom."[37]

There are numerous other cases in which the Supreme Court has addressed the right to know in one form or another. Together, these cases suggest three levels of the right of access to government information. The lowest level would simply prevent the government from interfering with the communication of facts and views about government affairs to the citizenry. The next level would obligate the government to comply with citizen demands for information. The highest level would impose an affirmative obligation on the government to inform the public. No unequivocal affirmation of the highest level of the right to know has yet emerged from the Court, and despite the various statutory attempts to shed light on the workings of government, there has been little support in the Court for a constitutionally enforceable right of access to government information. Only the prohibition of government interference with public communication seems to have been affirmed. The issue is no clearer today than it was fifty years ago, when a small band of press activists led a public crusade for open government and stirred Congress to seek a legislative basis for the public's right to know.

THE PRESS AS AGENT FOR THE PEOPLE'S RIGHT TO KNOW

In the years immediately following World War II, the American people anticipated the lifting of wartime secrecy and censorship, but the hopes of both the public and the press were quickly dashed. The Cold War led President Harry S. Truman to introduce a national security apparatus under the influence of what President Dwight D. Eisenhower would later call "the military-industrial complex," and anti-Communist hysteria produced an unprecedented umbrella of peacetime state secrecy which remains in place to this day.

By 1950 this atmosphere of national security paranoia and government information control had mobilized the press for the first organized campaign in support of the public's right to know. Kent Cooper, who spent forty-five years with the Associated Press and retired as its executive director in 1950, claimed to have first coined the phrase "right to know." In his book of the same name he wrote, "American newspapers do have the constitutional right to print. That is the so-called freedom of the press. But they cannot properly serve the people if governments suppress the news. To have that which the people are entitled to is a concept which long ago I first defined as 'the Right to Know.' " To support his claim to first use of the term, Cooper quoted a 1945 *New York Times* editorial that acknowledged his use of "a good new phrase for an old freedom."[38]

Cooper's definition of the right to know was tied to freedom of the press, but it was broad in concept and global in scope. It went beyond informing the American public and included support for democracy around the world. "My plea," said Cooper, "was for American newspaperdom to create and give momentum to a world movement that would make available to the people of all countries the blessed Right to Know."[39]

In the fall of 1945, Cooper had written to President Truman, suggesting that he require inclusion of this new form of press freedom in all postwar peace treaties. After Truman failed to heed his advice, Cooper urged the United Nations to expand the title of its declaration on press freedom from "freedom of information" to "the Right to Know," but the original wording was retained.

On the home front, Cooper said it was imperative to the maintenance of American democracy that the press be free and that full and complete information be available to Americans. "There must be no censorship except to the extent required by war necessity," he declared. "All channels of news must be kept open with equality of access to information at the source."[40]

Cooper decried the practice of using military censorship in wartime to suppress news of a nonmilitary character, but he was even more disturbed by the fact that political censorship during war was carried over by habit or design to suppress information in peacetime. Calling government secrecy and censorship a manifestation of the state's control of the conduct of its citizens, he complained that more and more officials at all levels of American government were operating on the assumption that public business was their own private domain, upon which newsmen were not expected to tread. Cooper believed that such secrecy was self-defeating because:

1. Confidence and loyalty thrive where people have the right to know.

2. Patriotism springs from the people's own convictions, based not upon government propaganda but on full information on all sides of every question.

3. Government power, backed by an informed citizenry, is unassailable, because through full availability to the news, an equal partnership between the government and the individual is established, based upon respect for the latter's right to know.

Many of Cooper's colleagues joined the fight against government secrecy. Throughout the 1950s, the American Society of Newspaper Editors (ASNE) and its Freedom of Information (FOI) Committee, under the direction of a series of dedicated committee chairmen, led the charge for the public's right to know. During his chairmanship in the late 1940s, Basil L. Walters of the Knight newspapers sounded the warning of official news suppression, saying that his work as chairman of the Freedom of Information Committee "frightened me very, very much because, for the first time, I really realized the perils that we face in this country."[41]

When James S. Pope, then managing editor of the *Louisville Courier-Journal*, succeeded Walters as chairman of ASNE's FOI Committee in 1950, he made that group into an effective national voice for the public's right to know. Pope declared, "Awakening to their responsibility, the first chairman of the Society's domestic Freedom of Information Committee . . . sounded repeated warnings that newspapers were permitting the people's right to information to go by default. The committee which succeeded his in 1950 took these warnings seriously. We had to. Editors were beginning to fight back against suppression of information, and the Committee began to receive requests for advice and assistance."

Pope admitted that he could not yet tell journalists how to gain access to public information. "Our Committee did not know," he said. "Each of us had some notion of how he would handle some issue for himself, but . . . we had only the foggiest idea of whence sprang the blossoming Washington legend that agency and department heads enjoyed a sort of personal ownership of news about their units. We knew it was all wrong, but we didn't know how to start the battle for reformation."[42]

Pope regarded the concept of freedom of information as "just an idealistic first cousin" of freedom of the press. "It is chiefly an inference," he declared. "[A]n inference that if the Founding Fathers wanted government to keep its hands off the press, they expected that government to be conducted openly. Otherwise, a free press would be unable to serve its intended purpose."[43] This view of the primacy of press freedom led Pope and others who followed him to assume a privileged role for the press as standard-bearer for the public's right to know.

Pope charged that many men in office propagated a creed that held that it was dangerous for news of government to leak out in any natural, unprocessed form. "Our committee has found instance after instance in which the people's right to know has been circumscribed or wiped out by 'regulation,' " he stated. "Almost all the administrative news of our Government is so controlled. Departmental records have been put into a privileged, quasi-confidential status under which there is no press or public inspection as a matter of right."[44]

Newspapermen were, of course, used to the nominal, sometimes ceremonial, struggle with government officials to gain access to information under their control, but Pope warned that the conflict had gone far beyond the simple ceremonial. "Only recently have most editors begun to realize that these familiar little guerilla skirmishes now are part of a broad-scale offensive against freedom of information—against the basic principle of a citizen's right to know, so that he may govern himself," asserted Pope. "[S]harp and critical disagreement has been found to exist between the country's newspaper editors and the officeholders who contrive much of its news. How much should the people know?"[45]

In an attempt to address this question in a systematic and scholarly way, ASNE retained Harold Cross, one of the top newspaper lawyers in the country and counsel for the *New York Herald Tribune*, to prepare a report on federal, state, and municipal information policies and practices. Cross's comprehensive report, published in 1953 under the title *The People's Right to Know*, confirmed the fears of newspapermen around the country that basic government information was being systematically denied to them and thus to the American people.

Though Cross characterized his report as a study of the state of the law governing the right of the people, not just the press, to freedom of information, he made it clear that the press must play the leading role in securing that freedom. He noted that some courts had held that the news function gives newspapers a "special interest" where that is required by statute for access to government records and a "proper purpose" for such access where that is necessary.

Cross claimed that in the absence of statute or common law to the contrary, the editor or publisher of a newspaper, or an authorized representative, has an enforceable legal right to inspect government records for a lawful or proper purpose. He noted that most of the reasons advanced for denial of the right of access in the cases of other applicants were absent in the case of newspapers. "The newspaper does not act out of mere or idle curiosity," stated Cross. "In a manner of speaking, when made by a newspaper, application of the right to inspect tends to circumvent, or at least dilute, the fear that if one citizen or other person be granted such right the rest of the community will march in upon the records, not as single spies but in battalions."[46]

Cross charged that the government's practice of withholding records had been aimed openly at newspapers, and he concluded, "Whatever may be said as to the merit of the trends or the newsworthiness of the prohibited matter, the challenge to the press at the threshhold of its functions is open, clear, intentional, unabashed."

In response to this challenge, Cross defined the battle line. "The public business is the public's business," he declared. "The people have the right to know. Freedom of information about public records and proceedings is their just heritage. Citizens must have the legal right to investigate and examine the conduct of their affairs. They must have a simple, speedy means of enforcement. These rights must be raised to the highest sanction. The time is ripe. The First Amendment points the way. The function of the press is to carry the torch."[47]

The press did indeed carry that torch in ways that were to light the path toward freedom of information for the public at large. James Russell Wiggins, the new crusading chairman of the ASNE Committee on Freedom of Information, recruited important political allies along that path. Wiggins used the documentation provided by Harold Cross to build a convincing case and forge a productive working relationship with members of Congress, particularly Representative John E. Moss (D-Calif.). This pragmatic political strategy would eventually move Congress toward legislative attempts to open the closed doors of government.

Wiggins did not believe that our system of government made an informed public inevitable or automatic, but he did believe that our democracy made it possible for private agencies, such as the press, to achieve that objective. Indeed, Wiggins defined the citizen's right to know in terms that were indistinguishable from freedom of the press: (1) the right to get information from the government, (2) the right to print it without prior restraint, (3) the right to print without fear of reprisal, so long as publication does not offend the laws, (4) the right to have access to printing materials, and (5) the right to distribute.[48]

In further clarifying the right to know, Wiggins asserted, "The right of one to speak is another's right to hear; the right of one to write is another's right to read. The right is not solely concerned with either one or the other aspects of this process, but with both of them. Together the two processes are indispensable to the people's right to know."[49]

GOVERNMENT MANAGEMENT OF THE NEWS

Despite the efforts of newsmen like James Pope, Harold Cross, and James Wiggins, the realities of government secrecy continued to frustrate the press and an increasingly concerned Congress. The Truman and Eisenhower administrations had maintained much of the wartime secrecy apparatus, and, to the dismay of the press, had introduced a new array of restrictive information policies. In November 1954, even as the nation's voters chose a Democratic Congress, Republican President Eisenhower chose to create the controversial Office of Strategic Information (OSI). The OSI was officially established by Secretary of Commerce Sinclair Weeks at the direction of the president and on the recommendation of the National Security Council. Weeks claimed the need for a central location within the government to work with the business community "in voluntary efforts to prevent unclassified strategic data from being made available to those foreign nations which might use such data in a manner harmful to the defense interests of the United States."[50]

The director of the new agency, R. Karl Honaman, described the OSI as a small fact-finding and policy-recommending group that would "cooperate" with the publishing world and industrial community. He stated that the OSI was concerned "only with the kinds of information and 'know how' a potential enemy could use to injure us, yet which cannot be properly handled by classification." Following Honaman's lead, the Defense Department cautioned defense industries to "exercise considerable caution" in releasing information that might assist America's enemies in determining our "strategic intentions."[51]

The OSI had thus introduced a new category of information over which the government had control. Now, in addition to Top Secret, Secret, and Confidential, the government would attempt to withhold unclassified "strategic information" from the public. The fact that strategic information had no definition led the press to conclude that there were no limits on the power of the OSI to control it. Newsmen were not reassured by the OSI's use of the term "voluntary" to describe its new censorship program. After all, the official censorship systems imposed during both world wars were nominally voluntary.

Rather than operating openly and informing the public of each act of voluntary news suppression, the OSI was inclined toward a confidential and private operation that exploited personal relations with individual newspaper editors. According to James Wiggins, "The Constitution may protect against the exercise of prior restraint on publication by congressional enactment, but what about prior restraint employed by executive agencies with the consent of the press? Many publications feared this might be involved in the Office of Strategic Information. . . . A government bureau, without a single statute to support it, in a time of fear and panic, no doubt could get nearly all publications to submit to restraints on publication of prescribed data."

Wiggins concluded, "[T]he constitutional immunity to prior restraint was not devised for the benefit of newspapers but for the information of the people. Such a consent to prior restraint would imperil their access to information as much as a legally enforceable censorship."[52]

On March 29, 1955, the government's secrecy policies were raised to a higher level when Secretary of Defense Charles E. Wilson issued a directive to government officials and defense contractors, asking them to curtail their public information activities. Wilson declared that henceforth, in order for an item to be cleared for publication, it not only had to meet security requirements, but must also make a "constructive contribution" to the Defense Department's efforts.

In response, the Associated Press Managing Editors Association adopted a resolution expressly condemning the withholding of information that was neither classified nor eligible for classification on the pretext that it was not "constructive" or that it might be of "possible use to a potential enemy." The association deplored "government secrecy that is withholding from American citizens facts about their Government that they are entitled to know" and concluded, "Whatever it is called, it is objectionable in a free society which hitherto has not had to look to Government for its approval or advice before distributing facts and information of a non-classified nature."[53]

Editorials published around the country were similarly opposed to the Eisenhower administration's new information policies. *Time* magazine commented, "Ever since Defense Secretary Charlie Wilson decreed that news put out by or extracted from the Pentagon must be 'constructive,' newsmen have been worried. Such a policy is just the thing for Government officials who want to cover up their own mistakes by withholding 'nonconstructive' news."[54]

Wilson added fuel to the fire when he named R. Karl Honaman, former chief censor at the OSI, as his deputy assistant in charge of public affairs. Honaman had never been a newsman, and aside from his OSI duties, his only press experience had been as director of publications for the Bell Telephone Laboratories.

In response to an inquiry from ASNE's Freedom of Information Committee, Honaman complained testily that press demands for information "take up the time of people with busy schedules" and "did not truly meet the requirements of being useful or valuable, nor yet very interesting to the public." When reporters protested this restrictive view of appropriate press coverage, Honaman suggested that editors should voluntarily refrain from publishing information that might be helpful to the Russians.[55]

J. R. Wiggins of the *Washington Post* stated, "The newspapers . . . will not join in a conspiracy with this or any other administration to withhold from the American people nonclassified information. . . . Honaman is asking them in effect to assume a censorship and suppression role which the Government itself is unwilling to undertake."[56]

Newsmen soon discovered that Honaman had sent censorship forms, called "balance sheets for strategic information," to all Army field commanders with instructions on how to use the forms to decide whether information requested by the press would be "helpful" or "harmful" to

U.S. interests. For example, one question on the form asked, "Does the information have much/little helpful/harmful effect on world opinion?" An Army officer admitted to a reporter that if he took the form literally he would have to turn down virtually all requests for information.[57]

The government regarded the mounting media furor as a press conspiracy. Public affairs deputy Honaman complained, "Practically all of this flurry traces back, directly or indirectly, to a campaign promoted by the chairman of the Freedom of Information Committee of the American Newspaper Editors [James Wiggins]. It was certain that in advance this group would read 'censorship' into any suggestion that editors should use their informed judgment to protect American strategic interests."[58]

THE MOSS SUBCOMMITTEE

The newly Democratic Congress had followed the Eisenhower administration's public skirmishes with the press with great interest. The highly publicized battles with bureaucrats like Charles Wilson and Karl Honaman may have actually precipitated the most important event on the path to a Freedom of Information Act: the creation of the Special Subcommittee on Government Information, called the Moss subcommittee after its chairman, Representative John E. Moss (D-Calif.).

According to congressional scholar Robert O. Blanchard, "The Honaman affair was a confrontation between a personification, on the one hand, of the new Eisenhower information policies—a former public relations man for the Bell Telephone Company—and, on the other side, a liberal, aggressive editor of a prestige newspaper in Washington who also happened to be chairman of the ASNE FOI Committee. It is difficult to measure precisely what effect the R. Karl Honaman–J. Russell Wiggins controversy had on Congressional decision-makers, but its relation to the establishment of the Moss Committee is clear. . . . [Subcommittee counsel Wallace] Parks used the Honaman affair to dramatize the need for an information subcommittee."[59]

On May 9, 1955, Wallace J. Parks, staff attorney for the House Government Operations Committee, wrote to Committee Chairman William Dawson calling attention to the negative press reaction to the Wilson and Honaman policies. Parks proposed that a new subcommittee be created to investigate the government's suppression of information. He discussed several possible committee projects with Representative John Moss, who showed great interest. Moss, in turn, told Parks to approach House Majority Leader John McCormack (D-Mass.) in an effort to solicit his support. As it turned out, McCormack was anxious to use Congress and its press allies to challenge the Eisenhower administration. According to David Glick, a Government Operations Committee staff member, "McCormack and others were pushed out of shape because the Administration was withholding information from Congress. He wanted to get the press aroused over the issue so he could pressure the Administration."[60]

With McCormack's strong support, the new House Subcommittee on Government Information was born on June 9, 1955, with Representative John Moss as its chairman.

In his letter establishing the subcommittee, Representative William Dawson (D-Ill.), chairman of the House Government Operations Committee, stated, "Charges have been made that government agencies have denied or withheld pertinent and timely information from those who are entitled to receive it. These charges include the denial of such information to the newspapers, to radio and television broadcasters, magazines, and other communications media, to trained and qualified research experts and to Congress."

Dawson concluded, "An informed public makes the difference between mob rule and democratic government. If the pertinent and necessary information on governmental activities is denied the public, the result is a weakening of the democratic process and the ultimate atrophy of our form of government. Accordingly, I am asking your Subcommittee to make such an investigation as will verify or refute these charges."[61]

The creation of the House Subcommittee on Government Information was applauded by the press as a significant, though long overdue, step toward open government. James Russell Wiggins, chairman of the ASNE's Freedom of Information Committee, said, "It will take a great many years to put a proper statutory foundation under the people's right to know about the executive departments of their government. Congress finally has made a tardy beginning by the selection of the Moss subcommittee."[62]

Moss himself told ASNE, "For 10 years, the American Society of Newspaper Editors and other newspaper groups have been fighting against restrictions on the flow of information from the Federal government. It was largely due to the ASNE that the House Government Information Subcommittee was created."[63]

The Moss subcommittee, a unique political hybrid, served the interests and used the methods of both politicians and journalists. The entire tone of the subcommittee's investigations into government secrecy was established by consultation with such press leaders as J. R. Wiggins, James Pope, Herbert Brucker, and James Reston. Perhaps most important, the subcommittee's own staff was composed largely of former newspaper reporters. The press-oriented staff collected information for the subcommittee through investigation, interview, and research and reported the results in clear, readable language, just as they had done while writing for their newspapers.

Harold Cross's seminal study of government secrecy was, of course, a powerful influence on the subcommittee. Cross also suggested journalists whom the subcommittee might consult. Among them was Jacob Scher, who was to become an important adviser and special counsel for the subcommittee until his death in 1961. The subcommittee staff was motivated by the conviction that there was indeed a constitutional right of public access to government information. Scher, a professor of journalism, claimed that the public's right to know about the workings of their government was part of the body of residual rights left to the people in the Ninth and Tenth amendments, "based on the experiences of the colonists as free-born Englishmen and their panoply of 'natural rights,' one of which was the right to report and comment on government."

Scher cited numerous provisions of the Constitution which support the public's right to know. He noted that Article 1, Section 5 provides that each House shall keep a public journal, that the Sixth Amendment provides for a public trial as a restriction on the arbitrary exercise of power, and that the Fifth and Fourteenth amendments contain due process clauses which speak of "liberty." Scher concluded, "The fact that a right has lain inchoate or dormant for a long time in no way is in derogation of that right. It may be brought to life by statutory enactment or by judicial construction."[64]

Like most legal scholars, Scher was unsure as to whether the right to know would have to come into practical existence through new legislation, or whether it was so fundamental that it could be enforced without legislative expression. He believed that the basic right was universally recognized in the language of the courts, though specific decisions had left the issue unclear. "Perhaps the crucible of experience, which is democracy, will provide in the future the proper tests so that the right becomes fully recognized," stated Scher. "A problem so important in big government's relation to the people cannot long remain unsolved. . . . If the news media persist, more significant advances are bound to come."[65]

Indeed, the press did persist, and advances were made. Subcommittee staff director Samuel Archibald, a former newspaperman, began the information-gathering process by meeting with James Wiggins, Lyle Wilson (United Press vice president and Washington bureau manager), Robert Hotz (editor of *Aviation Week*), and at least a dozen reporters who knew about specific instances of news suppression. In addition, freedom of information organizations, including the Associated Press Managing Editors, the American Newspaper Publishers Association, and Sigma Delta Chi, were contacted by mail.

The objectives and tentative plans of the subcommittee were communicated to such individuals and groups, and all of them offered their full cooperation. Archibald freely admitted that the first objective of the subcommittee staff was to gain the respect and trust of the press. "We knew in that day of McCarthy and the . . . congressional abuses of investigatory power, that we had to seek the active support of the press by demonstrating responsibility and restraint," declared Archibald. "At the same time, we had to convince the [House] leadership of the need of press support and, thus, of the priority of press information problems over that of Congress. We told them that without press support Congress could not attack agency restrictions with any effectiveness."[66]

The subcommittee often used personal communication to document examples of government secrecy. Moss would send a letter to the head of a federal agency outlining a particular practice of secrecy and demanding that the official explain and justify it. The letters were always in news story format, with the opening paragraphs covering the most interesting and important facts, as in the lead of a news story. Full background followed the lead. Sam Archibald, staff director of the subcommittee from its inception, recalled, "The subcommittee publicized the often-absurd government secrecy by demanding information, usually in a series of letters which were always available to the press. The policy of detailed investigations, full disclosure and complete cooperation with the press was established by Moss in one of his first staff meetings."[67]

The subcommittee had to ferret out specific examples of agency refusal to divulge information to the press. To prepare such case studies, the subcommittee first contacted reporters for tips and complete backgrounds on such instances. Only then would a staff member contact the uncooperative agencies for their explanations. Such authenticated instances were then used as the basis for the first subcommittee hearings, which would reveal the pattern of agency practices and policies in detail. A similar process was followed to document denial of information from Congress.

During the subcommittee's hearings, Moss was invited to dinner by prominent columnist Drew Pearson, who urged him to have his staff cleared for access to secret documents and then to release to the press those that did not deserve secrecy. Moss declined to follow Pearson's suggestion. According to Archibald, "Moss told his staff he did not want to follow McCarthy tactics; he wanted to do a slow and careful investigation of the government secrecy problem, then—and only then—publicize the facts of secrecy. The press would be on his side if he followed those careful tactics, Moss said, and the members of Congress also would support the study."[68]

Moss expressed the hope that he could determine the basic information policies of the agencies and discover whether there was arbitrary or capricious action. The "investigator-reporters" on the subcommittee were assigned particular agencies to study. They usually began with the public information officers, who could reveal the workings of the agency and the names of the officials who controlled the information. The investigators interviewed the responsible officials and filed reports which highlighted matters that would make good news stories.

Another part of the information-gathering process took place within Congress, and once again former journalists on the subcommittee staff worked closely with the press. Staffer J. Lacey Reynolds, another former newspaperman, conducted most of the in-Congress information gathering and got assurances from another former journalist/staffer, George Reedy (D-Tex.) (the right-hand man of Senator Lyndon Johnson) that the Senate would not provide any serious competition to Moss. Nonetheless, the high profile maintained by the press eventually became a partisan issue, and Representative Clare Hoffman (R-Mich.), the lone minority member on the subcommittee, complained about being "surrounded by publicity men." Hoffman declared, "One begins to suspect that the chairman does not wish to kill the white horse of publicity which a section of the press is feeding and grooming."[69]

By mid-1955, the subcommittee's journalist-staffers had completed their interviews with agency representatives and media sources. On August 18, 1955, Archibald issued a tentative program outline intended to guide the staff's decisions for the next few months. As part of the formal inquiry of government sources, agencies were given a four-page questionnaire asking them to disclose "whether information from government sources is sufficiently available to inform the people on the activity of their government." The subcommittee used the questionnaires to document the information policies and practices of each executive agency. Press releases, along with copies of the questionnaire, were distributed in the press galleries.

The first question posed to the government agencies was; "What categories and types of information possessed by your agency are not available to: (a) The press and other information media serving the general public? (b) The Congress? (c) Other federal agencies? (d) Business, trade and other groups with an economic interest in the information? (e) Research specialists, scientists, public affairs organizations and similar groups or individuals?" The follow-up question was, "On what do you base authority for denying access to or not making available such information?"[70]

Succeeding questions asked for details on the classification of information, who determines the classification, the declassification process, and the procedures for appealing restrictions on the free flow of news. Agencies were asked, "What consideration is given to the public's right to know and to the importance of an informed public in the successful operation of the democratic form of government?"[71]

When the questionnaires were retrieved and processed, a picture of blatant and arbitrary federal secrecy was revealed. Representative Moss described the results as startling evidence of the low regard federal officials had for the right to know.

The Moss subcommittee's first hearing, held in November 1955, brought together a panel of prominent journalists including Pope and Wiggins representing ASNE, Virgil Newton and Clark Mollenhoff of Sigma Delta Chi, Guy Easterly and Hugh Boyd of the National Editorial Association, Richard Slocum of the American Newspaper Publishers Association, William Beale of the Associated Press, James Reston of the *New York Times*, columnist Joseph Alsop, and, of course, Harold Cross.

The subcommittee had no need for press releases. Before each hearing, outlines of the subjects to be covered and background information on the witnesses were sent to reporters in the House press gallery. Indeed, the press was provided with the material prepared for the subcommittee.

In addition to his testimony, Harold Cross published articles in support of the Moss subcommittee. In one 1956 article, he applauded the work of the Moss subcommittee and affirmed its conclusion that the government had hidden many types of legitimate information. "In widespread areas having nothing whatever to do with national security or any other public necessity, the people, the Congress, and the press are being denied information essential to the formation of public opinion, to the formation of legislation, and to the function of their information media. They deny access to public records. They stamp 'secret' and 'confidential' on evidence of their action."[72]

In acknowledging the giant step taken by the Moss subcommittee, Cross nonetheless concluded, "On its face the law seems to be that, in the absence of general or specific acts of Congress affirmatively creating clear, legal right of inspection, there is no enforceable right of the people, including the press, to inspect any federal non-judicial record. . . . This much is clear: the Congress, to which alone the law-making power is entrusted by the Constitution, can legislate, if it will, far-reaching freedom for itself, the people, and the press without encroaching on actual powers of the President."[73]

Despite the highly publicized successes of the Moss Subcommittee, its future was by no means assured, since each successive Congress was required to reconsider its continuation. Having played the major role in creating the subcommittee, the press was forced to lobby for its continuation. James S. Pope's letter to Representative Dawson, chairman of the subcommittee's parent committee, was an example typical of such lobbying.

"I deeply believe the importance of the Committee's work cannot be exaggerated," wrote Pope. "It is absolutely essential that Congress continue to scrutinize the conduct of executive departments, boards and bureaus to make sure the people of this country are not being deluded and deceived. . . . You, of all people, probably understand all of this. But I did not want you to think the invaluable work of the Committee is being taken for granted. We who have seen the danger and the need are greatly heartened, and we would like to see the Committee's funds, its powers and its influence vastly expanded."[74]

REMOVING THE PAPER CURTAIN

With the help of its press allies, the Moss subcommittee had made government secrecy a major political issue. The 1956 Democratic party platform declared, "During recent years there has developed a practice on the part of Federal agencies to delay and withhold decisions affecting their lives and destinies. We believe that this trend toward secrecy in Government should be reversed and that the Federal Government should return to its basic tradition of exchanging and promoting the freest flow of information possible in those unclassified areas where secrets involving weapons development and bona fide national security are not involved. We condemn the Eisenhower administration for the excesses practiced in this vital area, and pledge the Democratic Party to reverse this tendency."[75]

Despite its political successes, it soon became clear that the Moss subcommittee was winning the publicity battle but losing the war. The Eisenhower administration had been forced to reveal publicly its restrictive information policies, but it showed little inclination to change its ways.

John B. Oakes, a member of the *New York Times* editorial board, wrote, "I believe most newspapermen would agree that during the past few years news has been censored at the source in various departments of government with increasing effectiveness. A kind of paper curtain has been set up by a multitude of government press agents."[76]

Reporters who testified before the Moss Subcommittee agreed that this "paper curtain" was screening government activity from the public. Author Dan Nimmo pointed out, "Behind this curtain lies an attitude novel to democratic government—an attitude which says that we, the officials, not you, the people, will determine how much you are to be told about your own Government. No single administration or political party is held responsible for such secrecy; the trend characterizes all administrations after World War II."[77]

Nimmo applauded the Moss hearings for spotlighting the journalists' argument against government secrecy. "Since the public has a 'right to know,' so do newsmen acting on behalf of the public," declared Nimmo. "Reporters appearing before the Moss subcommittee argued that the newsman is the agent of the citizen, for such a grant of authority is implicit in the the First Amendment of the United States Constitution. . . . Hence, refusal to inform the newsman is a refusal to reveal matters to a public which has a constitutional right to know about governmental affairs."[78]

J. R. Wiggins, the retiring chairman of the ASNE's FOI Committee, stated, "It is not a newspaper right for which we contend. We do not ask any access for ourselves that we do not concede belongs to any other citizen. We claim our rights to know about government business, not as editors and reporters, but as citizens entitled to the rights of all citizens in a democracy."[79]

Representatives of the press were losing patience with the Moss Subcommittee's focus on the voluntary release of government information. James S. Pope, of the Louisville *Courier-Journal* and former ASNE FOI chairman, wanted a broader examination of agency responsiveness to specific press requests. "If the people of the country are to be fully informed they should not be dependent on voluntary releases," declared Pope. "We are . . . concerned . . . with the attitude of officialdom, not only toward 'releases' but toward inquiries."[80]

The press was coming to believe that any system of obligatory agency response to public requests for executive information would require legislative leverage. *Editor and Publisher* joined in the call for legislation, declaring, "Citizens of a self-governing society such as ours must have the legal right to examine and investigate the conduct of its affairs, subject only to those limitations imposed by the most urgent public necessity."[81]

Press attorney Harold Cross sounded the call for legislative action. "Congress is the primary source for relief," he said. "In its *preoccupation* with other problems it has left the field wide open for executive occupation. The time is ripe for an end to ineffectual sputtering about executive refusals of access to official records and for Congress to begin exercising effectually its function to legislate freedom of information for itself, the public, and the press. The powers of Congress to that end are not unlimited but they are extensive."[82]

Cross was frequently called upon by the Moss subcommittee for legal advice and participation in hearings, a relationship that continued until his death in 1959. He believed that there was substantial basis for a right to know in the First and Fifth amendments, a view he felt would "ultimately prevail." Nonetheless, Cross was a practical man who supported immediate legislative action. He advised the subcommittee on a possible FOI statute, suggesting a simple requirement that "all records should be open except as otherwise provided by law."[83]

At its landmark meeting in April 1956, the American Society of Newspaper Editors declared, "It has become apparent that so far as federal secrecy is concerned, it is entrenched behind a host of statutes and regulations and the only real and lasting remedy is new legislation."[84]

NOTES

1. Thomas Cooley, *A Treatise on the Constitutional Limitations*, 8th ed., vol. 2 (Boston: Little, Brown, 1927), p. 822.

2. Louis Edward Ingelhart, comp. *Press and Speech Freedoms in America, 1619–1995: A Chronology* (Westport, Conn.: Greenwood Press, 1997), p. 10.

3. Ibid., pp. 15–16.

4. Ibid., pp. 16–17, 22.

5. John Adams, "A Dissertation on the Canon and Feudal Law," *Boston Gazette*, September 30, 1765, in *Papers of John Adams*, ed. Robert J. Taylor et al., vol. 1 (Cambridge, Mass.: Belknap Press of Harvard University, 1977), 108.

6. Ibid., pp. 120–21.

7. Ingelhart, *Press and Speech Freedoms in America*, p. 33.

8. Richard D. Brown, *The Strength of a People: The Idea of an Informed Citizenry in America, 1650–1870* (Chapel Hill: University of North Carolina Press, 1996), p. xiv.

9. Alexander Hamilton, *The Federalist Papers*, No. 84, ed. Clinton Rossiter (New York: Mentor Books, 1961), p. 513.

10. "Freedom and the Press," *The Progressive*, June 1962, p. 29.

11. Frank Luther Mott, ed. *Interpretations of Journalism: A Book of Readings* (New York: F. S. Crofts, 1937), p. 57.

12. James F. Stephen, *A History of the Criminal Law of England*, vol. 2 (London: McMillan, 1883), pp. 301–2.

13. William S. Holdsworth, *A History of English Law*, vol. 4 (London: Methuen, 1922–52), p. 499.

14. *De Libellis Famosis*, 3 Cokes Reports 254, 255 (1605).

15. Larry P. Eldridge, *A Distant Heritage: The Growth of Free Speech in Early America* (New York: New York University Press, 1994), p. 29.

16. Ibid., pp. 24–25.

17. Stanley N. Katz, Introduction to *A Brief Narrative of the Case and Trial of John Peter Zenger*, by James Alexander (Cambridge, Mass.: Belknap Press of Harvard University, 1963), p. 9.

18. Rodney A. Smolla, *Free Speech in an Open Society* (New York: Knopf, 1992), p. 29.

19. Katz, *A Brief Narrative*, pp. 70, 78–79.

20. *Near v. Minnesota*, 283 U.S. 697 (1931).

21. *Grosjean v. American Press Association*, 297 U.S. 233 (1936).

22. *Whitney v. California*, 274 U.S. 357 (1927) at 375–76.

23. *Grosjean v. American Press Association*, 297 U.S. 233 (1936).

24. *Writings of James Madison*, 6, Gaillard Hunt ed. (New York: Putnam, 1900–1910), p. 398.

25. *Writings of James Madison*, 9, Gaillard Hunt ed. (New York: Putnam, 1900–1910), p. 103.

26. Alexander Meiklejohn, "The First Amendment Is an Absolute," in *The Supreme Court Review*, ed. Philip Kurland (Chicago: University of Chicago Press, 1961), p. 257.

27. Wallace Parks, "The Open Government Principle: Applying the Right to

Know Under the Constitution," *George Washington Law Review* 26, no. 1 (October 1957): 9, 12.

28. Thomas I. Emerson, "Legal Foundations of the Right to Know," *Washington University Law Quarterly* 1976, no. 1 (1976): 2, 23–24.

29. Harold L. Cross, *The Right to Know: Legal Access to Public Records and Proceedings* (New York: Columbia University Press, 1953), pp. 131–32.

30. "Freedom and the Press," *The Progressive*, June 1962, p. 29.

31. *Lamont v. Postmaster General*, 381 U.S. 301, at 308 (1965).

32. *Griswold v. Connecticut*, 381 U.S. 479 (1965).

33. *Stanley v. Georgia*, 394 U.S. 557 (1969).

34. *Red Lion Broadcasting Co. v. FCC*, 395 U.S. 367, at 390 (1974).

35. *CBS v. Federal Communications Commission*, 49 LW 4891, at 4899 (1981).

36. *Virginia State Board of Pharmacy v. Virginia Citizens Consumer Council*, 425 U.S. 748 (1976).

37. *Board of Education, Island Trees Union Free School District No. 26 v. Pico*, 102 S. Ct. 2799 (1982).

38. Kent Cooper, *The Right to Know: An Exposition of the Evils of News Suppression and Propaganda* (New York: Farrar, Strauss and Cudahy, 1956), p. xii–xiii.

39. Ibid., p. 165.

40. Ibid., p. 180.

41. *Problems in Journalism*, Proceedings of the 1951 Convention of the American Society of Newspaper Editors. Washington, D.C.: American Society of Newspaper Editors, 1951, p. 170.

42. Cooper, *The Right to Know*, p. 283.

43. James S. Pope, "The Suppression of News," *Atlantic Monthly*, July 1951, pp. 50–51.

44. James S. Pope, "The Cult of Secrecy," *Nieman Reports*, October 1957, p. 8.

45. Pope, "The Suppression of News," p. 50.

46. Cross, *The People's Right to Know*, p. 123.

47. Ibid., pp. 12, 132.

48. David M. O'Brien, *The Public's Right to Know: The Supreme Court and the First Amendment* (New York: Praeger, 1981), p. 3.

49. James Russell Wiggins, "The Role of the Press in Safeguarding the People's Right to Know Government Business," *Marquette Law Review* 40 (1956): 74.

50. James Russell Wiggins, *Freedom or Secrecy*, rev. ed. (New York: Oxford University Press, 1964), pp. 102–3.

51. Miles B. Johnson, *The Government Secrecy Controversy* (New York: Vantage Press, 1967), pp. 32–33.

52. Wiggins, *Freedom or Secrecy*, p. 136.

53. "Editors Condemn Federal Secrecy," *New York Times*, November 19, 1955, p. 10.

54. "Censorship at the Pentagon," *Time*, July 4, 1955, p. 62.

55. Ibid.

56. Ibid.

57. Ibid.

58. Robert O. Blanchard, "Present at the Creation: The Media and the Moss Committee," *Journalism Quarterly* 49 (Summer 1972): 272–73.

59. Robert O. Blanchard, "The Moss Committee and a Federal Records Law (1955–1965)" (Ph.D. diss., Syracuse University, 1966), p. 217.

60. David Glick, quoted in Ibid., pp. 273–74.

61. U.S. House Subcommittee on Government Information, June 9, 1955, Letter from Representative William L. Dawson to Representative John E. Moss, Folder 1 of 2, File 84A-F.7.23, Record Group 233, National Archives, Washington, D.C.

62. Wiggins, *Freedom or Secrecy*, p. 91.

63. "Moss Has Hand on Knob to Open More Doors," *Editor and Publisher*, April 28, 1956, p. 56.

64. Jacob Scher, "Access to Information: Recent Legal Problems," *Journalism Quarterly* 35 (Winter 1960): 42–43.

65. Ibid., p. 52.

66. Blanchard, "Present at the Creation," p. 276.

67. Sam Archibald, "The Early Years of the Freedom of Information Act—1955 to 1974," *PS: Political Science and Politics* (December 1993): 727.

68. Ibid.

69. Blanchard, "Present at the Creation," p. 277.

70. Cooper, *The Right to Know*, p. 286.

71. Ibid., p. 287.

72. Harold L. Cross, "The Barricade of Secrecy," *Atlantic Monthly*, vol. 198, no. 6 (December 1956), p. 56.

73. Ibid., pp. 58–59.

74. Letter from James S. Pope, executive editor, *Louisville Courier-Journal*, to Representative William L. Dawson. File 2 of 2, 84A-F.7.23, Record Group 233, National Archives, Washington, D.C.

75. "Freedom of Information," *U.S. News and World Report*, August 24, 1956, pp. 102, 114.

76. John B. Oakes, "The Paper Curtain of Washington," *Nieman Reports*, October 1958, p. 3.

77. Dan Nimmo, *Newsgathering in Washington* (New York: Atherton Press, 1964), pp. 173–74.

78. Ibid., pp. 174–75.

79. "Editorial: ASNE's Unanswered Question," *Editor and Publisher*, April 28, 1956, p. 6.

80. Blanchard, "Present at the Creation," p. 276.

81. "ASNE's Unanswered Question," p. 6.

82. Cross, *The People's Right to Know*, p. 246.

83. Blanchard, "Present at the Creation," pp. 276–77.

84. "ASNE's Unanswered Question," p. 6.

CHAPTER 2

A Legislative Remedy

THE HOUSEKEEPING STATUTE

When it became clear that the federal executive would not willingly expose its business to the light of day, the press alliance with the Moss subcommittee turned to a legislative strategy. The Freedom of Information (FOI) Committee of the American Society of Newspaper Editors (ASNE) recommended three specific statutory changes and a dozen revisions in federal rules and policies. At the top of the list were amendment of the "Housekeeping" statute (5 U.S. Code 22) and the Administrative Procedures Act (5 U.S. Code 1001–1011), both of which had been identified by Representative John Moss (D-Calif.) as frequently cited authority for federal agencies to withhold information. Other recommendations included revision of President Dwight Eisenhower's Executive Order 10501 on national security information, reexamination of the Atomic Energy Act, an end to the suppression of unclassified information by the Office of Strategic Information, and a host of changes in federal policies.

Federal bureaucrats were indeed citing the obscure Housekeeping Act as authority for withholding government information. The 1789 statute had authorized department heads in George Washington's administration "to prescribe regulations, not inconsistent with law, for the government of his department, the conduct of its officers and clerks, and the custody, use and preservation of the records, papers and property appertaining thereto."[1] President Washington had never requested, nor had Congress intended, that the Housekeeping Act permit federal officials to impose secrecy on public information, but the law had been twisted by subsequent administrations as a justification for withholding a broad range of information from both the public and Congress. By exploiting the Housekeeping Act, federal departments and agencies had established their own restrictive procedures for disseminating information.

Encouraged by the Moss subcommittee, the press exposed the government's perversion of the Housekeeping Act. In 1958 the *Saturday Evening Post* pointed out "This 'housekeeping' regulation has been used, through bureaucratic interpretation, to justify closed-door Government. It has been used as authority for hiding everything from patronage lists, nonstrategic import-and-export data, Federal-building rentals, large Federal loans and a lot more. A recent study shows that the 'housekeeping' statute was being used to justify restrictions on public information by eight cabinet-level departments and three regulatory agencies. It has been used to keep facts from Congress and the Courts."[2]

The *Post* concluded, "The [Moss subcommittee] hearings . . . brought out the fact that neither citizen nor press has an enforceable legal right to inspect any federal nonjudicial record. There are still some sixty to eighty estimated further regulations which deny free access to government records. The House Subcommittee on Information still has a big job ahead."[3]

In an attempt to reduce the legislative authority for executive secrecy, Representative Moss and Senator Thomas C. Hennings (D-Mo.) cosponsored a so-called freedom of information bill, which made a modest but important change to the Housekeeping Act. Journalists James Pope and Clark Mollenhoff had proposed a simple amendment specifying that the Housekeeping Act "does not authorize withholding information from the public," and Moss embodied that wording in his bill: "This section does not authorize withholding information from the public or limiting availability of records to the public." The same wording was embodied in the Senate version of the bill, and the Moss-Hennings amendment, called the Freedom-of-Information Bill (H.R. 2767), soon passed the full Congress.

In explaining the significance of this simple legislative change, Representative Moss stated, "First, it means the removal of one crutch among the many which Federal officials have misused to withhold information from the public. Second, it demonstrates that the Congress is aware of the growing threat of improper secrecy in Federal departments and agencies which involve virtually every facet of American life. Thirdly, it serves notice to Federal officials that unless they have clear authority for withholding information, the right to know shall prevail."

Moss noted that each of the ten Cabinet departments in the Eisenhower administration opposed the amendment, and he warned, "Passage of the amendment is merely a first, limited step toward eradicating unnecessary Government secrecy. The new legislation merely eliminated one glaring violation of the right to know."[4]

Senator Hennings spoke with pride of the new legislation, but he placed it in the context of an expansive view of the public's right to know. "Freedom of information about governmental affairs is an inherent and necessary part of our political system," said Hennings. "Ours is a system of self-government—and self-government can work effectively only where the people have full access to information about what their Government is doing."

Hennings acknowledged that there was no explicit provision in the Constitution concerning the right to know, but said that, like many other fundamental rights, it was taken so much for granted by the Founding Fathers that it was deemed unnecessary to include it. "To argue otherwise . . . would be to say that since the Constitution does not specifically require it, the President is obliged to give *no* information to the public—a position which even the most ardent advocates of the 'Executive privilege' doctrine do not take."

Hennings concluded, "Since, under our theory of government, sovereignty resides in the people, it logically and necessarily follows that the people have a right to know what the Government—which they themselves established—is doing, and that government officials properly may interfere with the free exercise of that right only to the extent the people themselves consent."[5]

THE ADMINISTRATIVE PROCEDURE ACT

The White House was predictably cool toward the changes to the Housekeeping statute, regarding them as an incursion on executive authority. On August 12, 1958, when President Eisenhower signed the Freedom of Information Bill into law, he conspicuously stated, "It is . . . clear from the legislative history of the bill that it is not intended to, and indeed could not, alter the existing power of the head of an Executive department to keep appropriate information or papers confidential in the public interest. This power in the Executive Branch is inherent under the Constitution."[6]

The president did not clarify what government information could be kept "confidential," and he seemed to be mixing two different justifications for withholding information. On the one hand, his use of the phrase "in the public interest" to justify confidentiality was borrowed from a frequently claimed authority for government secrecy, the Administrative Procedure Act of 1946. On the other hand, his reference to executive authority "inherent under the Constitution" suggested the notion of executive privilege, an ill-defined and essentially arbitrary power claimed by many presidents throughout American history.

Senator Hennings denounced the administration's position as "poor law and poor policy" which was "completely contrary to the word and the spirit of the Constitution."[7] Nevertheless, the Eisenhower administration continued to rely on executive privilege and the Administrative Procedure Act as authorization to withhold information from the public. Because executive privilege was usually justified on the basis of the separation of powers concept, a matter to be judged by the courts in individual cases, Congress addressed the legislative component of Eisenhower's secrecy policies: the Administrative Procedure Act.

The act had been created innocently enough in 1946 in an effort to establish a comprehensive system to organize agency information. Indeed, it was ostensibly a public access statute, requiring the disclosure of federal records: "Except to the extent that there is involved (1) any function of the United States requiring secrecy in the public interest or (2) any matter relating solely to the internal management of an agency . . . matters of official record shall . . . be made available to persons properly and directly concerned, except information held confidential for good cause found."[8]

The misapplication of these minor exceptions soon made the Administrative Procedure Act the fountainhead of secrecy within government. Federal agencies exploited the vague provisions in the act requiring "secrecy in the public interest" or "for good cause," and also claimed the right to deny requests for information "relating solely to the internal management of an agency" unless the requestor was "properly and directly concerned." Armed with such implied authority, the government routinely denied public access to such aged and harmless materials as George Washington's intelligence methods and a Confederate general's memoirs.

Such arbitrary executive secrecy forced members of Congress like Senator Hennings and Representative Moss back to the legislative drawing board. Hennings made the amending of the Administrative Procedure Act the first point in what he called his "anti-secrecy program." He warned that the language of the act's public information section was loosely drawn, vague, and ambiguous. "These defects," said Hennings, "have enabled officials in the departments and agencies to point with some plausibility to the section as authority to withhold information, and some have not hesitated to use it."

Hennings further stated, "Proposed amendments are embodied in a bill which I have already introduced in the Senate. They would tighten the language of the section and replace the present vague and undefined terms and phrases with language of more definite meaning. These amendments should make the section the vehicle it was originally intended to be, and take away from the departments and agencies a secrecy weapon Congress never intended them to have."

During 1959 Hennings and Moss proposed amendments to the Administrative Procedure Act that would require all federal agencies to make public their regulations, policies of public information, and the availability of information they receive. The amendments defined "public records" to include at least "all applications, petitions, pleadings, requests, claims, communications, reports or other papers, and all records and actions by the agency," unless their availability to the public was limited by a published rule.[9]

Despite such efforts to tighten the language of the Administrative Procedure Act, no effective legislation was passed during the Eisenhower administration, and agencies continued to cite the act for withholding authority.

THE KENNEDY ADMINISTRATION

The election of President John F. Kennedy in 1960 was greeted with cautious optimism by Congress, the public, and the press, but the Kennedy administration carried over the secrecy practices of the Eisenhower administration. Under Kennedy, the public's right to know actually deteriorated, as new policies of secrecy and news control emerged. Not only did the Kennedy administration withhold government information from the public and press, it also asked the press to censor itself. On April 27, 1961, Kennedy told the American Newspaper Publishers Association that the Cold War required the press to exercise voluntary censorship to prevent disclosure of information that might help America's enemies. Kennedy acknowledged that such control of the news had customarily been restricted to wartime, but he noted that "in time of 'clear and present danger,' the courts have held that even the privileged rights of the First Amendment must yield to the public's need for national security."

Kennedy concluded, "If the press is awaiting a declaration of war before it imposes the self-discipline of combat conditions, then I can only say that no war ever posed a greater threat to our security. . . . Every newspaper now asks itself with respect to every story: 'Is it news?' All I ask is that you add the question: 'Is it in the interest of national security?' "[10]

The press was outraged. The *New York Post* asked, "Who is to define 'the interest of national security?' Will not some argue that 'the interest of national security' is damaged by any newspaper reports exposing economic and social injustice in our own country? These questions illustrate the hazards and ambiguity of the course proposed by the President."[11]

The *New York Herald Tribune* rejected Kennedy's call for news control by stating, "There is no need for further restrictive machinery. In days of peril especially the country needs more facts, not fewer. . . . In the long run, competent, thorough, and aggressive news reporting is the uncompromising servant of the national interest—even though it may be momentarily embarrassing to the Government."[12]

The *St. Louis Post Dispatch* took a similar position. "President Kennedy suggested the press submit itself to a system of voluntary censorship under Government direction, as has been customary in shooting wars. This, we believe, would undermine the essential mission of the press, which is to inform, interpret, and criticize."[13]

In late 1962, Assistant Secretary of Defense Arthur Sylvester defended the Kennedy administration's information policies, claiming that the control of news by the government was "one weapon in a strained situation." A *New York Times* editorial responded, "The American press, which is made by this means the unwilling servant of the government, will also have a reduced credibility at home and abroad. These are high prices to pay for getting the results which Mr. Sylvester thinks justify the use of news and access to news as a weapon."

The *Times* editorial concluded, "There is no doubt that 'management' or 'control' of the news is censorship described by a sweeter term. There is no doubt that it restricts the people's right to know. There is no doubt that public positions upon great national issues cannot be intelligently formed unless the facts are available. There is no doubt that a democratic government cannot work if news of and about that government is long suppressed or managed or manipulated or controlled."[14]

The Kennedy administration's information policies further energized the Moss subcommittee, which continued to use its trailblazing surveys and reports on government information to document the need for freedom of information legislation. In its fourteenth such report, covering 1961 and 1962, the subcommittee addressed specific examples of restrictions on access to government information with two stated objectives in mind: to remove the restrictions documented and to urge administrative action or legislation to prevent their recurrence.

The report documented a number of success stories in which "the barriers of secrecy erected by Government agencies gave way to congressional pressure," but it concluded: "[N]o Government agency should be complimented for informing the citizenry. One unnecessary secret is one too many. To withhold information from the public is contrary to the basic principles of a democratic society; to inform the public is the Government's fundamental responsibility. . . . The increasing readiness of the Congress to assert its right to know has become a vital counterpressure against the bureaucratic penchant for secrecy."[15]

In December 1962, the ASNE, joined by the National Editorial Association and the American Newspaper Publishers Association, issued a report on the relation of a free press to national security. The report asserted that the security of the nation could be maintained only by full reporting of all the truth that is not directly harmful to our military interest. "We are concerned," stated the report, "lest Government go beyond a legitimate suppression of strictly military information and look upon news of what the government is doing not as an honest report of what happened but as a means to some desired end."[16]

The report concluded that the real danger to national security came when the government regarded news as "a weapon or other instrument of national policy."[17]

The *New York Times*, praising the ASNE report, declared, "The kind of governmental news management, restriction, control and censorship of which there have been disturbing indications in recent weeks could not fail, if continued, to threaten our form of representative democracy. The people's 'right to know' is not just a glittering phrase; it is a foundation stone of our society. A democracy is impossible unless the people are informed. A secret government leads to certain tyranny."[18]

The press continued to protest the Kennedy administration's information-control policies, right up to the months before Kennedy's assassination. Arthur Krock of the *New York Times* said that, after almost fifty years of reporting and editing, he was forced to make two critical judgments of the Kennedy administration. "1. A news management policy not only exists, but in the form of direct and deliberate action, has been enforced more cynically and boldly than by any previous Administration in a period when the U.S. was not in a war or without visible means of regression from the verge of war; 2. In the form of indirect but equally deliberate action, the policy has been much more effective than direct action in coloring the several facets of public information, because it has been employed with subtlety and imagination for which there is no historic parallel known to me."[19]

Author Hansen Baldwin warned of the serious consequences of government control of the news: "The fundamental case against the kind of news management, restriction, control and censorship which has been practiced recently is quite simply, that it impairs the constitutional rights of a free press, and hence poses a potential danger to our form of democratic and representative government. No people can be really free if its press is spoon-fed with government pap, or if the news which provides a democracy with the rationale for its actions is so controlled, restricted, managed, or censored that it cannot be published."[20]

Just weeks before President Kennedy's untimely death, Sigma Delta Chi, the professional journalistic fraternity, stated in the *New York Times* that freedom of information was at "the lowest ebb in history" because of "the blanket of secrecy over the records of government."[21]

THE FREEDOM OF INFORMATION ACT

Congress now realized that minor changes to existing statutes would never deter executive secrecy. In concert with the press, the Moss subcommittee searched for a more comprehensive legislative remedy—a new Freedom of Information Act (FOIA).

Sam Archibald, staff director for the Moss subcommittee throughout its eleven years of work toward the FOIA, recalled that Moss selected his journalist-staffers without regard to party affiliation. "Even the lawyers had newspaper experience," said Archibald. "While the rhetoric of the subcommittee's reports and pronouncements emphasized a general public right of access to government documents, the reality was that the pillars of the press had to be convinced to join the political fight for the FOIA or there would have been no law."[22]

Jacob Scher, a professor of journalism at Northwestern University, led the Moss subcommittee members and staff in discussions of possible legislation, and members of the press, such as Harold Cross and James Russell Wiggins, were often included in such discussions. In 1960 Scher recommended legislation that recognized the right of any individual to request government information and, where access is denied, to appeal to the judiciary.

According to Archibald, "At first Scher suggested defining the specific 'public records' which should be open to the press and the public, but no one could come up with an acceptable definition. Over the years and through the subcommittee hearings, various ideas and legal vehicles were developed, and both the possibility of legislation and the glow of publicity attracted the U.S. Senate."[23]

Senator Thomas Hennings, chairman of an important Senate judiciary subcommittee, began working closely with the Moss subcommittee, and joint discussions developed preliminary legislation which was introduced in both the House and Senate. Moss proposed broader legislation stipulating that "every agency shall, in accordance with published rules stating the time, place, and procedure to be followed, make all its records promptly available to any persons," except in "certain specific cases." These "specific cases" or exemptions included the right of the executive branch to withhold information when secrecy was required "in the interest of national defense or foreign policy" or where secrecy is authorized under a specific law. Also exempted were certain raw investigatory files or files that involved invasion of privacy.[24]

There was, however, a major sticking point between the House and Senate bills. Because his subcommittee was part of the House Government Operations Committee, Moss attached his bill to the Housekeeping statute that he had amended in 1958. The Senate bill, on the other hand, was an amendment to the Administrative Procedure Act of 1946, because the Senate Judiciary Committee, which handles freedom of information issues, had legislative jurisdiction over that act. Consequently, when the Senate Judiciary Committee oversaw the passage of its bill in 1964, it sent the bill over to a subcommittee of the House Judiciary Committee. Unlike the more supportive Moss subcommittee, the House judiciary subcommittee showed little interest in the bill, and it died in committee.

During the next Congress, an almost identical freedom of information bill was introduced in the Senate and House. Again it passed the Senate, but, without the stewardship of Representative Moss, it again died in the House. In the process, however, several changes were made on the Senate floor that would be retained in subsequent bills. Senator Hubert Humphrey (D-Minn.) exempted federal agencies that supervise banks from the provisions of the bill, and Senator Everett Dirksen (R-Ill.) added a similar exemption for federal agencies overseeing oil and gas exploration.

In February 1965, the bill with the Humphrey and Dirksen changes passed the Senate on a voice vote as S. 1160 and was again sent to the House as an amendment to the Administrative Procedure Act. This time Moss convinced Senate Judiciary Committee chairman Emanuel Celler (D-N.Y.) to permit the bill to be referred to the Moss subcommittee, rather than a subcommittee of the Judiciary. The tactic took the executive branch by surprise. Because the Johnson White House had assumed that the latest freedom of information bill would meet the same fate as its two predecessors, it had supported the third Senate bill. It now appeared that a freedom of information bill actually had a chance for passage.

Moss knew that if the bill were open to amendments, it would be weakened or destroyed at the bidding of the executive branch; therefore, he worked out a plan with other members of his subcommittee to permit absolutely no amendments to the Senate bill as it passed through committee hearings and floor debate. The agreement to prevent amendments to the bill was achieved with one condition: the Justice Department must be included in negotiations with the Moss subcommittee.

Tensions with the White House and the Justice Department ran high, forcing Moss to maintain a low public profile. "Negotiations were very rough," Moss later confided. "I recall that the assistant attorney general would walk out and say, 'All right, there'll be no bill, then.' "

Moss admitted, "[President] Johnson was not enthused about this legislation. . . . I knew and he knew that I didn't have two-thirds to override a veto."[25]

Since Justice Department lawyers were in the forefront of the fight against public access to federal records, they provided weakening language for the House report, which became an important part of the subsequent interpretation of the bill. Due to Department of Justice's drafting, the House report did not always reflect the true intent of the designers of the bill. Indeed, it was not only frequently at odds with the more faithful Senate report, but in disagreement with the simple text of the law. The subsequent attorney general's memorandum on the act compounded the confusion by ill-advised reliance on the House report. "A comparison of the reports on the identical legislation which passed the

Senate and the House shows the difference between the Senate staff-created explanation of the new law and the House staff-created, emasculating compromise with the government lawyers,"[26] said Sam Archibald.

Even with the weakening language, the House Committee on Government Operations refused to consider the bill until the following year. On June 20, 1966, the House finally approved the Senate bill on a unanimous vote, 308 to 0, with 125 not voting. Having passed both Houses of Congress, the Freedom of Information Act was ready for the president's signature. After eleven years of valiant struggle for the FOIA, Representative Moss anticipated a formal signing ceremony, with his press allies present. There was no such event. On July 4, 1966, President Lyndon Johnson signed the Freedom of Information Act into law while vacationing at his Texas ranch. Johnson's staff had prepared a press release to be issued from the Texas White House, but at the last minute it was withdrawn. Members of the press present at the signing were told that no statement was available, leading the *New York Times* to report that the first government information withheld under the FOIA was the White House statement on the act itself.

The president's brief statement, subsequently released by the White House staff, dealt overwhelmingly with Johnson's concerns about the FOIA's imposition on executive prerogatives. In less than a page, he found room to declare that the FOIA should disclose only "information that the security of the Nation permits," that the rights of individuals "may require that some documents not be made available," that as long as threats to peace exist "there must be military secrets," that a person must be able to provide confidential information to the government without fear of "being required to reveal or discuss his sources," that "information in personnel files be protected from disclosure," and that government officials "cannot operate effectively if required to disclose information prematurely or to make public investigative files and internal instructions."

Johnson elaborated on the need to maintain some degree of executive secrecy despite the FOIA's disclosure requirements, claiming that both were "vital to the welfare of our people." He was also careful to add the broad claim that "this bill in no way impairs the President's power under our Constitution to provide for confidentiality when the national interest so requires." The president concluded, "I am hopeful that the needs I have mentioned can be served by a constructive approach to the wording and spirit and legislative history of this measure."[27]

President Johnson's attorney general, Ramsey Clark, evinced little of Johnson's concern about the FOIA in his memo to executive departments and agencies. His 1966 memo on implementation of the FOIA began, "If government is to be truly of, by, and for the people, the people must know in detail the activities of government. Nothing so diminishes democracy as secrecy. Self-government, the maximum participation of the citizenry in the affairs of state, is meaningful only with an informed public. How can we govern ourselves if we know not how we govern? Never was it more important . . . that the right of the people to know the actions of their government be secure."

Clark made it clear to all executive agencies that the FOIA "leaves no doubt that disclosure is a transcendent goal, yielding only to such compelling considerations as those provided for in the exemptions of the act." He advised agency heads that the law was "not wholly self-explanatory or self-executing" and its efficacy was therefore "heavily dependent on the sound judgment and faithful execution of those who direct and administer our agencies of Government."

Clark also expressed his "concerns" about the act, but they were diametrically opposed to those expressed by President Johnson. Clark's memo stated:

This law was initiated by Congress and signed by the President with several key concerns:

• that disclosures be the general rule, not the exception;
• that all individuals have equal rights of access;
• that the burden be on the Government to justify the withholding of a document, not on the person who requests it;
• that individuals improperly denied access to documents have a right to seek injunctive relief in the courts;
• that there be a change in Government policy and attitude.

It is important therefore that each agency of Government use this opportunity for critical self-analysis and close review. Indeed this law can have positive and beneficial influence on administration itself.[28]

In a recent interview, Clark capsulized the difference between his and the president's approaches. "The principle underlying FOIA which is essential to democracy and limitations on government power is expressed in the first three sentences of my forward," Clark revealed. "President Johnson's signing statement limited that principle by the phrase 'that the security of the nation permits.' I believed, and still do, that the security of the nation is far more threatened by secrecy than by disclosure."

Clark, who recently referred to the FOIA as "one of my loves," moved on from government service to public interest law, including FOIA litigation. Indeed, he would later argue the first FOIA case before the Supreme Court, *Mink v. EPA* (1973) (see Chapter 4).

Was there really a conflict between Attorney General Ramsey Clark and President Johnson over the FOIA? Clark recently told me that, in principle, Johnson shared his hopes for the FOIA. "Everything I knew about the man tells me that he favored the FOIA," he said. "Throughout his years in Congress, Johnson had such difficulty getting information out of the government that I'm sure he favored some kind of open records law. But during the passage of the FOIA he was very distracted by the Vietnam War, and I was being isolated because of my opposition to the war, which didn't help matters. For these reasons, my contact with the President became sporadic. His involvement with the FOIA was very limited, not because he wasn't supportive, but because he was distracted."

Clark then reflected, "You know, I don't even remember a signing ceremony. President Johnson loved signing ceremonies because he regarded them as milestones, but I don't remember one."

Clark was right, of course. And he had a good laugh when I told him of the *New York Times'* claim that the first information withheld under the FOIA was the White House statement on the Freedom of Information Act.

Though Clark was respectful in his recollection of President Johnson's role in the passage of the FOIA, he was explicit in describing the bureaucratic resistance to his request for full agency compliance with the statute. "It was an easy proposition for me," he said, "because I believed it was government's purpose to serve the people, not to hide things from them that they need to know. But it was difficult to convince the bureaucracy. I would say every agency opposed the FOIA, though they probably felt that they could manipulate it. I told the agencies to work hard at complying with the FOIA, but they were almost uniformly offended by the statute itself. They thought it implied that they weren't trusted and they feared that the FOIA would force them to work in a gold fish bowl, observed by the public."[29]

This initial agency suspicion produced bureaucratic intransigence and an early record of abominable government compliance with the FOIA.

STRENGTHENING THE FOIA

Despite its many inadequacies, America's FOIA is recognized worldwide as trailblazing legislation. It established for the first time the statutory right of *any* person to access government information. Consumer advocate Ralph Nader recently declared, "One way to look at it is, it's the best FOIA in the world, because, in effect, it gives private right of action. It gives the citizen the right to challenge the withholding of information and have judicial review. Most freedom of information acts in other countries have little or no judicial review."[30]

Initially, there was widespread public support for the FOIA and the philosophy of open government that spawned it, but because it was immediately opposed by the federal bureaucracy, the law did not really work. It contained no deadlines for compliance and no penalties for violation. Many federal agencies instituted crippling delays in compliance with requests, and others imposed high fees as a means of discouraging requestors.

Ralph Nader, a strong advocate of the FOIA, was perhaps the most vocal critic of the government's poor compliance with the act, but he did more than just carp on the sidelines. In 1969 Nader organized a group of 100 student aides, working in study groups coordinated by Nader, to visit federal agencies and analyze their compliance with the FOIA. Nader subsequently released a statement that said, "After three months of exploring the frontiers of the Freedom of Information policy of several federal agencies . . . I have reached a disturbing conclusion: government officials at all levels in many of these agencies have systematically and routinely violated both the purpose and specific provisions of the law. These violations have become so regular and cynical that they seriously block citizen understanding and participation in government. Thus the Act, designed to provide citizens with tools of disclosure, has been forged into a shield against citizen access."[31]

By 1972 the House Government Operations Subcommittee on Foreign Relations and Government Information, the successor to the old Moss subcommittee, concluded that the act had been hindered by five years of foot-dragging by the federal bureaucracy.

A Library of Congress study of the first four years of the FOIA revealed:

1. It took an average of thirty-three days for federal agencies to respond to requests for information under the act and many additional months for the requester to get the material when the answer to a request was "Yes."

2. Heavy fees were charged by the government to copy requested records. For example, the State Department charged $10 a page to copy a mimeographed pamphlet.

3. Individuals requesting records under the FOIA were required to provide massive detailed descriptions of the material they wanted before the agency would even process the request.

4. When a small piece of a file—a paragraph or page—qualified for withholding under one of the nine exemptions, agencies withheld the entire file.

5. Under the FOIA, the courts had no authority to review the secrecy judgments of the Pentagon.

6. Many agencies claimed that any information related to an investigation could be withheld forever, even if that investigation had long ago been closed or settled in court.

The many compromises negotiated with Department of Justice lawyers before the passage of the FOIA left it so vulnerable that even the courts were of little help. Indeed, in cases like *Mink v. EPA* (1973), the Supreme

Court expressed open exasperation with the FOIA as the justices reluctantly confirmed the government's right to arbitrarily withhold information under the statute (see Chapter 3). In response to the glaring inadequacies in the FOIA, a new House Information Subcommittee, chaired by Representative Bill Moorhead (D-Pa.), and the Senate's Administrative Practice and Procedure Subcommittee, chaired by Senator Edward Kennedy (D-Mass.), drafted legislation to ease restrictions on access and make the act a more workable tool of participatory democracy.

Thomas Susman, counsel on Senator Kennedy's subcommittee during this period, recalled the organized effort made to strengthen the FOIA. "One of the things that fell under my jurisdiction on the subcommittee was keeping up with freedom of information," said Susman. "It soon became quite clear that the FOIA wasn't working very well. The House had a series of oversight hearings that were quite good, and they led to a legislative effort. The Watergate scandals certainly helped mobilize public and congressional support for open government. There was no question that distrust of the FBI [Federal Bureau of Investigation] and doubts about the use of executive privilege contributed to popular support for the FOIA."

Organized lobbying was essential in building support for the proposed legislation. "Ralph Nader was a great spokesperson," said Susman. "People like Ron Plesser and Mark Lynch were lobbyists for Nader, and they were very effective. The ACLU [American Civil Liberties Union] was involved in the legislative side, and John Shattuck was very active. Various press groups, editors, publishers, and representatives from radio and television were very active and very effective."

Susman recalled the frenzied activity on Kennedy's subcommittee to come up with a bill that would fix the FOIA while maintaining the support of both houses of Congress. "I actually drafted the amendments on the Senate side," said Susman, "and we worked with staffers on the House side. We staff peons, we know our place. I did the writing, but Senator Kennedy was the one who spent the time and energy to get the legislation through and put his name on the line. It's interesting, the House began with very aggressive oversight of the FOIA, but when it came to writing legislation, we on the Senate side took the initiative. The teeth in the 1974 bill were Senate initiatives."[32]

An FOIA reform bill was introduced in the House in early 1973, and a companion bill was offered in the Senate. During hearings, no department or agency witness expressed support for the bill, but it was reported from committee in February 1974 and conferees were named to reconcile the differences between the House and Senate versions.

The proposed amendments were not a direct response to the growing Watergate scandal, but they gained more and more support as congressional investigators revealed the details of Watergate. While congressional conferees were deliberating on the House and Senate amendments to the FOIA, President Richard Nixon resigned in disgrace. Vice President Gerald Ford, succeeding to the presidency, communicated his unhappiness with the wording of the amendments, but the conferees pressed on and submitted their report for approval. On October 1, 1974, the Senate unanimously approved the conference report on the amendments by voice vote, and six days later the House registered an overwhelming bipartisan vote of 349 to 2 in favor of the amendments. The measure was promptly sent to the White House for President Ford's signature.

The president vetoed the legislation, citing his objections to the authority of the courts to inspect classified documents, the weakened confidentiality of law enforcement records, penalties for agency noncompliance, and the requirement that agencies meet specific time frames in processing FOIA requests. Ford concluded his veto message by declaring, "It is only my conviction that the bill as enrolled is unconstitutional and unworkable that would cause me to return the bill without my approval. I sincerely hope that this legislation which has come so far toward realizing its laudable goals, will be reenacted with the changes I propose and returned to me for signature during this session of Congress."[33]

Congress had no intention of enacting Ford's changes. On November 19, 1974, Representative Moorhead, chairman of the subcommittee that guided the 1974 amendment through the House, criticized Ford for following Nixon's Watergate strategy of using "national security" to cover his opposition to the public's right to know. "Such unwarranted and illogical action," said Moorhead on the House floor, "coming on the heels of the President's pledge to the American people of an 'open government,' forces us to recall all of the sordid happenings of his predecessor's administration that were first spawned and then covered up by abuses of Government secrecy. Excessive Government secrecy, whether to hide criminal action by Government officials or to prevent the public from knowing about embarrassing policy mistakes, has undermined the faith of millions of Americans in our governmental institutions."[34]

Moorhead declared that the FOIA amendments would contribute to truly open government, "badly needed as an antidote after the Watergate mess." He stated further, "If ever any veto deserved to be overriden . . . it is this one. The veto message itself is filled with missatements of fact, incoherent inaccuracies, legal mythology, and shows an amazing lack of understanding of the operation of the Federal judicial system and the Freedom of Information Law."[35]

Moorhead concluded, "Let our voices here today make clear to the doubting citizens of America that Congress, at least, is totally committed to the principle of 'open government.' By our voices to override this veto we can put the needed teeth in the freedom of information law to make it a viable tool to make open government a reality in America."[36]

On November 20, 1974, the House voted 371 to 31 to reject the president's veto. On the following day, the Senate voted 65 to 27 to override, an action characterized by Senate Kennedy as "a visible and concrete repudiation by Congress of both the traditional bureaucratic secrecy of the federal establishment and the special antimedia, antipublic, anti-Congress secrecy of the Nixon administration."[37]

Having acquired the two-thirds majority required to override the veto, the amendments became law and took effect on February 19, 1975.

The following improvements were made to the FOIA: agencies could now provide documents to requesters without charge or at reduced cost if the material was in the public interest; courts were allowed to conduct in camera review of contested materials to determine whether they were properly withheld; a judge could award attorney fees and litigation costs when a complainant had "substantially prevailed" in seeking records; a court could take notice of "arbitrary and capricious" withholding of documents and require an investigation to determine whether disciplinary action against agency officials was warranted; any record containing segregable portions of exempted material must be released after the necessary deletions; exemptions pertaining to classified information and law enforcement materials were narrowed; the definition of agencies covered by the FOIA was expanded and clarified; and specific response times were established for agency action on initial requests, appeals, and lawsuits.

Consumer advocate Ralph Nader's lobbying operations had been crucial to the override of President Ford's veto in the Senate, where the vote was 65 to 27, just three votes more than the two-thirds required. Nader had suggested a provision of the amendment requiring penalties to be imposed on government employees who violate the FOIA, and President Ford had cited the Nader provision as one of the reasons for his veto.

In a recent interview, Nader discussed his lobbying efforts on behalf of the FOIA amendments. "We were the main outside factor on Capitol Hill on this issue," said Nader. "The media liked the idea, but they weren't really lobbying on it. We had people from our Congress Watch organization, myself, Joan Claybrook, and others lobbying for it. We tried to take advantage of the Watergate reform atmosphere, which had put words like secrecy, coverup, hush money, etc. in the headlines. We pointed out to Congress that the culture of secrecy in the executive branch would taint the legislative branch as well by allowing abuses to fester, at which time Congress would be blamed along with the guilty department or agency.

"Still, the amendment was resisted in the White House and it was jeopardized in the Senate. We had a now-historic meeting with Senator Kennedy, and he agreed to play a very prominent role supporting the amendments and getting them through. He was a critical ally. Of course John Moss was essential, and Don Edwards was an important ally. Phil Burton was also a champion of FOIA. There were a lot of congressional allies, most of whom are gone now, and there were people from the consumer protection and environmental movements along with worker safety allies."[38]

FOIA allies had one more strengthening amendment up their sleeves. The government had been interpreting Exemption 3, which originally protected information "specifically exempted from disclosure by statute," as applying to statutes that simply gave agencies broad discretion over whether the information *could* be withheld. In 1976, when the Supreme Court's decision in *FAA Administrator v. Robertson* accepted the use of such discretionary statutes under Exemption 3, Congress passed an amendment to the FOIA to overcome the *Robertson* decision. Exemption 3 now authorizes nondisclosure of information "specifically exempted from disclosure by statute . . . provided that such statute (A) requires that the matters be withheld from the public in such a manner as to leave no discretion on the issue, or (B) establishes particular criteria for withholding or refers to particular types of matters to be withheld."[39]

Under the 1976 amendment, agencies could not withhold information simply because another statute gave them discretion to do so. If a statute did not specifically require them to deny information requested under the FOIA, agencies were obligated to release it.

REVERSE FOIA

From 1975 into the 1980s, there was an explosion of FOIA requests, due in part to the enactment of the 1974 and 1976 amendments, but also because of increased awareness of the usefulness of the FOIA by interest groups, individuals, and businesses. During 1975, FOIA requests quadrupled. Requests to the Food and Drug Administration (FDA) increased fivefold, typifying the growing use of the FOIA by businesses requesting information about other businesses. Ironically, the dramatic increase in corporate requests was accompanied by increased corporate concern over the kind and extent of business information being made public under the FOIA. Corporations began sueing the government to prevent the release of confidential business records to third parties. These suits came to be known as reverse-FOIA suits.

Corporations initiating reverse-FOIA suits cited the provisions of the FOIA itself, and often relied on the Trade Secrets Act and the Administrative Procedure Act as well. Through these suits, the federal courts, acting as a virtually independent force determining business-disclosure practices, decided whether to provide a requester with business information. Initially, the courts had relied on the House interpretation of the FOIA, exempting business information from disclosure if it was given to an agency in confidence. This "promise of confidentiality test" was soon abandoned by the courts on the grounds that it was too subjective. The new standard, based on the original Senate reports on the FOIA, became the "expectation of confidentiality test."

In 1979 the Supreme Court further clarified a different aspect of reverse-FOIA litigation. In *Chrysler v. Brown*, the Court decided that neither the Trade Secrets Act nor the Freedom of Information Act provided a legal basis for enjoining government agencies from disclosing information submitted by businesses. The FOIA, said the Court, was a disclosure statute, and unless Congress chose to amend it, the FOIA could not be used to prevent disclosure. The Trade Secrets Act, on the other hand, was ruled to be an appropriate statute under which the government could withhold information, but it did not constitute private grounds for corporate action against the government and hence could not be used in reverse-FOIA suits. In the wake of the *Chrysler* decision, the business community had only the Administrative Procedure Act to rely upon to enjoin government disclosure of confidential information.

In *National Parks and Conservation Association v. Morton* (1974), the D.C. Circuit Court of Appeals clarified the legal test for the confidentiality of business information, establishing that such information should be withheld if its disclosure would (1) impair the government's ability to obtain necessary information in the future or (2) cause substantial harm to the competitive position of the person from whom the information was obtained. That standard was modified later in *Critical Mass Energy Project v. Nuclear Regulatory Commission* (1992), a landmark case that significantly reduced the amount of business information available to the public.

In *Critical Mass*, the public interest group Public Citizen sought access to safety reports submitted to the Nuclear Regulatory Commission after the Three Mile Island nuclear power plant accident. In denying access to those reports, the D.C. Circuit Court distinguished between information submitted voluntarily to the government, as were the safety reports, and information submitted under regulatory requirements. If submission was mandatory, said the court, the information should be disclosed to the public unless it would cause substantial competitive harm to the company. However, the court allowed the government to withhold information that was voluntarily submitted, so long as the submitter did not customarily release it.

Political support for the reverse-FOIA cause has always rested primarily with Republicans in the White House and Congress. During the 1980s, President Ronald Reagan was particularly aggressive in advocating policies to protect the property rights of companies submitting business information. Toward that end, Attorney General William French Smith revoked the previous Department of Justice FOIA guidelines and replaced them with rules that would discourage the release of business information. At the same time, some members of Congress attempted to establish a legislative basis for reverse-FOIA suits. Senator Orin Hatch (R-Utah) introduced a bill that would guarantee anyone who submitted confidential business information both the right to notification and the opportunity to object to the release of the information. It also provided a judicial-review process that would give submitters the same de novo rights as information requesters. Similar bills in the House mandated predisclosure notification to submitters of information and provided a statutory basis for reverse-FOIA cases.

Congressional support for the business-related provisions of these proposed FOIA amendments gradually waned, overshadowed by a desire to strengthen agency authority to withhold law enforcement records. Under pressure from the FBI and the Central Intelligence Agency (CIA), Congress and the Reagan White House conducted a full-scale assault on the FOIA that submerged the issue of business confidentiality.

WEAKENING THE FOIA

Under the leadership of President Reagan, the tide turned dramatically against the public's right to know during the 1980s, and the FOIA suffered in the process. The CIA played a major role in drafting Reagan's 1982 Executive Order 12356, which eliminated the need for government agencies to consider the public's right to know when deciding whether to release information. It increased the ability of government agencies to withhold information under the "National Security" exemption [(b)(1)] and permitted officials to reclassify documents during the FOIA review process in order to deny requests for them. Executive appointees slowed the processing of FOIA requests while virtually eliminating releases of exempt material as a matter of government discretion. They also began to reduce the amount of information routinely disseminated by government and increased the cost of whatever information they released.

In March 1981, the CIA repeated an earlier request for a specific legislative exemption from all of the FOIA's disclosure provisions. Deputy CIA Director Max Hugel claimed that the FOIA hindered the agency's ability to perform its mission, but rarely produced any information of public interest. "While we do not question the principle that U.S. citizens should have the right to know what their government is doing and has done in the past," said Hugel, "we firmly believe that an exemption should be made in the case of the CIA."[40]

On May 4, 1981, Attorney General Smith announced that the Reagan administration had initiated a formal review of the FOIA to assess the need for legislative reform. He said that such a review was necessary because of the FOIA's administrative costs and its "impediments to effective government." At the same time, Smith rescinded the existing administrative guidelines governing FOIA suits. In the past, the Department of Justice defended in court only those FOIA denials in which the disclosure of information would be "demonstrably harmful" to the national interest. Now the government would be free to defend any and all agency denials in court.

The Reagan administration formally submitted its proposed FOIA amendments in October 1981. In testimony before Congress, CIA Director William Casey demanded that the files of the CIA, the Defense Intelligence Agency, and the National Security Agency be totally exempted from the FOIA. Among other changes proposed was an increase of fees to cover all costs for the processing of FOIA requests, including the salaries of officials reviewing documents, and limitations on judicial review of agency denials. Congressional opposition stalled the legislation, eventually focusing the proposed CIA exemption on operational files. CIA lawyers also compiled a list of twenty-three pending FOIA lawsuits against the agency that could be dismissed under the new legislation. The list included twelve actions that sought CIA files on the assassination of John F. Kennedy. These provisions to dismiss pending lawsuits became part of the House bill, sponsored by Representative Romano Mazzoli (D-Ky.), titled "The CIA Information Act, Legislation to Modify the Application of the Freedom of Information Act to the CIA."

On February 8, 1984, Representative Mazzoli held a little-reported hearing on the CIA Information Act, during which the CIA and the American Civil Liberties Union were the prominent voices. Mark Lynch of the ACLU testified, "[O]ur position on this bill is that if, in fact, it will not result in the loss of any meaningful information to the public, and if it will result in expedited processing, it will be a plus for the public, and it is something that we would support."[41]

Lynch was willing to accept the dismissal of some of the FOIA lawsuits against the CIA in order to help reduce the agency's FOIA backlog, but concern about imposing an ex post facto law caused Mazzoli to later remove that section of the bill. Mazzoli submitted his bill, H.R. 5164, to Congress on March 15, 1984, and on September 19 the House considered the CIA Information Act. Despite the CIA's claims that passage of H.R. 5164 would not deny any significant information to the public, some in the House had their doubts. Representative Theodore Weiss (D-N.Y.) pointed out that the FOIA had been responsible for revealing such CIA excesses as spying on Martin Luther King, Jr. and the Black Panthers, as well as the CIA's continued involvement with the National Student Association.

"Enactment of the CIA Information Act (H.R. 5164) . . . will make future discoveries of this nature and others that quickly come to mind more difficult—if not impossible," concluded Weiss. "Only a few months ago the CIA was caught withholding vital information from congressional Intelligence Committees regarding the mining of Nicaragua's harbors and at this very moment appears to have violated congressional prohibitions on transferring airplanes to the Contras for use over Nicaragua. I believe the CIA requires not less, but even closer oversight by the Congress, the courts, and the American people. I urge my colleagues to join me in voting against an unjustified increase in secrecy."[42]

Despite such warnings, the House passed H.R. 5164 by a vote of 369 to 36, and the bill moved on to the Senate, where Senator Barry Goldwater (R-Ariz.) spoke forcefully in its favor. "H.R. 5164 will effectively end a debilitating waste of resources without significantly diminishing the proper public release of information about the CIA," said Goldwater. "It will enable the CIA to respond more quickly and more efficiently to Freedom of Information Act requests. This legislation will also positively contribute to security in the conduct of intelligence activities."

Even Senator Patrick Leahy (D-Vt.), a strong FOIA supporter, accepted the CIA's assurances about H.R. 5164. "The Central Intelligence Agency will be relieved of the obligation to search and review its sensitive operational files, from which it almost never releases information in response to Freedom of Information Act requests," stated Leahy. "At the same time, relief from this obligation will enable the CIA to respond in a more timely way to FOIA requests not involving its operational files. Thus, both the CIA and the user of FOIA will benefit."[43]

On September 28, 1984, the Senate overwhelmingly passed the CIA Information Act, making a significant portion of the CIA's files fully exempt from the FOIA. The ACLU had explained its acceptance of the act on the basis of the need to moderate legislation that would have passed over its objections. Despite the CIA's earlier assurances that the legislation would not reduce the amount of information made available to the public, the CIA Information Act limited the power of FOIA litigation against the CIA as well as the authority of judges to conduct in camera inspection of CIA files.

The campaign to weaken the FOIA was not over. Having insulated the CIA from the FOIA, the Reagan administration sought to do the same for the FBI. Vice President George Bush formed the cabinet-level Task Force on Combatting Terrorism which made the FOIA one of its prominent targets. The task force issued a report recommending the repeal of the 1974 FOIA amendments on the grounds that terrorists might now be using the strengthened FOIA. "Members of terrorist groups may have used the Freedom of Information Act to identify FBI informants, frustrate FBI investigations, and tie up government resources in responding to requests," stated the report. "This would be a clear abuse of the Act that should be investigated by the Department of Justice and, if confirmed, addressed through legislation to close the loophole."[44]

The FBI soon proposed that the (b)(7) FOIA exemption [law enforcement investigative records] be rewritten to allow law enforcement agencies to have final say over the release of records. Under the proposed change, the scope of (b)(7) was to be vastly expanded to shield large segments of FBI records, including some political spying files, from FOIA access and judicial oversight. Under certain conditions, the FBI would be allowed to treat the records as not subject to the requirements of the FOIA. The proposal would also allow the FBI to conceal information supplied by state, local, foreign, and private agencies, which are themselves outside the range of congressional oversight, thus allowing the FBI to use surrogates to gather intelligence secretly.

In concert with conservative members of Congress, the FBI succeeded in drafting several bills to rewrite the FOIA comprehensively, but press and public interest groups worked to bottle them up in Congress. During 1981–1982, Senator Hatch repeatedly introduced FOIA amendments that were beaten back by liberal Democrats. John Podesta, who served as the Democrat's minority counsel on the Senate Subcommittee on the Constitution during this period, characterized the struggle to protect the FOIA against such amendments as "the most bruising FOIA battle of the last decade." Podesta described one amendment that Hatch worked out with the Justice Department. "If enacted," said Podesta, "it would have gutted the Act [FOIA]. I was serving as Counsel to Senator Leahy who took up the cause and attacked virtually every feature of the bill."

At Leahy's insistence, the Judiciary Committee reported a bill that amended every section of the Hatch bill, but Randy Rader, then counsel to Senator Hatch, had written a report on the bill prior to the Leahy changes. According to Podesta, "What followed was a six-month staff battle, filled with screaming, swearing (on my part only), table-thumping meetings, over how the draft had to be changed to fairly reflect the Committee bill. The result, Senate Report No. 97–690, was the shortest report in Senate history. . . . It said in total, 'The text of the bill speaks for itself.' "[45]

Indeed, of all the amendments proposed during the 1980s to weaken the FOIA, the only bill that was accompanied by an actual committee report was S. 774, and it never passed. Introduced by Hatch in 1984, S. 774 would have modified the language of Exemption 7 for law enforcement records, excluded informant records requested by a third party, and excluded records of an organized crime investigation generated within five years of the date of an FOIA request. The amendment failed to pass the 98th Congress, but its provisions were reintroduced in September

1986 when Hatch attached them to a bipartisan anti–drug abuse bill (S. 2878).

Senator Leahy succeeded in negotiating a floor amendment with Hatch that deleted the "organized crime records" provision, added "exclusions" for records related to certain classified investigations, and added provisions revising fee policies. Representative Glenn English (D-Okla.), chairman of the House subcommittee with jurisdiction over the FOIA, made several minor changes to the Senate-passed FOIA provisions on behalf of the House, and these were also accepted by the Senate.

As Congress rushed toward adjournment, both houses of Congress passed the FOIA amendments as part of the Anti–Drug Abuse Act of 1986. Members of Congress voted for the amendments without ever seeing a copy of what they were voting on. The new FOIA provisions which became effective on the date of enactment, October 27, 1986, applied to any request for records, whether or not made prior to that date.

Specific changes in the wording of Exemption 7 [law enforcement records] included the substitution of the broad phrase "records or information" for "investigatory records" as the threshold qualification for exemption from disclosure and the substitution of "could reasonably be expected to" for "would" as the standard for risk of harm. Such harm could now be considered with respect to "any individual" rather than only "law enforcement personnel." The meaning of "confidential source" was also expanded to include state, local, and foreign agencies, as well as private institutions.

In addition to the Exemption 7 changes, new "exclusions" were created giving limited authority to agencies to respond to a request without confirming the existence of the requested records. This was contrary to normal FOIA practice, which required an agency response stating whether there existed records relevant to the request, even when such records were exempt from disclosure. Under the new exclusions, agencies could treat three categories of exempt records as if they were not even subject to the FOIA. Requests for such records would produce an agency response that there were no disclosable records responsive to the request. Since these exclusions are applicable only to information that is otherwise exempt from disclosure, some FOIA supporters claim that they do not broaden the authority of an agency to withhold documents.

The first of these exclusions concerns records related to an ongoing and undisclosed criminal investigation, where the disclosure of the *existence* of such records could reasonably be expected to interfere with the investigation. The second exclusion applies to informant records maintained by a criminal law enforcement agency under the informant's name or personal identifier. The third exclusion applies to FBI records pertaining to foreign intelligence, counterintelligence, or international terrorism. Again, when the *existence* of such records is classified, they may now be treated as not subject to the requirements of the FOIA.

An important provision added to the 1986 amendments by FOIA supporters concerned fees and fee waivers. First, fees for records requested for commercial use were to be limited to reasonable charges for document search, duplication, and review. Only duplication costs would be charged for noncommercial requests from (a) educational or scientific institutions whose purpose is scholarly research or (b) representatives of the news media. A full waiver of fees would be granted if disclosure of the requested records is likely to contribute significantly to public understanding of the operations or activities of the government. Other minor changes in fees included general limitations on the amounts of fees and court review of waiver determinations.

The unusual circumstances surrounding the passage of the 1986 FOIA amendments left a considerable difference of opinion over its practical significance. The last minute deal between Senators Hatch and Leahy had significantly modified Hatch's original proposals. Further confusion resulted from the fact that Hatch had tacked the amendment onto the Anti–Drug Abuse Act of 1986 without hearings or press coverage, leaving Republicans and Democrats to argue over what had actually been accomplished. In the absence of hearings and committee reports, floor statements provided the only explanation of the purpose and effect of the FOIA changes.

In particular, there were conflicting interpretations of the new informant exclusion. The only relevant committee report was the three-year-old Senate Judiciary Committee report on S. 774, the early Hatch amendment from which the 1986 changes in Exemption 7 and the informant record exclusion were derived. In its report on S. 774, the Judiciary Committee had interpreted the earlier version of the informant exclusion to mean that agencies had no obligation to acknowledge the existence of such records in response to a request. Senator Leahy and Representative English interpreted the exclusion to authorize a "*Glomar* response": a refusal to confirm or deny the existence of the requested records. Senator Hatch, on the other hand, said the exclusion differed from the *Glomar* response in that agencies would invoke it without the specific knowledge of the requester.

Many legislators and lobbyists claimed that the 1986 amendments provided no substantive new withholding authority for federal agencies and that, overall, the press came out ahead because of the generous fee waivers. On the other hand, the FBI felt that most of its legislative demands had been met, and Attorney General Edwin Meese began advising FOIA supervisors throughout the government to "be mindful of the greater latitude" to withhold documents, some of which could be treated "as if they did not exist."[46] The Justice Department, the FBI, and Senator Hatch claimed that records on foreign intelligence, counterintelligence, and international terrorism were now outside the scope of the FOIA. If their interpretation proved correct, the amendment could inhibit the disclosure of the FBI's controversial domestic programs, a frightening possibility given the fact that only the FOIA had been able to expose domestic excesses like the bureau's notorious COINTELPRO program.[47]

Ultimately, the ambiguities in the 1986 amendment to the FOIA were left in the hands of the courts in case-by-case judgments. To date, the results are mixed, but some of the judgments have been disturbing. Three days after President Reagan signed the 1986 amendments, they were invoked to prevent further release of documents on Fred Wilkinson, head of the watchdog National Committee Against Repressive Legislation, who had sued for their release in 1980. The presiding judge in the Wilkinson case ruled that the relationship of an informant to the FBI can be kept secret forever, even after the informant's death. In another case, U.S. District Judge Thomas Flannery adopted the FBI's interpretation of the amendments when he cited "the newly amended statute and the broader category of information that is protectable" when he blocked the release of documents related to the assassination of President Kennedy.[48]

THE ELECTRONIC FOIA AMENDMENTS OF 1996

On September 17, 1996, the U.S. House of Representatives voted 402 to 0 to pass H.R. 3802, the Electronic Freedom of Information Act Amendments, popularly known as "E-FOIA." The following day, when the Senate voted overwhelmingly to pass the amendments, Senator Leahy, the major sponsor of the E-FOIA, said, "As the Federal government increasingly maintains its records in electronic form, we need to make sure that this information is available to citizens on the same basis as information in paper files. Enactment of the Electronic Freedom of Information amendments of 1996 will fulfill the promise first made thirty years ago in the FOIA that citizens have a right to know and a right to see the records the government collects with their tax dollars."[49]

Effective March 31, 1997, the E-FOIA mandated that agencies make certain previously requested records available without a request and that they provide indexes to help requesters formulate requests. The 1996 amendments confirmed that electronic records are subject to the FOIA and required agencies to honor requesters' preference for special formats. Agencies are also required to increase the amount of information available on-line. Finally, beginning in October 1997, the E-FOIA modified deadlines and procedures for the expedited processing of FOIA requests and encouraged the reduction of backlogs and delays.

Prior to the E-FOIA, agencies were required to publish some records and make others available in public reading rooms. Now, the materials that must be made available without a FOIA request have been expanded to include records previously requested under the FOIA and those that "have become or are likely to become the subject of subsequent requests for substantially the same records," if those records were created after November 1, 1996. Such frequently requested records must be made available for public inspection and copying at agency reading rooms and, effective November 1, 1997, in electronic reading rooms as well. Congress and the administration have a strong preference that agencies fulfill this requirement by making the records available over the Internet, but if an agency does not have the means to do so, it must employ some other electronic form.

Agencies are also required to make available a general index of previously released records that are likely to be requested in the future. In addition to assisting requesters, this requirement was intended to assist agencies in reducing processing time. The index will initially be available in regular agency reading rooms, but it must be available on-line by December 31, 1999. The E-FOIA also requires that agencies make available "reference guides" that would include: (1) an index of all major information systems of the agency, (2) a description of major information and record locator systems, and (3) a handbook for obtaining various types of agency information.

The E-FOIA amendments define "records" to include any information "maintained by an agency in any format, including an electronic format." Prior to the amendments, there were disputes over whether an agency could satisfy its obligations under the FOIA by providing a paper printout, even if the requester wanted access to the electronic format. Now, even if the agency does not maintain the record in the format desired by the requester, the agency is required to provide it in the desired format if it is "readily reproducible" from the agency's records. The E-FOIA also requires that agencies make "reasonable efforts to search for the records in electronic form or format." However, no such search is required if "such efforts would significantly interfere with the operation of the agency's information system."

If an agency claims that the records are not "readily reproducible" in the requested format, or if it fails to indicate the extent of redacted material on the grounds that it is not "technically feasible" to do so, the E-FOIA accords substantial weight to the agency's claim. This mandate to defer to the agency makes it difficult to challenge such agency determinations, although it does not require courts to accept the agency's claims if they are shown to be inaccurate.

Under the E-FOIA, agencies must expand the information in their annual reports to Congress and make these reports available to the public through a computer network or other electronic means. Agencies must report the number of days it takes them to process particular types of requests and must publish information regarding denials of requests, appeals, the statutes upon which information is withheld under exemption (b)(3), the number of backlogged requests, the amount of fees collected, and the funds and staffing devoted to processing FOIA requests. The attorney general and the director of the office of Management and Budget (OMB) were required to develop reporting guidelines for the annual reports by October 1, 1997, but the Justice Department interpreted E-FOIA to require that the first reports need not be filed until February 1, 1999.

One of the intentions of E-FOIA was to reduce agency delays in responding to FOIA requests by improving internal housekeeping efficiency. For example, E-FOIA encourages agencies to use computer technologies to redact information from records before release. However, this often makes it difficult for the requester to determine the amount of material that was withheld. Generally speaking, the delays in agency response to FOIA requests have been inherent in the labor-intensive nature of the work and the inadequate staffing and funding in FOIA offices. This had made the previous statutory requirement of ten-day turnaround time virtually meaningless, because agencies were permitted to ignore the limit on response time if they had substantial backlogs. The 1996 E-FOIA amendments double the ten-day limit, encourage agencies to employ better management systems to expedite processing, and prohibit agencies from relying on routine backlogs as a reason for delay.

Agencies are now required to promulgate regulations to authorize expedited processing of requests if the requester demonstrates a "compelling need" for a speedy response. The requester must show that expedition is appropriate because (1) failure to obtain the records within an expedited time frame could pose an imminent threat to an individual's life or physical safety or (2) the request is made "by a person primarily engaged in disseminating information" and the requester demonstrates "urgency to inform the public concerning actual or alleged Federal Government activity."

Even for requests that do not qualify for expedited processing, the E-FOIA amendments encourage "multi-track processing," through which small requests are processed separately from the larger ones. Agencies may offer requesters faster processing if they are willing to limit the scope of their requests.

Despite its provisions to expedite processing and reduce agency backlogs, the E-FOIA permits agencies in "unusual circumstances" to extend for a maximum of ten working days the twenty-day statutory time limit for response to an FOIA request. Agencies may invoke this extension only after notifying the requester in writing and only if the delay results from the volume of records requested, the need to collect records from multiple offices, or the need to consult other components of an agency. E-

FOIA specifies that if an agency fails to respond to an FOIA request within the initial twenty-day deadline or the ten-day extension, the requester may bring suit. However, if the agency shows that "exceptional circumstances" justified its original delay and that it is subsequently exercising "due diligence" in an effort to respond, the courts will almost always give the agency additional time.

Will Ferroggiaro, the FOIA coordinator at the National Security Archive, believes the Electronic FOIA amendments of 1996 have increased popular interest and professional support for the FOIA. "The changes in the law, along with Clinton's Executive Order on national security information, have encouraged the belief that the FOIA can be made to work better," he said. "The most immediate change that we have seen here at the National Security Archive is the tendency of agencies to process requests into queues. The simpler requests are processed a lot more quickly and come back in a shorter period of time. Public Citizen has just filed a lawsuit concerning agency compliance with the E-FOIA. They sued because many agencies haven't put their indexes and related materials on their Web sites yet. Many people were watching to see whether the agencies would meet their obligations and have such material up and ready to go as required. Few of them did, and even those were in shell-form."[50]

Indeed, FOIA watchdog groups like Public Citizen were quick to complain about spotty agency compliance with the requirements of the E-FOIA. In December 1997, Ralph Nader's Public Citizen organization brought suit, claiming that many agencies had failed to comply with statutory provisions, such as the obligation to post information about their records on the Internet. In early 1998, Mike Tankersley, the Public Citizen attorney primarily responsible for the suit, pointed out, "The lawsuit, filed on December 4, is to enforce the requirements of 552 (g) of the E-FOIA amendments, which requires agencies to prepare and make available to the public a handbook and descriptions of their major information systems. We've sued the Office of Management and Budget and a number of the more prominent cabinet department agencies for failing to comply with this requirement."

When Tankersley was asked to specify which agencies had failed to comply, he said, "Virtually everybody. There are a few that I would say are in substantial compliance, but many agencies don't have a handbook and about 90 percent haven't made available a comprehensive list of their major information systems."

Tankersley thinks the likelihood of success for his suit is high. "The requirements of the statute are unequivocal, and it's pretty clear that what the agencies have done so far doesn't comply with those requirements. Under the FOIA or the Administrative Procedure Act, there's not really any kind of penalty for failure to comply on time, but it will be a matter of setting deadlines for compliance with these requirements. The law gives the government 60 days to respond to the complaint."[51]

In April 1998, while Public Citizen's suit was still in its preliminary stages, the watchdog group OMB Watch issued a report characterizing government compliance with the E-FOIA as "overwhelmingly inadequate." After surveying eighty-four agencies and 136 government Web sites, OMB Watch concluded that, as of January 1, 1998, not one agency had met all of the E-FOIA requirements, and thirteen agencies had no E-FOIA presence at all. Even at the agencies attempting to comply, on-line information was "unorganized, unrelated and difficult to find."

OMB Watch blamed the poor agency compliance on the low priority placed on it by the agencies, inadequate congressional funding, and lack of guidance from the OMB, which is assigned by statute to assist federal agencies in implementing the E-FOIA. Indeed, some of OMB's advice was actually misleading and reflected "a pattern of apathy toward public access to government information."[52]

THE FOIA EXEMPTIONS AND THEIR LEGAL INTERPRETATIONS

The full text of the Freedom of Information Act is contained in Appendix 1 of this book, but a brief description of its disclosure requirements would be useful at this point. As amended in 1974, 1976, 1986, and 1996, the act contains six subsections, the first of which, subsection (a), establishes categories of information that the government must automatically disclose. Subsection (a)(1) requires publication in the Federal Register of descriptions of agency organizations, functions, procedures, substantive rules, and statements of general policy. Subsection (a)(2) specifies that materials such as final opinions in the adjudication of cases, specific policy statements, and certain administrative staff manuals must be made available for public inspection and copying. These materials, commonly referred to as "reading room" materials, are required to be indexed to facilitate public inspection.

The E-FOIA amendments of 1996, described above, expanded the definition of such materials and required some of them to be included in electronic reading rooms.

Subsection (a)(3) of the act makes all records not covered by (a)(1) and (a)(2) or exempted/excluded from disclosure by subsections (b) and (c), subject to disclosure upon an agency's receipt of a proper access request from any person.

Subsection (b), as amended, contains the nine basic exemptions from disclosure under the act, summarized as follows:

Exemption 1: *Matters specifically authorized by Executive Order to*

*be kept secret in the interest of national defense or foreign policy and
are properly classified pursuant to such an order.*

Exemption 1 of the FOIA is tied to the executive orders that define
national security information. Throughout the history of the FOIA, numerous litigants have challenged the government's classification of documents and have requested in camera review by the courts in order to
obtain disclosure. Nonetheless, the courts have usually upheld agency
classification decisions, according little weight to the opinions of persons
other than the agency classification authority.

Prior to 1986, no appellate court had ever upheld, on the merits of
the case, a decision to reject an agency's classification claim. In 1986 the
Court of Appeals for the Second Circuit upheld a district court disclosure
order, finding that the FBI had inadequately described the withheld documents and was unconvincing as to any potential harm that would result
from disclosure. The plaintiff subsequently withdrew his request for the
classified records in exchange for the government's agreement not to
seek to vacate the Second Circuit's opinion in the Supreme Court.

In 1995 the Court of Appeals for the Ninth Circuit affirmed a district
court disclosure order for classified information concerning the FBI's investigation of the free speech movement during the 1960s. The district
court grounded its decision on its belief that the information requested
was likely to have been public knowledge. Upon review, the Ninth Circuit
held that the government had not demonstrated why classification was
warranted. It rejected the FBI's argument that the lower court had failed
to show "substantial deference" to the government's classification decisions, declaring that "the FBI had failed to make an initial showing which
would justify [such] deference."

As agencies were increasingly compelled to submit in camera affidavits
justifying the withholding of documents under Exemption 1, they developed a response that refused to confirm or deny the existence of requested records. This came to be known as the *"Glomar* response," after
the court's acceptance in *Philippi v. CIA* (D.C. Cir. 1976) of the government's claim that even the confirmation or denial of the existence of
records pertaining to the *Glomar Explorer* submarine retrieval ship
would pose a threat to national security.

Exemption 2: *Matters related solely to the internal personnel rules
and practices of an agency.*

Exemption 2 of the FOIA has been interpreted by the courts to encompass two categories of information: internal matters of a relatively trivial
nature and more substantial internal matters whose disclosure would risk
circumvention of a legal requirement.

Exemption 3: *Matters specifically exempted from disclosure by statute, providing that such statute leaves no discretion on the issue or
establishes particular criteria or types of material for withholding.*

Exemption 3 of the FOIA originally covered only information "specifically exempted from disclosure by statute," but after the Supreme Court interpreted the exemption much more broadly in 1975, Congress amended the exemption in 1976 to narrow its application.

At one time, the question of whether the Privacy Act of 1974 could serve as an Exemption 3 statute was unsettled, but in 1984 Congress explicitly provided that the Privacy Act was not an Exemption 3 statute.

Exemption 4: *Trade secrets and commercial or financial information that is privileged or confidential.*

Exemption 4 of the FOIA has been interpreted by the Court of Appeals of the District of Columbia to overlap the Trade Secrets Act, a criminal statute. The court concluded that it need not attempt to define the outer limits of the Trade Secrets Act because the FOIA itself would provide authorization for the release of information falling outside the scope of any exemption.

Exemption 5: *Inter-agency or intra-agency communications which would not be available by law in litigation with the agency.*

Exemption 5 of the FOIA has been interpreted broadly by the Supreme Court to encompass both statutory privileges and those recognized by case law. Exemption 5, more than any other FOIA exemption, is at the very core of federal government operations, and it should not be invoked without a clear and compelling government need to do so.

Exemption 6: *Personnel and medical files and similar files the disclosure of which would constitute a clearly unwarranted invasion of personal privacy.*

Exemption 6 of the FOIA has been interpreted by the courts to cover the personal, intimate details of an individual's life, information which, if disclosed, might cause the individual involved personal distress or embarassment. Courts have regularly upheld the nondisclosure of information concerning marital status, legitimacy of children, welfare payments, family fights and reputation, medical details and conditions, date of birth, religious affiliation, citizenship data, social security numbers, criminal history records, sexual inclinations or associations, and financial status.

Exemption 7: *Records or information compiled for law enforcement purposes, when the revelation of such records could: (a) interfere with enforcement proceedings, (b) deprive a person of a right to fair trial or impartial adjudication, (c) constitute an unwarranted invasion of personal privacy, (d) disclose the identity of a confidential source or confidential information furnished by the confidential source, (e) disclose investigatory techniques or procedures for law enforcement investigations or prosecutions, (f) endanger the life or physical safety of law enforcement personnel.*

Exemption 7 of the FOIA was significantly broadened by the 1986 amendments to the FOIA, allowing the government greater authority to withhold law enforcement records. The exemption's original use of the phrase "investigatory files" was replaced with the extremely broad wording "records or information," and the original requirement that disclosure "would" cause harm was replaced with the phrase "could reasonably be expected to" cause harm.

Exemption 8: *Matters related to reports prepared by, on behalf of, or for the use of an agency responsible for the regulation or supervision of financial institutions.*

Exemption 8 of the FOIA has been interpreted by the courts to have two major purposes: (1) to protect the security of financial institutions by withholding from the public reports that contain frank evaluations of a bank's stability and (2) to promote cooperation and communication between employees and examiners. Given the breadth of this exemption and its purely institutional nature, there is good reason to expect significant numbers of discretionary disclosures by agencies under the "foreseeable harm" standard of the Clinton administration.

Exemption 9: *Geological and geophysical information and data, including maps, concerning wells.*

Exemption 9 of the FOIA has been rarely invoked by agencies or interpreted by the courts.

The nine FOIA exemptions define areas within which agencies *may* withhold information. These heavily wielded exemptions are not the FOIA's only barriers to the public's right to know. The weakening amendments of 1986 created three new "exclusions," described earlier, authorizing federal law enforcement agencies to treat records related to ongoing investigations, informants, foreign intelligence, counterintelligence, or international terrorism as not subject to the requirements of the FOIA.

These exclusions are not to be confused with the *Glomar* response described earlier. The exclusions produce a response to the requester that there exist no records responsive to the request, even when there are such records. A requester, if he were familiar with the exclusion mechanism, could seek review in an effort to pursue his suspicions and have a court determine whether an exclusion, if used, was appropriately employed. However, since the very purpose for the exclusions was to prevent a requester from learning that records exist, administrative appeal in cases where an exclusion *was* properly invoked will simply result in a statement that the appeal was without merit. Such responses are stated in a way that does not indicate whether an exclusion was in fact invoked.

Exclusion issues in court cases are handled similarly. Judicial review of a suspected exclusion is handled ex parte, and requesters are unable to determine whether an exclusion was employed.

THE PRIVACY ACT

The Privacy Act of 1974, which became effective on September 27, 1975, attempts to regulate the collection, maintenance, use, and dissemination of personal information by federal government agencies. The act was passed in great haste during the final week of the Ninty-Third Congress, and no conference committee was convened to reconcile differences in the House and Senate bills. Instead, staff members of the respective committees prepared the final version of the bill that was ultimately enacted. The act's limited legislative history, imprecise language, and outdated regulatory guidelines have made it difficult to apply, and even today numerous Privacy Act issues remain unresolved or unexplored.

Although the FOIA and the Privacy Act both establish procedures for gaining access to federal records, the FOIA is exclusively a disclosure statute, whereas the Privacy Act authorizes both information disclosure and protection. In 1974 Congress was concerned with curbing the government's illegal surveillance and investigation of individuals, including the activities that were exposed during the Watergate scandal. There was also concern with potential abuse of the government's rapidly growing use of computers to store and retrieve personal data. In this context, the Privacy Act sought to balance the government's need to maintain information about individuals with the rights of individuals to be protected against unwarranted invasion of their privacy from federal collection, maintenance, use, and disclosure of personal information about them.

The Privacy Act has four basic policy objectives: (1) to restrict *disclosure* of personally identifiable records maintained by agencies, (2) to grant individuals increased rights of *access* to agency records maintained on themselves, (3) to grant individuals the right to seek *amendment* of such records upon a showing that the records are not accurate, relevant, timely, or complete, and (4) to establish a code of *"fair information practices"* requiring agencies to comply with statutory norms for collection, maintenance, and dissemination of records.

Because the second objective of the Privacy Act overlaps the purposes of the FOIA, individuals requesting information about themselves under either act often specify *both* acts in their requests. Indeed, regardless of which statute is cited in a request, most federal agencies will automatically release requested information if it can be disclosed under either the FOIA or the Privacy Act. For this reason, and because the Privacy Act does not address the workings of our government in the way that the FOIA does, we have provided only a brief discussion of that act.

STATUTORY LIMITS TO THE RIGHT TO KNOW

We began this book by describing the constitutional origins of a citizen's right to know about the workings of government. We have seen that many of this nation's founders warned of the danger of attempting to specify the inherent rights of the people. Leaders like Alexander Hamilton opposed even the Bill of Rights on the grounds that the Constitution granted specific powers to the government, leaving *all* other rights to the people. To begin enumerating the rights of the people, Hamilton warned, whether through amendments to the Constitution or through specific statutes, would suggest that any right unspecified is denied to them.

Today's advocates of open government have not forsaken the constitutional rights of the people for an imperfect set of statutes. They maintain a fundamental belief in the citizen's right to know, beyond and independent of any freedom of information statute.

In a recent interview, Ralph Nader decried the poor implementation of the FOIA and affirmed his belief in the Constitutional right of American citizens to know about their government. "I think the right to know is implied in the right to petition," he said. "What good is the right to petition if citizens are kept ignorant of the kinds of government activity about which to petition?"[53]

Indeed, it was no coincidence that the Bill of Rights coupled the rights to freedom of speech and press with the rights to assemble and petition. Nader's view can be found in Supreme Court opinions dating back to the nineteenth century. In *U.S. v. Cruikshank* (1876), the Court interpreted the right of assembly and petition very broadly: "The right of the people peaceably to assemble for the purpose of petitioning Congress for a redress of grievances, *or for anything else connected with the powers or the duties of the national government*, is an attribute of national citizenship and as such under the protection of and guaranteed by the United States" (emphasis added).[54]

Will Ferrogiarro, FOIA coordinator for the National Security Archive, pointed out, "We assume the public has a right to know. We don't consider the FOIA to be the end all and be all of freedom of information. It's a tool, a useful tool, but our pursuit of information does not end with that statute. It's an access law fraught with all kinds of problems and difficulties, and it's at the mercy of the bureaucracy."[55]

Kate Martin, general counsel for the National Security Archive and director of the Center for National Security Studies (CNSS), believes that, even without the FOIA, Americans would still have a right to government information. "The right to know is included in the First Amendment protection for freedom of speech," she stated. "If you look at it functionally, perhaps the most basic purpose for protecting free speech is to encourage the informed citizenry necessary for a democracy, and information about the workings of their government is the most basic information necessary for an informed citizenry. In fact, international treaties, starting with the United Nations Declaration of Human Rights, explicitly acknowledge the right of free expression *and* the right to information as basic human rights. The United States is a party to these international treaties which recognize the right to know."

Martin pointed out that all of the freedom of information statutes, the FOIA, the Privacy Act, the government in the Sunshine Act, the Federal Advisory Committee Act, and so on were constitutionally based, but she acknowledged that people do not sue for information on the basis of the First Amendment. They sue under the statutes. Does that suggest that without the statutes, requests for government information would be unavailing, that the right to know does not exist without a statutory basis? Martin does not think so.

"The First Amendment wasn't really enforced by the courts until the late 1950s and early 1960s," said Martin, "the same period during which the FOIA was drafted and enacted. If there had not been a Freedom of Information Act, you would probably have seen the development of a body of law concerning the right to know about government activities. Today, people don't sue directly under the First Amendment for access to information because they don't have to."[56]

NOTES

1. 5 U.S.C. 22.

2. "We've Made a First Move to End Government Secrecy," *Saturday Evening Post*, December 27, 1958, p. 10.

3. Ibid.

4. John E. Moss, "Anti-Secrecy Law Is Hailed by Moss," *New York Times*, August 17, 1958, p. 66.

5. Thomas C. Hennings, Jr., "Constitutional Law: The People's Right to Know," *American Bar Association Journal* 45 (July 1959): 669.

6. White House press release, August 12, 1958, "Constitutional Law: The People's Right to Know," *American Bar Association Journal* 45 (July 1959): 667.

7. "Hennings Protests Information Policy," *New York Times*, February 2, 1959, p. 7.

8. 5 U.S.C. 1002.

9. Thomas C. Hennings, Jr., "Secrecy—Threat to Freedom," *Progressive*, April 1959, p. 23.

10. "President Urges Limits by Press," *New York Times*, April 28, 1961, p. 14.

11. "Press Is Divided on Kennedy Talk," *New York Times*, April 30, 1961, p. 68.

12. Ibid.

13. Ibid.

14. New York Times editorial, "Editorial Comment on Pentagon News 'Weaponry,' " *Aviation Week*, November 12, 1962, p. 156.

15. House Committee on the Judiciary, Fourteenth Report by the Committee on Government Operations, *Availability of Information from Federal Departments and Agencies (Progress of Study September 1961–December 1962)* (Washington, D.C.: U.S. Government Printing Office, 1963), pp. 9–10.

16. "Government and News," *New York Times*, December 15, 1962, p. 6.

17. Ibid.

18. Ibid.

19. Arthur Krock, "Mr. Kennedy's Management of the News," *Fortune*, March 1963, p. 82.

20. Hansen Baldwin, "Managed News: Our Peacetime Censorship," *Atlantic Monthly*, April 1963, p. 53.

21. "Newsmen Score Federal Secrecy," *New York Times*, November 27, 1960, p. 68.

22. *The Freedom of Information Act: A 25th Anniversary Retrospective* (Lynchburg, Va.: Access Reports, 1991), p. 3.

23. Sam Archibald, "The Early Years of the Freedom of Information Act—1955 to 1974," *PS: Political Science and Politics* (December 1993): 728.

24. Miles Beardsley Johnson, *The Government Secrecy Controversy* (New York: Vantage Press, 1967), p. 123.

25. George Kennedy, "How Americans Got Their Right to Know," *American Editor*, October 1996, p. 13.

26. Archibald, "The Early Years," p. 729.

27. U.S. Department of Justice, Ramsey Clark, Attorney General, *Attorney General's Memorandum on the Public Information Section of the Administrative Procedure Act* (Washington, D.C.: U.S. GPO, June 1967), p. II.

28. Ibid., pp. III–IV.

29. Ramsey Clark, telephone interview with author, May 14, 1998.

30. Ralph Nader, telephone interview with author, March 16, 1998.

31. Ralph Nader, "Freedom from Information: The Act and the Agencies," *Harvard Civil Rights–Civil Liberties Review* 5, no. 1 (1970): 2.

32. Thomas M. Susman, telephone interview with author, May, 5, 1998.

33. Peter Hernon, *Federal Information Policies in the 1980s*: Conflicts and Issues (Norwood, N.J.: Ablex Publishing, 1987), p. 61.

34. *Congressional Record*, House, Proceedings and Debates of the 93rd Cong., 2d sess., November 19, 1974, p. 36593.

35. Ibid., p. 36599.

36. *Congressional Record*, House, Proceedings and Debates of the 93rd Cong., 2d sess., November 20, 1974, p. 36624.

37. *Congressional Record*, Senate, Proceedings and Debates of the 93rd Cong., 2d sess., November 21, 1974, p. 36865.

38. Nader, telephone interview with author.

39. 5 U.S.C. 552.

40. House Permanent Select Committee on Intelligence, Subcommittee on Legislation, *Hearing on H.R. 5164, CIA Information Act, Legislation to Modify the Application of the Freedom of Information Act to the CIA*, 98th Cong., 2d sess., February 8, 1984, p. 2.

41. Ibid.

42. *Congressional Record*, House, Proceedings and Debates of the 98th Cong., 2d sess., September 19, 1984, p. H26059.

43. *Congressional Record*, Senate, Proceedings and Debates of the 98th Cong., 2d sess., September 28, 1984, pp. 27788–89.

44. *Public Report of the Vice President's Task Force on Combatting Terrorism* (Washington, D.C.: U.S. Government Printing Office, 1986), p. 26.

45. *The Freedom of Information Act: A 25th Anniversary Retrospective*, pp. 20–21.

46. Angus MacKenzie, *Secrets: The CIA's War at Home* (Berkeley: University of California Press, 1997), p. 150.

47. COINTELPRO was a secret and largely illegal FBI program begun in 1967 and discontinued in the early 1970s. It had two components: (1) COINTELPRO–New Left, which targeted people who opposed American involvement in the Vietnam War and related government policies; and (2) COINTELPRO–Black Nationalist, which was directed at civil rights organizations.

48. *Allen v. Department of Defense*, 658 F. Supp 15, 23 (D.D.C. 1986).

49. *Congressional Record*, Senate, Proceedings and Debates of the 104th Cong., 2d sess., September 18, 1996, p. S10894.

50. Will Ferroggiaro, telephone interview with author, May 19, 1998.

51. Mike Tankersley, telephone interview with author, April 22, 1998.

52. "Arming the People: Report on the Implementation of the EFOIA Amendments," OMB Watch Report, April 1998, available on Web site http://ombwatch.org/www/ombw/info/efoiareport.pdf.

53. Nader, telephone interview with author.

54. *U.S. v. Cruikshank*, 92 U.S. 542, 552 (1876).

55. Ferroggiaro, telephone interview with author.

56. Kate Martin, telephone interview with author, June 28, 1998.

CHAPTER 3

Government Compliance with the FOIA

EXECUTIVE RESISTANCE

It has been virtually a matter of principle for American presidents to op-pose the Freedom of Information Act (FOIA). Even Lyndon Johnson, who signed the FOIA into existence in 1966, buried his perfunctory paeons to open government under a mountain of cautionary criticism. This persis-tent executive hostility toward the FOIA derives from a constitutional concern about legislative encroachment upon the executive branch as well as a practical desire to protect the confidentiality of White House communications.

The farther down the executive chain of command one goes, the less obstinate is the opposition to the FOIA and the more likely that it is seen as an administrative law that requires compliance within the limits of staff time and resources. Among most FOIA officers, the individuals who pro-cess the requests and authorize the disclosures, there is, in fact, a genuine respect for the FOIA. Even some high-level White House officials have been FOIA advocates. Anthony Lake, former national security adviser for the Clinton administration, has also been associated with the National Security Archive, a private FOIA support group and archive of documents released under the act. During a recent conference appearance with Scott Armstrong, founder of the National Security Archive, Lake described his ambivalence about the FOIA. "I have been on both sides of this issue," he said. "When I was on the non-governmental side, it was as a board member of the National Security Archive when Scott was there. I was subsequently sued in my official capacity [at the White House] by the National Security Archive, so I've literally seen it from both sides.''

As a private citizen and author, Lake has made good use of the FOIA. With tongue in cheek, he recently gave an amusing description of his unique method of pressuring an intransigent agency to release material under the FOIA.

"I had an unusual experience with the Freedom of Information Act when I was working on a book on American policy toward Nicaragua," said Lake. "I had put in a number of requests that the Archive helped me with, and the only thing I received was a 500-page document in Spanish. I don't speak Spanish. I was charged for the document and xeroxing costs, and none of the material I really sought was released to me. So I wrote the book unencumbered by facts, and forgot about my FOIA requests. Five years later, just after I had joined the White House, I received a letter from the National Security Council Staff at the White House, stating that after going through all of my FOIA requests, they could now provide a final response: 'denied, denied, denied, denied, denied, denied,' and then two documents were provided which were almost completely blacked out. The accompanying letter said that if I wished to appeal this decision, I could write to the Executive Secretary of the National Security Council staff, stating my grounds for the appeal. I couldn't resist writing to the Executive Secretary saying, 'I hereby appeal your ruling and the grounds are that you work for me.' I was denied again, of course."[1]

No one, in or out of government, can deny the oppressive delays in agency response to FOIA requests, but this varies from agency to agency and is often due to the refusal of the executive branch to provide adequate funding and staffing for its FOIA sections. Indeed, there is considerable evidence that the career professionals overseeing the implementation of the FOIA in federal agencies have, for the most part, accepted the principle of the public's right to know. This attitude can be seen most clearly in the work of an association of FOIA professionals, within which agency bureaucrats and FOIA requesters work in close and amicable cooperation.

THE AMERICAN SOCIETY OF ACCESS PROFESSIONALS

The American Society of Access Professionals (ASAP) is an independent, educational, nonprofit association founded in 1980 by concerned federal government employees and private citizens working in the fields of information access through the Freedom of Information Act, the Privacy Act, and related statutes. ASAP is dedicated to bringing government FOIA and Privacy Act personnel into touch with the requester community, whether it be private citizens, law firms, businesses, nonprofit organizations, or the media. Its lengthy "Statement of Principles" begins by declaring that all "access professionals" have the responsibility to:

facilitate and advance effective methods, procedures, and techniques of administering statutes pertaining to the availability of records or information contained therein or open meetings;

promote improved liaison, communication, and education among persons whose positions require an understanding of such statutes, sometimes called "access laws" (i.e., freedom of information, privacy protection, sunshine, fair credit reporting, etc.);

enhance understanding and appreciation of principles of fair information practice;

promote and facilitate citizen observation of and participation in government decision-making through open official meetings or hearings; and

cooperate with government agencies, private organizations, and legislative committees in seeking creative solutions to problems inherent in such laws or legislative proposals.

The ASAP membership of more than 300 access professionals in the United States and Canada represents a wide cross-section of individuals in both public and private sectors who are concerned with the effective and responsible administration of access laws. About 85 percent of ASAP members work in federal agencies that are FOIA information providers; the other 15 percent represent the requester community. Virtually every major federal agency or one of its components is represented among the ASAP membership, although ASAP members serve as individuals, not as formal representatives of the agencies or organizations for which they work. The traditional adversarial relationship between the executive branch and FOIA advocates is not evident among ASAP professionals. They recognize that they are all players in a difficult game, not of their making, and that their joint efforts to clarify the ambiguity of the FOIA statute, the court opinions, and administrative guidelines can only improve things for all concerned.

The candid and cooperative working relationship between the members of ASAP derives in part from one of its cofounders, Russell Roberts, the legendary and outspoken former head of the FOIA division at the early Department of Health, Education and Welfare (HEW), later renamed Health and Human Services (HHS). In a recent interview, Roberts, now retired and living in South Carolina, described the contentious origins of ASAP in Washington, D.C. "The first thing I did," recalled Roberts, "was to call a meeting of FOIA specialists across town. I sent out memos asking that we get together in the [HHS] Department's auditorium to discuss the idea of an organization. The first issue that we had to face was whether we were going to limit our membership to agency FOIA

officers. There were those of us who felt that we shouldn't place any sort
of restriction on membership, that if we limited ourselves to agency FOIA
officers we would all be singing from the same sheet music about those
bad people who had the temerity to submit FOIA requests and take up
our time. Initially, the membership was exclusively agency people, but
soon the seven founders made the decision to open it up to the requester
community as well. It was the best thing that we ever did, because it gave
us a much broader perspective on things.''

In those early days, not every agency was anxious to join ASAP. "Today,
most of our members just want to make the law work," said Roberts,
"but in the beginning, outfits like the FBI [Federal Bureau of Investiga-
tion] and CIA [Central Intelligence Agency] refused to join. The Department of Justice initially explained their reluctance on the basis of ASAP's
heavy dependence on funding from their annual symposia and regional
seminars. They thought this was an inappropriate use of federal funds.
Justice eventually joined ASAP and even served on our board of directors,
but some other agencies were quite hostile. I don't know what the attitude these days is at IRS [Internal Revenue Service], but they were initially
so resentful of the statute itself that they couldn't accept working with
the requesters who forced them to give up records. Later, even the IRS
was well represented in ASAP, but never the Secret Service, FBI, CIA,
National Security Agency and those folks. They considered it anti-
American.''

Occasionally, Roberts organized ASAP programs that rubbed some
agency heads the wrong way. His choice of one luncheon speaker, Susan
B. Long, a professor at the John Marshall College of Law in New York,
caused a minor rebellion in ASAP's ranks. "She and her husband had
sued the IRS to obtain manuals and other materials, and though they
won all eleven of their lawsuits, they never got the first page," recalled
Roberts. "I brought her to speak to agency FOIA officers about the kinds
of problems she had with such a stiff-necked approach to administration
of the Freedom of Information Act, but there was great opposition. That
was the only luncheon speech that was boycotted. I mean, people stayed
away in droves. Of course, none of the people from IRS came. They just
didn't want to hear criticism of their administration of the statute."[2]

Such disputes became rare as ASAP's membership diversified. Indeed,
the last two ASAP presidents have been from public interest organizations, a portion of the requester community that had never before been
represented in the presidency. Two earlier presidents had come from the
commercial sector, and all others had been chosen from the government
sphere. Will Ferroggiaro, the current ASAP president, is the FOIA coordinator at the National Security Archive, and he regards ASAP's acceptance of leadership from the requester community as an encouraging
sign. "Certainly the public interest community sees ASAP as an important

vehicle to further openness within the agencies," he said. "They have found that this organization welcomes them, that the government employees are not bitter or antagonistic toward the people on the outside. ASAP has a titular presidency, but the board really functions in a collegial manner. The important point is that the membership, which is predominantly government people, accepts public interest people as legitimate colleagues with whom they are easily able to work."

When asked about the early friction in the organization, including the boycott described by Russell Roberts, Ferroggiaro said, "I haven't seen that sort of thing in the years that I have been involved. At a given symposium there are probably individuals who vote with their feet and don't attend a talk, but I've never heard of anything like a boycott or any organized disapproval. I think the organization has played a role in reducing that kind of antagonism. Our current board composition is about evenly split between agency people and requesters. At the training seminars and symposia there is a good airing of views, and people don't always agree, but I don't think it could be regarded in any way as a split. The requester community has especially come to see how things work on a day to day basis and, in a way, empathize with FOIA officers who are often not in a priority position within their agencies. Once you begin to see what happens on the inside, the picture becomes much more complex. It's also been helpful for government people to see that requesters can be much more reasonable when they are armed with information. The organization has helped to reduce suspicion on both sides."

Despite the increasingly collegial atmosphere of ASAP, some of the more secretive agencies are still reluctant to become formal members. "They attend conferences," said Ferroggiaro. "Some just come as government employees and don't indicate their agency affiliation. I know the CIA people today sign up for our programs as CIA. They're much more open about how they appear in such forums. But in my old membership directory, I don't see anyone listed under CIA or NSA [National Security Agency], for example. They may be concerned about revealing institutional affiliation, though that is not required."

Ferroggiaro was asked if he was aware of any discomfort among the members with the concept of freedom of information and open records statutes. "I would say that everyone accepts the FOIA as law and the need to make it work," he said. "If you're a member of this organization, you're a professional and you're inclined toward promulgation and implementation of the law. The ASAP membership is the cream of the crop of the federal information apparatus, and, either out of self-interest or in support of the agency's mission, they are there to fulfill the requirements of the law or of the current Executive Order. There are no loose cannons here. You just don't meet people like that. They work very much by the book, attempting, often under difficult circumstances, to live up to the requirements of the law and their agency regulations. Because they are forward-looking people, you won't see ideological battles in here. The kind of people who would attempt to subvert the FOIA are probably not going to join ASAP, because the organization serves the entire information process."[3]

AGENCY RESPONSIVENESS TO FOIA REQUESTS

Though the FOIA staff in federal agencies have generally embraced the letter and spirit of the FOIA, full compliance with the act is frustrated by underfunding and, in some agencies, by clear hostility at the policy level. A 1990 report prepared by the Society of Professional Journalists (SPJ) expressed the disappointment of the press with agency responsiveness. The report, based on questionnaires and interviews with journalist and nonjournalist users of the FOIA, concluded. "Together, the responses to these inquiries create a graphic mosaic of agencies routinely violating the FOIA, robbing the public of needed information and jeopardizing good government." Among the report's principal findings were: (1) Federal agencies consistently failed to meet the response times required by the statute; (2) Information was withheld, not because the law exempts it, but because it might embarrass government officials; (3) those charged with handling FOIA requests are often improperly or inadequately trained.[4]

The reporters who responded to the survey filed an average of ten FOIA requests per year, and 53 percent of them reported that the agency to which they had most recently submitted a request took more than thirty days to respond. Eighty-nine percent of these journalists said they would use the FOIA more often if requests were granted more quickly.

"I often call the Freedom of Information Act the 'Freedom to Delay Act,' " said Eric Nalder of the *Seattle Times*. "Using the Act often means that the government will take longer to send the information"[5]

Lloyd Pritchet, a reporter at *The Sun* in Bremerton, Washington, said he was still waiting to receive materials that he requested from the Department of Energy in 1988. "It's hellacious," he said. "The lady I talked to at the office said to me, 'You think you have it bad. One person has been waiting since 1883.' "[6]

Royal Calkins, an investigative reporter at the *Fresno Bee*, complained that agencies sometimes release documents to private individuals but deny them to the press in an attempt to avoid public revelations. He described one case in which the Department of Defense blacked out most of a document provided to him, but released the same document intact to a private individual. "I was amazed at what was deleted from the document that was sent to us," said Calkins. "I compared the two, and what they blacked out clearly didn't fit any of the FOIA exemptions. It was clear that the agency was trying to protect itself from political embarrassment."[7]

The SPJ study found that agency responses to the same or similar requests often varied within and among agencies. For example, information requested by a reporter from the *Detroit Free Press* was denied by the FBI and CIA but routinely provided by the Federal Aviation Administration. One television reporter described a request that was denied by the CIA but provided by the FBI. Reporters also complained that agencies treated mid-size and smaller news organizations less favorably than the larger organizations closer to Washington, D.C.

The society's study found that many journalists do not use the FOIA, in large part because the excessive delays render the requested information useless. "Generally, I avoid FOIA at all costs," said Royal Calkins. "I don't have a lifetime to wait."[8]

David Rossmiller, a staff writer for the *Phoenix Gazette*, declared, "Requesting information through the Freedom of Information Act is sometimes more trouble than it's worth. It's a far better thing for me to get information . . . by making friends within the agency."[9]

Many of the journalists who do use the act have been forced to devise strategies to bypass the bureaucratic delays. One frequently used strategy is to communicate directly with the FOIA officer handling the request. "We have to [call the officers] every couple of months to let them know that this information is important to us," said Natalie Phillips, a reporter for the *Colorado Springs Gazette Telegraph*. "Also, we want to keep them on their toes. I often find out that rules tend to change with the people."[10]

The journalists polled by the SPJ cited many causes for the delays they experienced, including loopholes in the FOIA, agency desire to protect government officials from embarrassment, inadequate training of FOI officers, and a first-in, first-out system that contributes to agency backlogs.

Since the publication of the SPJ report, there has been little improvement in agency delays. Journalist Terry Anderson has complained of his inability to acquire information for a book describing his experiences as a hostage of Islamic Jihad in Lebanon. Upon his release in 1991, Anderson attempted to assemble relevant government files through the use of the FOIA. "Like many others before me who have tried, I have found the Freedom of Information Act to be badly misnamed—a joke or an insult, I'm not sure which," wrote Anderson. "The Government has persistently refused me access to records and files about my capture and incarceration in Lebanon. Its lack of cooperation has been at times comical, at times unbelievable."

Anderson had sent FOIA requests to thirteen agencies requesting files on himself, his wife, two other hostages, and his captors, Islamic Jihad. Most agencies denied his requests on national security grounds, but Anderson's favorite response came when he asked the Drug Enforcement Agency (DEA) for information on his captors, nine terrorists cited by name. Anderson was informed that he would need to acquire a privacy waiver from the terrorists before the DEA could disclose information about them. Otherwise, said the DEA, disclosure would be an unwarranted invasion of the terrorists' privacy.

Shortly before publication of of his book, *Den of Thieves* (1993), Anderson wrote, "I've given up on getting any substantial information in time for my book. What I find more difficult to accept is that I may have to wait longer for my files than I did for my freedom."[11]

Author and reporter Steve Weinberg espressed similar complaints: "After 21 years of using the Freedom of Information Act as a newspaper reporter, magazine writer and book author, I continue to be incredulous at the delays. I have always believed, however vainly, that information is the backbone of a free society, and that the bureaucrats who collect that information are the public's servants rather than the public's masters. Yet it is the rare custodian of information who subscribes to that formula." Weinberg explained that FOIA staff often refuse to return telephone calls, fail to answer letters, and take months or years to perform tasks that should take hours or days. Still he concluded, "Despite all the frustrations, I refuse to be deterred from using the FOIA."[12]

Though critics complain that federal compliance with the FOIA leaves much to be desired, they agree that responsiveness varies dramatically from agency to agency. A comprehensive examination of the FOIA operations of all federal agencies would itself fill an entire book, and a large one at that, but we can review some significant departments and agencies that are representative of the mainstream and reveal the good and bad aspects of the information-providing function of our government. Toward that end we present in-depth interviews with FOIA staff members from the Department of Health and Human Services, its component Food and Drug Administration (FDA), the Department of Defense (DOD), and the Department of Justice (DOJ). We then conclude with an examination of the FOIA operations of three secret agencies: the FBI, CIA, and NSA.

The Department of Health and Human Services and the Department of Defense together represent more than half of the FOIA activity in the entire federal government, and those two departments are widely regarded as the federal government's most responsive agencies to FOIA requests. The Department of Justice ranks third among all federal departments in total FOIA requests processed, but more important, it provides an advisory and oversight function for the entire executive branch. The FBI, CIA, and NSA, who represent the dark face of government secrecy, are, of course, the FOIA bad boys.

THE DEPARTMENT OF HEALTH AND HUMAN SERVICES

The Department of Health and Human Services (HHS) administers the Public Health Service, the Food and Drug Administration, the Health Care Financing Administration, the Office of Human Development Services, the Social Security Administration, the National Institutes of Health, the Center for Disease Control, the Alcohol, Drug Abuse, and Mental Health Administration, the Office of Child Support Enforcement, and the Office of Community Services. A number of these functions had a long history before HHS, particularly under the Department of Health, Education and Welfare, which functioned from 1953 to 1980, and the earlier Federal Security Administration (1939–1953).

HEW was created in 1953 under reorganization legislation requested by President Dwight D. Eisenhower. The new HHS was established in 1980 with Patricia R. Harris as its first secretary. HHS regional offices are located in Boston, New York, Philadelphia, Atlanta, Chicago, Dallas, Kansas City, Denver, San Francisco, and Seattle. Its National Institutes of Health concentrate on individual problems, such as drug abuse, arthritis, cancer, lung ailments, and dental concerns. The Health Care Financing Administration, created in 1977, focuses on long-term care, including Medicare and Medicaid. The Center for Disease Control, established in Atlanta in 1973, is dedicated to both the prevention and control of disease.

The assistant secretary for public affairs administers all Freedom of Information Act and Privacy Act requests made to the department and is the secretary's principal public affairs adviser, reviewing and approving all departmental publications and communicating on behalf of the department with the public, special interest groups, news media, and other government agencies. Over the past decade or so, HHS, along with its various components, has handled more FOIA requests than any other federal agency, yet most requesters give it good marks. To explain this apparent success story, I interviewed three FOIA directors at HHS, covering the operation of that division from the passage of the FOIA in 1966 to the present.

Russell Roberts is the grand old man of FOIA. This outspoken, often hilarious champion of open government headed the FOIA division at HEW/HHS from 1969 until his retirement in 1989. He was the first full-time FOIA officer in the federal government, and he set the standard, not only for those who followed him at HHS, but for all other federal agencies as well. Upon his retirement, Roberts reaffirmed his FOIA philosophy: "The requester is *not* the enemy," he said, "and the most effective way to deal with FOIA requests is to bite the bullet, do the work and try to be helpful. . . . From the bureaucrat's perspective, the tendency too often is to be defensive and to deal with any FOI request—particularly from the media, but also from advocacy or watchdog organizations—as a worrisome, unnecessary burden."[13]

In early 1998, I asked Roberts to recall his days as FOIA officer for HHS. "I came to the old Department of Health, Education and Welfare (HEW), the predecessor to HHS, in 1963," he said. "I was a public affairs officer with a news reporter background (the *Washington Evening Star*), and I immediately ran afoul of the newly appointed Assistant Secretary for Public Affairs under HEW Secretary [Casper] Cap Weinberger. Republicans always thought that anyone who had been with the agency prior to their taking it over couldn't be a loyal Republican and therefore had to be disposed of as quickly as possible."

I asked Roberts how he managed to survive in such an atmosphere and eventually come to head HEW's FOIA division. "I had done some charitable work for about ten years," he explained, "through which I raised money, clothing and toys for inner city folks at Christmas time. I used to play Santa Claus, taking anywhere from two to three weeks of my annual leave to play that role. Elliot Richardson, Weinberger's predecessor as Secretary, had presented me with the first 'Volunteer Award' for such services, and I guess that helped to protect me. Also, the *NIH Record*, their in-house newsletter, did an article about me titled 'Santa Claus under Fire.' All of those things helped when the Assistant Secretary for Public Affairs shook his finger in my face and said, 'Your job is not safe.' "

Despite the protective cover that Roberts's community work provided him, the assistant secretary still wanted to fire him, so Roberts sought refuge at the National Institutes of Health (NIH). "I went out to NIH as a way to hide," said Roberts. "The Deputy Assistant Secretary, a fellow named Jim Holland from Alabama, had called me and said, 'Russ, we're going to want you to find another job.' They stripped me of all duties and took away my parking space. I went to the doctor at NIH and said, 'Doc, I need a place to hole up for a while.' He said, 'How long are you going to need?' I said, 'Another month.' He said, 'You've got it.' I had been accepted in a clinical study, so I stayed out there until the storm blew over."

When Roberts finally returned to HEW in Washington, his public affairs job had been taken over by a new man. Roberts wandered the halls, renewed acquaintances in the personnel office, and inquired about his rights as a civil servant. "By this time, the Freedom of Information Act was in existence," said Roberts, "but it was being administered part-time by someone, as something to do with his left hand. I met with Assistant Secretary Louis Helm, who was being pressured to get rid of me, and Jim Holland's deputy. It was a very friendly meeting, unlike the last one, at which Lou shook his finger in my face and threatened my job. The head of the personnel office had advised Helm, 'Don't screw with this guy, don't screw with Santa Claus. Find something for him to do.' So Lou said to me, 'Russ, I think this Freedom of Information Act is going to continue to grow. Would you be interested in taking it over full-time?' I said, 'Yeah, I'd be very interested in that,' so I became the government's first full-time Freedom of Information Officer."

Roberts's responsibilities included responding to all FOIA requests addressed to the Office of the Secretary of HEW and its components, including the Office of the Inspector General, and to oversee the response to requests submitted to the FDA, NIH, Social Security, the Welfare Administration, and other units of the department. Like FOIA directors today, Roberts had to use ingenuity to fund his operation. "I would resort to rhetoric when it came to budget time," he said. "I would say things like, 'Look, we're walking the razor's edge. We have an outstanding reputation as a responsive agency, but I don't know how long I can maintain that reputation.' " Roberts ended up with six staff members in addition to himself.

I asked Roberts when he decided to take a hands-on approach to the administration of the FOIA. "From the very beginning," he said. "I encouraged reporters and others to call me if they needed help figuring out what their rights were under the statute or in phrasing a request. I told them we didn't want to dump a truckload of stuff on them that they were not really interested in, and I suggested that we talk about the requests and see if we could focus them. We had broad requests from the tobacco industry, among others, asking for every document that related to smoking and health. I called them and said, 'Look, we've got a warehouse full of documents on that subject that we've been compiling over the years. I'm not going to stand in front of a photocopy machine to get it to you. You bring your own copying machine and plug it into our electricity and you can go from file to file to file, copying whatever you want."

The department never completely accepted the way Roberts administered the FOIA. "In a staff meeting," recalled Roberts, "one of the General Counsels told her lawyers that Russ Roberts would give away every piece of paper that the Department has. She didn't like me much, but, again, I was simply interpreting the statute accurately. When there was a question, I took it to a branch office in the General Counsel's office that specialized in administration of the FOIA and interpretation of legal issues. In fact, that branch head and I actually wrote the regulation implementing and administering the FOIA. I was able to get the Secretary to sign it, but OMB sent it back about three times saying it was not acceptable. OMB [Office of Management and Budget] said, 'You can't do it this way. Where's the legalese?' I told them we didn't want any damn legalese in it. We wanted it in plain English. It was meant to be understandable by the in-house administrators and the FOIA requesters. This was enough to make the people in Washington look at me like I was crazy. After OMB had sent it back the third time, I told them, 'I've been able to get the Secretary to sign it three times, and I'm not taking it back to him a fourth time to tell him you won't accept it.' "

Many FOIA officers have complained about the increased workload that came with the 1974 strengthening amendments. Not Roberts. "It increased my business," he said, "but it also broadened my authority. For that reason, I never believed that it made things more difficult for me."

On August 2, 1988, Roberts was asked to testify before the Senate Subcommittee on Technology and the Law, which was investigating agency compliance with the FOIA. The committee was concerned with the lack of responsiveness from the Justice Department, the FBI, and the CIA, so it summoned their FOIA officers as well as reporters and authors who had trouble dealing with those agencies. Roberts, on the other hand, was summoned to represent the *right* way to administer the FOIA.

"Senator Patrick Leahy (D-Vt.), the subcommittee chairman, had asked for my personal testimony on behalf of HHS," recalled Roberts, "rather than having an Assistant Secretary sent over, which was the way requests for testimony had been handled in the past. The CIA and FBI and so forth were the 'bad guys' and I was the knight in shining armor brought in as the alternative."

One of the witnesses from the media was the editor and publisher of Senator Leahy's small hometown newspaper, who had submitted FOIA requests to the CIA in an effort to learn about their practice of recruiting on college campuses. The CIA had refused to extend the FOIA's press benefits to the editor, claiming that he was not part of the working press. According to Roberts, "It was obvious that they didn't understand that on a small town newspaper the editor does the editorial page and often the news, so this man was obviously a member of the 'working press.' But the CIA told him that since he was not a representative of the news media, they would need $600 up front before they could even consider his FOIA request. The editor testified to all of this, and that didn't go over too well with the subcommittee. Senator Leahy then asked me how I would have responded to the same FOIA request. I said the first thing I would have done was to recognize simply from the letterhead and the signature block that this was a representative of the news media and should be so treated under that portion of the statute. And if I had any questions about it, I would have picked up the phone and called him. Leahy then shot back to the CIA representative, 'Did you ever think of that? Did you ever think of picking up the phone and talking to a requester?' "

Roberts says that after the hearings, Dick Huff, the codirector of the Justice Department's Office of Information and Policy, came to him and said, "You know Russ, we might be able to use that idea of yours about phone calls to clarify requests, because, as it is, we engage in long and expensive correspondence that could be avoided with a single phone call."

Russ Roberts left HHS and federal employment on July 1, 1989. "I assured myself that my successor would be the fellow who had been my deputy, Carl Coleman," said Roberts. "He died a year and a half ago from a heart attack. Carl's background was as a newspaper reporter and broadcaster, and he understood the need for effective administration of the Freedom of Information Act. Carl and I were not only philosophically attuned with respect to the Freedom of Information Act, but our personal relationship was that of best friends."[14]

Carl Coleman, Roberts's hand-picked successor at HHS, showed the same kind of hands-on approach to the FOIA as did his mentor. Coleman tried to tutor requesters on how to get the information they sought, whether through FOIA or other sources. In an interview in 1993, Coleman advised researchers, "Use your congressman or senator and their access to the Library of Congress. Certainly use newspaper morgues and congressional hearings. Make yourself familiar with the agency's FOIA regulations. Meet those regulations in any way you can. Be familiar with the law and demand your rights under the law. Push these agencies to the wall. Just the mere filing of a lawsuit will sometimes turn an agency around. Here at HHS, we honestly try to shove everything we can out the door."

Coleman described the process for handling requests under his administration at HHS. "First they are stamped in, the tracking process. Second, a case number is assigned on the computer. Information is then transferred to a folder. The folder file has significant events written on it, phone calls, dates, etc., the basic history of the processing. When the final letter of determination is sent out, we write CLOSED on the folder. If it is subsequently appealed, we will reopen it. Sometimes one of our FOIA specialists will respond in writing, sometimes we use the phone. Finally, if the program folks say the material can be released, we just let it go, because we're advocates for disclosure. We then decide whether to charge fees. Legitimate scholarly research would never have a problem with fee waiver if I'm administering the law correctly. Waivers of copying costs or reductions in fees are based on whether the public is going to benefit and it is not a commercial interest. Sometimes we will waive fees if we've taken a long time, or if we conclude, my God, this person has been through enough. If someone thinks they've been treated unfairly, or if I think we've been misunderstood, I try to reach them by phone."

Like Russ Roberts before him, Coleman would frequently call requesters to clarify their needs and see how much they really wanted. He also had suggestions for making request letters more effective. "To figure out where to send your letter, start with the U.S. Government Manual," he said. "It can take months for a FOIA request to go through channels if the letter is sent to the wrong agency. Also, use a little psychology in the request letter. Don't be arrogant. Treat people like human beings. Don't tell us what we already know, and don't make it sound like we're a bunch of dumb bureaucrats. Don't use 'legalese.' Be specific and direct in describing what you want. The more you can narrow it down, the better off you are. Requests should have clarity and meaningful detail. Include your phone number. Show us up front a contract for a book, etc., to get a fee waiver. Let us know if you have a deadline. It would speed things up."

The kinds of records that were most often withheld at HHS during Coleman's watch were matters of personal privacy, medical records, general counsel opinions, open investigative files, closed investigative files if privacy was involved, contracts, trade secrets, cost proposals, confidential commercial proposals, and so on. The most commonly invoked exemptions were Exemptions 4, 5, and 6. However, just because material was exempt from release under the FOIA did not necessarily mean that Coleman would withhold it. "Even if something is exempt," he said, "as a practical matter, if a requester makes a strong case for discretionary release, we may release it."[15]

When Carl Coleman retired in 1993, his successor as FOIA director, Ross Cirrincione, quickly demonstrated that he would continue in the tradition of Roberts and Coleman. In December 1997, I asked Cirrincione how HHS's enviable record of responsiveness to FOIA requesters had been established. "I think the credit for that has to go to one of my predecessors," he said, "a fellow named Russ Roberts, who was one of the first people to recognize that communication with the requester was an essential part of making this statute work. He would pick up the phone and call the requester and say, 'I'm sorry, we don't understand what you're looking for.' Or, 'What you've asked for is quite extensive. Can we help you focus your request so we can answer it more quickly and better satisfy your need?' He was very proactive in terms of bringing the requester into the process. He never looked at the requester as an antagonist or someone with whom he was engaged in a battle of wits to see who could outsmart the other. He took a very cooperative and outgoing approach to the whole business, and that has permeated this office for all of the years since he has been gone, and it's had a very positive effect on the rest of the Department and other parts of the federal government."

The administrative connection between Cirrincione's office and the other FOIA components of HHS, such as the FDA and the Health Care Financing Administration (HCFA), is quite loose. "We provide, if you will, the broad framework," he said. "We write the basic regulations, and we write them as broadly as we can, so that folks like Food and Drug and Health Care Financing can write their regulations to apply more specifically to their kinds of records. I think it would be presumptuous to say that I oversee their operations. I talk to them frequently. We meet, I try to communicate information about the Department of Justice's position on things. Of course, I make sure that they understand HHS policy. For example, we're going to meet soon on the format for the Electronic FOIA report which we will be doing in January 1999."

Cirrincione feels that the best FOIA officers come up through the program ranks. "I'm certainly not in the majority when I say I think FOIA officers should be program analysts rather than administrative specialists. They need to learn what can happen in a program environment. I worked as a program analyst in the Medicaid program where I came to understand the sensitivities of the states, the problems of the state legislatures, what happened when one state felt it was being treated differently from another state. It fine-tunes you to a whole series of things that, surprisingly, are important when you're doing this job."

I asked Cirrincione if he had trouble handling the heavy volume of FOIA requests at HHS. "Yes," he said emphatically. "We and all the components of HHS are overwhelmed with requests. The Health Care Financing Administration in Baltimore has on occasion gone as high as 60,000 FOIA requests in a year. It's a tremedous workload, but fortunately much of the requested material has been reviewed many times before, so large quantities of it can be released without further review. Whatever they do to this statute and whatever they do to the hardware, they're never going to change the fact that freedom of information is a labor intensive activity. Even when you get the fancy hardware that allows you to scan in the record and then read it and redact it electronically, you still need somebody to run the blasted machine. And you need somebody who understands both the statute and the nature of the work that the organization is involved in. We're not heavily budgeted at HHS. A lot of HHS's money is committed before we even get it, and we don't even have a budget line for FOIA."

Like his predecessors at HHS, Cirrincione had advice for requesters: "Any FOIA officer in the government will tell you that the more specific the request is, the easier it is for us and the more likely that you will get exactly what you want in a shorter period of time. Include a phone number in your letter so we can call, if necessary, to clarify your request. It never hurts to be courteous. Every agency gets its share of irate requesters, but they were usually angry before they submitted their request. In that sense, it's not the FOIA's problem, except that we all have to learn to be very thick-skinned and not take any of the comments personally."

The kinds of records that HHS tends to deny today under the FOIA are roughly the same as they were under Roberts and Coleman. "This agency has a very high level of sensitivity regarding personal privacy," said Cirrincione. "The Food and Drug Administration, of course, has a deep-seated concern about proprietary business information. Those are the areas that most often require withholding records. Whereas four or five years ago every agency did a fair amount of withholding under the deliberative process exemption, the Clinton and Reno memos in October 1993 have changed that somewhat. The memos have succeeded in getting more information out to people, and we can no longer categorically deny every draft of a document, which was pretty much the practice prior to the articulation of the openness policy. In the past, we would get a stack of three or four different versions of memoranda, all stamped 'DRAFT,' and we wouldn't even have to read them. We can still deny what's predecisional, but it's not as simple as before."

I asked Cirrincione if he considered the 1996 Electronic FOIA amendments to be good law. "In terms of clarity, enforceability, and so on, the FOIA itself was never good law," he said candidly. "It's a great concept. I've always believed in it and I love to remind people that it came out of the Federalist Papers, in which John Jay, Alexander Hamilton and James Madison articulated the idea that an informed constituency is necessary for the proper conduct of a representative form of democracy. It just took us 200 years to get around to putting that in the statutes. As far as the Electronic FOIA is concerned, I think it has blurred some traditional lines. In the effort to be proactive, they've put us in the position of being not just FOIA officers, who can focus on documents and the interpretation of the statute, but public affairs officers as well. There have been fears expressed about the Electronic FOIA, but so far most have proved to be groundless. The public has been reasonable when requesting electronic versions of documents, and more often than not they include the qualifying phrase 'if it is available.' "

Indeed, Cirrincione welcomes the electronic revolution and the use of the Internet. "Our 'Guide to Information Resources' on the HHS Home Page directs interested parties to the various FOIA, publication, and general information offices throughout the Department, as well as other Web sites," he explained. "I'm sure this has saved many people time and helped them get to the right source quickly. A lot of my work has been eased by the fact that the Departmental Appeals Board has gone electronic. This is a quasi-judicial organ which reviews decisions made regarding grants, monies made available to the states under our cooperative programs, things like that. Their records are public and have always been made readily available when requested, but now they're on the Net. So all I have to do when someone writes me requesting a particular Departmental Appeals Board decision is refer them to the Net, which is a lot easier than collecting the records, reading them and mailing them out."

As in the past, HHS frequently makes discretionary releases of requested material even though it may be exempted. "We may release exempted material if we believe no harm is done," says Cirrincione, "We would ask the program people if this is going to hurt someone or create a problem. If not, we'll usually let it go."[16]

THE FOOD AND DRUG ADMINISTRATION

Though the FDA is a component of the HHS, it is such a large and autonomous unit with such a high volume of FOIA requests that it deserves a separate discussion. The FDA traces its history back to President Abraham Lincoln's appointment of chemist Charles Wetherill to head the Chemical Division of the new U.S. Department of Agriculture in 1862. Within five years, Wetherill had begun investigating food adulteration. The modern era of the FDA began with the passage of the Food and Drugs Act of 1906, which the FDA's predecessor, the Bureau of Chemistry, was charged to uphold. That agency's name was changed to the Food, Drug, and Insecticide Administration in 1927 and to its current name in 1930, and though the 1906 law has long since been replaced, the FDA's core mission to protect the public health has remained intact since 1906.

The FDA was part of the U.S. Drug Administration (USDA) until 1940, when it was moved into the new Federal Security Agency (FSA) with other health agencies. When the FSA was dissolved, the FDA became part of the Department of Health, Education, and Welfare in 1953 and ultimately joined HHS in 1980. Today, the FDA oversees most food products other than meat and poultry, as well as human and animal drugs, biological medicines, medical devices, and radiation-emitting products for consumer or professional use, cosmetics, and animal feed.

The FDA's principal components are the Center for Drug Evaluation and Research, the Center for Biologics Evaluation and Research, the Center for Devices and Radiological Health, the Center for Food Safety and Applied Nutrition, the Center for Veterinary Medicine, the National Center for Toxicological Research, and the Office of Regulatory Affairs, which manages the five regional offices. Additional offices are devoted to legislative, health, public, and consumer affairs, planning and evaluation, and legal issues.

Ross Cirrincione, current head of the FOIA division at HHS, stated, "In a normal year the FDA handles 45,000 FOIA requests, and it can go up much higher than that. They use the technical expertise of their program people because the nature of their records requires someone who is steeped in the program activity to be able to understand what's being requested and to recognize what might do commercial harm to someone whose drug application is pending. The FDA is extremely sensitive to FOIA. They have been in the business a long time, and they make as much information available as possible and as quickly as possible, but they're always going to have a tremendous backlog because of the time it takes to review those drug applications. Once an application is filed, competitors are interested in knowing what's in it, so they will ask for whatever is releasable, often at about the same time that the agency is beginning to look at the application. Because that is a very lengthy process, there's usually nothing ready for FOIA review for quite some time."[17]

The FDA has FOIA offices in each of its centers. There is, however, a central FOI Staff Office which coordinates FOIA work in the agency. In a 1993 interview with Gerry Deighton, then head of the FDA's FOIA Staff Office, I discovered that the FDA took the same affirmative approach to the FOIA as did the HHS FOIA office. Deighton's office always worked with the requester to avoid sending a formal denial. They encouraged requesters to communicate, to make telephone calls, and to reach the right person. It made their jobs easier and ensured that the requesters received more records in a shorter period of time. Deighton added that most people were appreciative of their efforts to find the requested records.

When an FOIA request came into Deighton's office, it was almost always for a record not generally available to the public. His routine for processing requests went as follows: If the request came into one of the district offices or one of the centers, it was sent on to Deighton's office, logged in as an FOIA request, and assigned to whoever in the agency had the requested records. If the request was from a historian, it was sent to John Swann in the History Office, particularly if it involved older records. None of these requests had to mention the FOIA. They only had to request "records." If they simply asked for "information" and Deighton's office didn't think there were records responsive to that request, it would refer such requests to whatever part of the agency could best answer them.

Requests that were received by the FDA press office or called in to the general information number were usually referrred to the FOIA office. Most of the requesters were regular customers who knew what they wanted and what they were entitled to. For every request that Deighton received, he generated a printout showing who the requester was and what was requested. It was like a shopping list that was itself much in demand and frequently requested under the FOIA. Deighton said it was requested every day, either in hard copy or on computer disk, by a dozen different requesters, law firms, consultants, FOIA services, and so on.

Most of the requests that came to his office concerned topical and current health issues, such as silicone breast implants and Prozac. Very few requests were strictly historical, and those were usually funneled to the History Office. Deighton averaged over 40,000 requests a year, and less than 1 percent were historical.

When Gerry Deighton retired in 1996, his successor, Betty Dorsey, continued the tradition of hands-on FOIA service. In December 1997, I spoke with Les Weinstein, deputy director in Dorsey's FOI Staff Office. He advised, "If you are in doubt about how to word your request, call the FOIA office and say, 'This is the kind of information that I need, but I can't identify the specific document. Can you help me?' We welcome such calls. Together we can figure out how to phrase the request so that the agency can be as responsive as possible. Make your request as specific as possible, and try not to use phrases like 'any and all documents' regarding such and such. Eliminate those catch-all phrases, because you may end up having to pay for voluminous amounts of documents that you really don't need."

Weinstein described the kinds of requests most frequently received at the FDA. "The press represents only 14 percent of our requesters, while 34 percent come from industry," he said. "Those are usually commercial requests. About 28 percent of our requests come from what we refer to as 'FOI Service Companies,' who are probably acting on behalf of commercial requesters. Lawyers make up 20 percent of our requesters, private individuals 2 percent, public interest groups 1 percent, and 'others' 1 percent. Only written requests qualify as FOIA requests. If a FOIA request is attempted by phone, we will provide the individual with our address and ask them to mail the request to us. When we get requests for information, rather than records, we categorize them as 'general correspondence,' which are not tracked as FOIA requests. They are sent to whatever office in FDA could be most responsive to them. That could include, for example, the Office of Consumer Affairs or, if the question concerns policy, it could be sent to a policy office. In any case, it would be sent to an office that could sit down and write a response tailored to the request."

Like the FOIA officers at HHS, Weinstein had advice for requesters. "Number one," he said, "I would advise going to the Internet first. We have a home page now at www.fda.gov. Congress recently passed the Electronic Freedom of Information Act Amendments of 1996, which require, among other things, that agencies create what are called 'Electronic Reading Rooms.' These must be accessible on the Internet, if the agency has Internet access, or on some other electronic medium if they do not have Internet access. Agencies must place in their Electronic Reading Rooms all of their documents that have become 'frequently requested.' This is a new category of Reading Room documents that we determine have been or are likely to be frequently requested under the FOIA."

Weinstein said this new electronic access to government information was serving the public's right to know, but it was not yet clear whether it would result in a net increase or decrease in FOIA workload for the agencies. "The Electronic Reading Rooms made things more difficult for us initially because we had to involve a lot of people, including computer types, in our work in order to figure out what to get up on the Web and how to do it. But we're hopeful that, by putting a lot of information on the Web, we will reduce the number of individual FOIA requests we get, and I think that was the intent of Congress in passing these amendments. I'm not sure whether it will help us in the long run. Some agencies think that they have experienced an increase in the number of requests received, because people searching their Electronic Reading Rooms realize for the first time the extent and kind of documents available in that agency. So they file a FOIA request. Some agencies actually include a message on their Electronic Reading Room saying, 'If you would like to request some information, type your name here and submit your request electronically.' "

I asked Weinstein if FDA received many historical requests, rather than requests for current information. "I do know that we get a lot of requests that say, 'I'd like to see all of the inspection reports for such and such a company back to 1989,' for example, or 'all of the applications for a particular company back forever,' " he said. "But most of the purely historical requests go to the FDA's History Office."[18]

THE FDA HISTORY OFFICE

'The FDA's History Office is an important complementary component to its FOIA offices. Whereas requests to the FOIA offices deal primarily with current topics and short deadlines, the History Office deals overwhelming with scholarly research involving longer deadlines. Their informative booklet *Guide to Resources on the History of the Food and Drug Administration* is designed to familiarize researchers, policy makers, and the general public with information available in the agency as well as in public sources.

There is no direct administrative link between the FDA's FOI Staff Office and its History Office, but their functions are interconnected. The History Office is located administratively in the FDA's Office of Regulatory Affairs, but it has an agency-wide function.

"We basically exist to promote and interpret FDA history," said FDA historian John P. Swann. "We have a small office here with three full-time staff. We also have two part-time oral historians who do oral history interviews with agency employees who are retiring. Part of our mission is to encourage and promote an informed and accurate history of the Food and Drug Administration. We try to accomplish that in many ways, by researching, documenting and interpreting the history of the agency on our own, while doing what we can to assist those on the outside to do the same. One of our functions here is to search FOIA requests as public information officers, but we do a lot of general information work as well. We try to lead people to the right source to answer their questions. We handle a lot of phone queries that are totally outside of the FOIA process. When the queries are more involved and require the use of agency records, we ask them to submit a formal FOIA query. When we're dealing with a FOIA request, it's usually a combination of initial phone work and then correspondence. There's a lot of e-mail as well."

At FDA, virtually any FOIA request dealing with history is routed to the History Office. "Our office tends to deal with long term projects," said Swann, "with the scholar, the historian usually, researching subjects like drug approval, chloramphenacol, vitamins, Coca-Cola, etc. We try to work with the scholar as historian to historian to determine what is really needed and how the query can best be focused. FOIA kicks in for us when the information being requested really requires investigation into FDA records. Using all the knowledge we have of our records systems, we advise requesters to ask for particular types of records, and we advise the FOIA officers on what kinds of records would be appropriate to the request. People on the outside are often unaware of some of the best records for their particular research. I try to give them an appreciation of the variety of records available inside FDA, but I also inform them of published sources on the outside that are freely available to researchers. Most of the historical requests we receive are from graduate students working on their theses or dissertations or from established scholars working on books or papers. In the context of the FOIA, we do not generally deal with reporters, who are on much tighter deadlines. They usually work directly with the Press Office."

The History Office is not in the business of denying FOIA requests. "We do not typically handle decisions about what to withhold," said Swann. "We generally do not do the review work, the redacting and so on of the FOIA requests. That's still the responsibility of the FOIA Office, of Betty Dorsey's office, or of one of the other FOIA offices in the agency. For example, if someone is interested in looking at, say, sensitive information in a new drug application, I would work with the scholar in the field, but the decision to release or withhold that information would be made by the FOIA Office in the Center for Drugs. What is redacted is identified by law. They don't need our advice on what to redact. What they need our advice on is which records to pull for review, because the FOIA officers may not be aware of the existence of certain historical records. There have been cases in the past where a requester has filed a historical request without being aware of our office. After the fact, we may discover that the records received by that requester were not the most pertinent to his research question. That's the sort of thing that we would like to prevent, to make sure that the FOIA Officer in charge of that request is considering the most relevent records."

I asked Swann to mention some recent publications that made significant use of the FOIA through his office. "Historians don't usually write quickly," said Swann. "Everything is done very slowly and methodically. James Harvey Young has used a lot of our records. Harry Marks of Johns Hopkins University published a paper on cortisone that relied on our records. Thomas Maeder, a researcher in Philadelphia, published a book on the history of chloramphenicol, which made use of many records at the agency, including old establishment inspector's reports. There's another book that Princeton published a couple of years ago by Rima Apple, a historian at the University of Wisconsin at Madison. The book is titled *Vitamania*, and discusses food supplements. It utilized many agency records. All of these projects made good use of the FOIA, and as professional historians we made use of our familiarity with the records of the agency to advise these researchers on what to request through the FOIA."

The Internet has already affected Swann's operation. "We're on the Web," he said. "There's a history section on the FDA Web site, where we've put up things like brief biographies of the FDA commissioners, a selected bibliography, the milestones of food and drug law, and so on. Our office just did an organizational and functional history of the Center for Drugs, and that will go on the Center for Drugs Web site. We will eventually put our full Guide on the Web, with illustrations. We've already reached the point where virtually the first thing we tell callers is to check the Web site."

Swann was thoughtful in expressing his personal view of the FOIA. "I think the FOIA speaks for itself," he said. "The Freedom of Information Act was passed to let the people know more about how their government operates, and some agencies have been much more responsive to the Act than others. Even our agency generates complaints about responsiveness. People on the outside don't always understand how much the agency tries to work with requesters, and they may think the agency is simply trying to find ways to avoid revealing information. That's not consistent with what I've seen here. The FOIA is supposed to be an open records law, but from an agency point of view there are inherent conflicts in the law. I think this agency has historically done a very good job in interpreting that law and trying to work with requesters as much as possible. The FOIA has to coexist with other laws, such as the 1938 statute that explicitly prohibits divulging certain information about companies. The FDA has itself promulgated certain regulations prohibiting the identification of investigators. As a historian, I have an interest in getting information to the public, but I am also an employee of the Food and Drug Administration."[19]

THE DEPARTMENT OF DEFENSE

The Department of Defense is responsible for providing the military forces needed to deter war and protect the national security. The successor agency to the National Military Establishment, created by the National Security Act of 1947, the DOD was established as an executive department of the government by the National Security Act Amendments of 1949. The DOD, headed by the secretary of defense, is composed of the Office of the Secretary, the military departments and services, the chairman of the Joint Chiefs of Staff, the Joint Chiefs of Staff, the combatant commands, the defense agencies, the DOD field activities, and such other offices or activities as may be established by law or by the president or secretary of defense.

The Department of Defense and HHS together handle more FOIA requests than all of the rest of the federal government agencies put together. Due to its size and complexity, the DOD's FOIA program is decentralized among the several DOD components, which operate their own FOIA offices and respond directly to the public for their own records. The office of the Directorate for Freedom of Information and Security Review, under the direction of the assistant secretary of defense for public affairs, is responsible for responding to requests for records from the Office of the Secretary of Defense and the chairman of Joint Chiefs of Staff. Charlie Talbott, the directorate's FOIA staff specialist, handles those high-level FOIA requests and also provides oversight for DOD's entire FOIA program.

In January 1998, I asked Talbott why DOD consistently receives such a high volume of FOIA requests. "We're the largest organization in the government," he said. "That's the first reason. We're even larger than HHS. The second reason, I suspect, is that we're involved in everything that happens around the world."

I asked what kinds of people were submitting all those requests. "A lot of media," responded Talbott. "A lot of research groups, historians, and a lot of non-profit, watchdog-type groups who monitor government activities. We get a lot from law firms too, dealing in acquisition for contracting. You see, because DOD is so big, we have a tremendous contracting base which represents dollars to the outside community. We also receive a lot of FOIA requests from contractors trying to see each other's bids, that kind of activity."

DOD's FOIA office provides oversight for the department's various components. "We are decentralized into what we call 'defense components,'" Talbott explained, "and we've broken that out in certain ways. The three big ones, Army, Navy and Air Force, are all separate components, and we have separate defense agencies as well. They actually receive their own FOIA requests directly, answer them, take their own appeals, and defend themselves with Justice in litigation. As the largest service component, the Army receives the largest amount of requests. All DOD components perform their function under the aegis and oversight of this office and the regulations that we write. We have the FOIA policy oversight responsibility for the whole department, and, in addition, we process FOIA requests and appeals for the Office of the Secretary of Defense and the Chairman of the Joint Chiefs of Staff. This is all contained in DOD's FOIA Regulation, which may be found on the World Wide Web, [http://web7.whs.osd.mil/pdf/foi597.pdf.]."

Given the size and complexity of the Department of Defense, it is not unusual for FOIA requests intended for DOD components to come to Talbott's office. "They come in by mistake virtually every day," he stated. "We correct the address and ship them out to the appropriate component."

The kinds of FOIA requests most often denied by DOD are, predictably, those dealing with national security information. "Classified information is the most obvious exemption invoked at DOD," according to Talbott, "but there's a lot of 'deliberative process' material that gets taken out as well. There's also a lot of privacy information (b)(6), withheld, as well as a bit of Exemption 7 on the investigative side for the Inspector Generals. There's a small amount of (b)(3) for statutory exemptions and a lot of (b)(4) for contracting and proprietary concerns, because there is so much contracting done here. This office and the entire department actually use all of the exemptions except 8 and 9."

When I told Talbott about my intention to write about the salutory effect of the work of the ASAP on the use of the FOIA, he spoke approvingly of the organization and mentioned his own involvement. "I was on the board of directors for two years and served one year as president," he said. "I'm all for it. I think it does a good job. I encourage the people who work for me to go to the meetings and join the association, and they do. I believe that most FOIA staffs in most agencies take their responsibilities seriously and regard them as a public obligation. They do the best they can with what they've got. We all struggle with insufficient funds, insufficient staff, and too many requests to handle in a timely fashion. The people who run the daily mission programs in the agencies find it hard to devote the time to FOIA. These are the same old problems, and nothing has changed for the better. In fact, we're downsizing here, losing people, and that's a big problem. We've lost several people here who used to handle FOIA requests, and it's getting worse. At the same time, our work burden is at least as great as in the past, if not greater."

Given these continuing bureaucratic burdens, I wondered how Talbott's office, and the others, could get the work done. "We get slower," he said. "That's the irony of this whole situation. The 1996 Electronic FOIA amendments were designed to expedite the processing of requests, but these are labor intensive operations. Some agencies are getting money, but we're not. I doubt if we'll get any money, because we're so decentralized. There's no line item funding for FOIA here. We've taken personnel cuts, and reorganization of staffs may actually result in misplacement of documents."

I asked Talbott whether the 1996 Electronic FOIA amendments had significantly affected his operation. "Not a whole lot," he said. "For the most part, we were pretty much doing things as the new statute requires. We've known for a long time that electronic records are subject to the FOIA, so we haven't fought it. In fact, many of the changes in the statute were modeled on agency procedures. You can recognize them. We talked to the people who wrote the statute, and they listened, so it has been no sea change for us thus far. The only significant change over the earlier FOIA is that we have to take electronic FOIA requests now, but even that is no big deal. E-FOIA didn't actually require that, but it's a simple matter of logic that you can't say no."

Talbott frequently interacts with other agencies, or even private organizations, in an effort to meet the needs of requesters. He recalled that Scott Armstrong, founder of the National Security Archive, a private repository for declassified FOIA materials, once told him, "Some day you'll be sending people to me." Today Talbott admits, "We have been known to send people over to that organization, because they do have a vast repository of information there."

The various presidential libraries also work cooperatively with DOD on FOIA requests. "Requesters can FOIA the library and they will send documents to us for review," he said. "It will be a lot quicker. Mandatory classification review works that way too. You can simply go to a Presidential Library and ask for declassification of some of the presidential documents, and they'll send them to the appropriate agency for review."

Like all FOIA officers, Talbott had advice for requesters. "Be as specific as possible about what you want," he said, "and don't ask for the world. The ones who hurt us the most are the ones that say, 'Give us any and all records on. . . . ' That just sweeps in the world. You should also offer to pay if you are a paying customer. And a little courtesy never hurts. Be polite and you'll get politeness back. We've received some very nasty letters, and we try to stay above that. Being courteous, polite and professional is the key for our staff."[20]

THE DEPARTMENT OF JUSTICE

The Office of the Attorney General was established in 1789 to prosecute and conduct all federal suits in the Supreme Court and to provide advice to the government on questions of law. Not until 1870 did the Attorney General administer a Department of Justice. Today, the DOJ may be viewed as the largest law firm in the nation—one that represents the people in enforcing the law in the public interest. Through its thousands

of lawyers, investigators, and agents, the DOJ works to protect the public
from crime and subversion, ensure healthy business competition, safeguard the consumer, and enforce drug and immigration laws. The attorney general supervises and directs these activities and those of the U.S.
attorneys and marshals throughout the country.

Because the Department of Justice is the lead agency on FOI implementation, it maintains the FOIA Counselor Service to advise all executive
agencies on the wide variety of unique FOIA issues. The counselor hotline
was provided by the DOJ to assist agencies in resolving FOIA problems
that they have been unable to resolve in consultation with their own FOIA
officers. In addition to advising agencies on particular problems, the
Counselor Service provides guidance on FOIA case law and the "Openness initiative" that originated in 1993 with a series of memos from Attorney General Janet Reno and President Bill Clinton.

The Office of Information and Privacy (OIP) in the Department of Justice has an umbrella function similar to that of the offices headed by
Charlie Talbott in the DOD and Ross Cirrincione in HHS, but the OIP's
responsibility is even broader, including advice and counsel to the entire
executive branch. In my conversations with various people at the OIP,
their support for Attorney General Janet Reno was clear. She was described as open and approachable, someone who was down in the caf-
eteria without an entourage during her first week on the job, talking to
people and listening to them. This respect for the attorney general was
particularly significant for the FOIA personnel, who were expected to
embrace her openness initiative, which asked FOIA personnel in all agencies to make greater efforts to release information to the public.

Ironically, though the Justice Department issued the regulations encouraging greater openness in government, its own responsiveness has
received mixed reviews from the FOIA community. In my recent conver-
sation with Peggy Irving, deputy director of the Department of Justice's
Office of Information and Privacy, I asked whether the FOIA personnel
in Justice had the same commitment to full compliance with the FOIA
that was described by Talbott and Cirrincione in Defense and HHS. "Absolutely," said Irving. "It's in their nature. You'll see that when you talk
to people like Charlene Thomas, for example. They believe in the idea
that the public should be informed, and they work very hard with the
requester community to make sure that they meet their needs. Charlene
has received countless letters thanking her for her assistance. Many are
from media types. One was a Canadian author, who praised her for her
cordiality throughout a complex process."

Some critics of the FOIA have charged that President Clinton's much
publicized openness initiative has been unable to turn around the bureaucratic behavior established by twelve years of Reagan-Bush restrictive
information policies. Irving disagreed. "I see nothing to characterize

these FOIA professionals as being partisan either way," she said. "They're professional careerists, and whatever the policy is, they will administer it. It's not their job to make political decisions, and I think they're very comfortable with the Attorney General's guidelines."

Like other FOIA officers, Irving admitted that the OIP's resources were often inadequate to meet its administrative needs. "We're short on staff and funding," she said, "but that's reflective of the entire government. Part of the problem is, FOIA work is a very labor intensive process. For example, in our office when we examine a requested document it is rare that we are not required to sit down and talk to the author of that document and find out their views regarding disclosure. So, by its very nature, it takes time, even if you had a lot of staff. We're inundated with FOIA requests that require us to examine voluminous records or to search multiple offices or records. One such FOIA request can, on its own, hold up many, many other requests behind it. One of the things that the E-FOIA contemplated was to separate such requests and place them on a slower track, allowing us to proceed with another track for the so-called quick hits. But at some point you still have to process the bigger cases. Those types of cases are particularly frustrating, requiring a lot of communication with the requesters. The process of 'opening up the bureaucracy' for requesters goes a long way in reducing the number and scope of these requests, but they continue to play a major role in preventing us from responding in a timely fashion. I would say such requests are more responsible for our backlogs than the shortage of staff."

There have been complaints from the FOIA community about the DOJ's inadequate follow-through on the Clinton-Reno openness initiative, but Irving sees no lack of support from her staff. "I've not seen a problem," she said, "but I'm in a difficult position to answer that question. When I talk to people, I'm speaking on behalf of the senior offices. So when I say, 'This is what the Attorney General wants,' it's hard for me to imagine a person being so foolish as to tell me, 'I really don't like this policy.' Having said that, I can tell you that I have seen no opposition. Quite the opposite. I'll give you one example. The Criminal Division, which deals with criminal law enforcement matters, is very comfortable dealing with the policy of discretionary disclosures. They look at the records, and they really do say to themselves, 'Would a harm occur if we release this?' They are accepting disclosures of attorney work product, deliberative process, and they are making attempts to be clean and clear in withholding information relating to a confidential source. That's the way the paper work is coming to me, and it suggests that they have no problem with the Attorney General's guidelines."[21]

Charlene Thomas, chief of the Initial Request Unit in the Office of Information and Privacy, compared the OIP with offices like Charlie Talbott's in the DOD and Ross Cirrincione's in HHS. "Our office's function is a little different from theirs," she said, "because the OIP is responsible for ensuring compliance and providing guidance and counsel throughout the entire Executive Branch, including, for example, HHS and DOD. Of course, within the Department of Justice, we have the role of providing that guidance and counsel to each of the components. The DOJ has a decentralized FOIA processing operation. The Office of Information and Privacy has a dual function. It responds to FOIA requests on behalf of several of the leadership offices, such as the Offices of the Attorney General and Deputy Attorney General, but the OIP primarily adjudicates administrative appeals on behalf of departmental components."

Thomas explained that the DOJ places a heavy emphasis on training FOIA staff. "We try to train all of our employees to be responsive," she said. "We know what it's like to call an organization and get passed from one person to another. By the time you reach the right person, you're not a happy camper. We send out acknowledgement letters as soon as we can. We try to provide the information the requester is seeking within the required 20-day time limit, but if we can't provide the information, at least we try to get a letter out providing our phone number, our fax number, and the statement, 'If you have any questions, give us a call.' Often we will call the requester on our own. We've actually tried to get the phone numbers of requesters through directory assistance so that we can talk to them as soon as possible. We try to help them frame the request. It makes it easier for us to clarify the search parameters, so we don't consider it an extra step."

I asked whether an information request that fails to cite the FOIA would be returned for resubmission if the statute was required for the release of the requested records. "Oh no," said Thomas. "We would not do that. I receive a lot of letters that don't cite the FOIA, but I process them as FOIA requests because they would have greater access to the information under the FOIA. When we acknowledge such requests, we say that we're interpreting them to be FOIA requests under 5 U.S.C. 552. I've never had someone call back and say, 'Oh no, please don't do that.' "

Thomas has mixed feelings about the effect of the Electronic FOIA legislation. "I certainly welcome its automation aspects, including the requirement that agencies devote time and resources to updating a lot of the government computer systems. I also appreciate the increase in the amount of time provided to agencies for processing requests, but, still, we've only been able to handle between approximately 40 to 60 percent of our requests within the statutory time limit. The fact that a requester may immediately sue if a request is not processed within the time limit forces us to litigate, which also slows up the process."

I wondered if the E-FOIA had actually increased her workload. "It's hard to say," answered Thomas. "The increase in work load includes getting staff up to speed, comprehending the new requirements and explaining them to the staff and the requesters, getting regulations published and getting them online. So there's going to be some lost time in preparing for implementation. All of this is a good thing, but, in terms of reducing backlogs, you can't process a request and put information online at the same time. There's a lot to do in a short period of time, but the staff is getting it done. Indeed, their commitment to the FOIA is even stronger because of the attention being given to it."

Like Peggy Irving, Thomas saw positive results from the openness initiative of Janet Reno and President Clinton. "It's had a great impact on us," she said, "because the Office of Information and Privacy has such a broad responsibility for FOIA administration. We have disseminated subsequent memoranda instructing DOJ components to grant discretionary disclosures whenever possible. There's also been an effect on the performance appraisal system because the Attorney General has added a new element to the appraisals of all officials who have any dealings with the FOIA. The timeliness within which they respond to FOIA matters, whether it be with respect to record searches or making final determinations, is something on which they are evaluated. So the impact has been great and I see full compliance."

Thomas saw little difficulty in reversing the restrictive policies of the Reagan and Bush administrations. "I believe the bureaucracy has made the change," she said. "I think the bureaucratic structure is layered with professionals who simply want some clear direction, and that's what Attorney General Reno's memorandum provided. Many folks here in the FOIA office have been in FOIA work through many administrations, and they're very flexible."

I asked Thomas whether the requester community had noticed an improvement in FOIA policy. "All I can say is that this office always seems to want to argue for disclosure," she said. "The big difference made by the Attorney General's memo is that now we can argue for disclosure, even when there is an exemption present. We can say to agency officials, 'Yes, the document clearly falls within this exemption, but we can't articulate the foreseeable harm.' "

When I inquired about the FOIA policies of the FBI, Thomas suggested that a representative of the bureau's FOIA office would be better able to speak on that matter. She did say, however, that even the FBI had been affected by the openness initiative of the Clinton administration. "For example," she said, "I've noticed in processing paper for the FBI that if there was a document that involved FBI and Attorney General information, the FBI's analysts have been disclosure-oriented."[22]

THE FEDERAL BUREAU OF INVESTIGATION

Up to this point, our survey of agency responsiveness has relied on the voices of agency FOIA officers. The following examination of the three traditionally secretive agencies—the Federal Bureau of Investigation, the Central Intelligence Agency, and the National Security Agency—is based primarily on the views of their critics.

Charlene Thomas at the Department of Justice may have been correct in characterizing FBI FOIA analysts as "disclosure-oriented," but complaints from the requester community are directed primarily at the FBI's information policies, not at its FOIA staff. The FBI maintains its own FOIA office, and though the DOJ's Office of Information and Privacy provides loose oversight, the bureau's FOIA practices appear to be unique and independent. Harry Hammitt, editor of *Access Reports*, the premier FOIA journal, said recently, "The FBI has more serious FOIA problems than virtually any other federal agency."[23] Those problems, which include extraordinarily long processing times for FOIA requests, derive from the bureau's historic opposition to the FOIA.

The origins of the FBI date back to 1908, when Congress banned the standard Department of Justice practice of using part-time Pinkerton agents or Secret Service agents as its law enforcement officers. In response, the DOJ hired nine former Secret Service agents on a permanent basis, and the Bureau of Investigation (BI) was born. Renamed the Federal Bureau of Investigation in 1935, the bureau today has responsibility for investigating all violations of federal law, except those that have been assigned to another federal agency. Its jurisdiction covers a broad range of the criminal, civil, and security fields, but priority has been assigned to six areas: organized crime, drugs, counterterrorism, white-collar crime, foreign counterintelligence, and violent crime.

During the Cold War, Congress mandated FBI investigations as part of a massive federal employment security system, which eventually led the bureau to conduct general intelligence investigations on subversive individuals or organizations that had committed no crimes. Such investigations were predicated on presidential directives, which were often secret. The FBI, acting as the intelligence arm of the White House, has also provided personal information about the administration's critics.

The FBI has always vigorously opposed congressional attempts to provide public access to its records. When the Administrative Procedure Act of 1946 threatened the FBI's absolute control over any information leaving the bureau, FBI officials convinced Assistant Attorney General S. A. Andretta that any rules governing compliance with the new legislation should follow Departmental Order 3229 of May 2, 1939, which states, "All official records of the FBI are regarded as confidential and cannot be disclosed except on the authority of the Attorney General, the Assistant to the Attorney General, or an Assistant Attorney General acting for him."[24]

During the late 1950s, as Congress began to work on the comprehensive amendments that led to the Freedom of Information Act, FBI Assistant Director John Mohr recommended that, should legislation be passed, the FBI's congressional liaison should "take steps to have all the Bureau's records exempted" from its provisions. FBI Director J. Edgar Hoover told Deputy Attorney General William Rogers that "all of the records and files of this Bureau are confidential and must be protected."[25] As congressional support for the FOIA grew, Hoover protested that the proposed national security and law enforcement exemptions were "by no means so comprehensive and clear as to give this Bureau all the protection which it needs, and that this fact, taken with the philosophy of the bill that information not clearly protected must be made publicly available, suggests the possibility of problems arising in a number of areas."[26]

After the passage of the FOIA in 1966, Hoover advised National Archives officials that the new statute should have no effect on restrictions against access to FBI data in records under National Archives control unless cleared with the bureau. During the 1970s, as Congress began to work on the FOIA amendments to increase access to the records of federal intelligence agencies, acting FBI Director L. Patrick Gray complained, "These changes raise serious questions concerning the protection available to investigative files compiled for general intelligence purposes and we strongly object to such modifications." Gray stated that instead of broadening the FOIA to allow greater access, the Justice Department should seek an amendment "to provide an express exemption for FBI files."[27]

FBI officials expressed concern that the release of FBI files could cause the bureau to suffer irreparable loss of public confidence. Indeed, the FBI claimed that its "very existence as an investigative agency is based on our ability to instill confidence in the public," and this required preserving the "sanctity of our files." The bureau opposed the release of *any* information, regardless of age, warning that it could provoke "a clamor from the public once it was aware there was even a small hole in the dike."[28]

Intense lobbying by FBI and Justice Department officials could not prevent the passage of the 1974 FOIA amendments allowing public access to FBI records. The bureau promptly volunteered its assistance to sustain President Gerald Ford's veto, and when Ford's veto was overridden, the FBI immediately sought strategies to limit the effects of the FOIA. The bureau prepared a number of responses to the new power of the FOIA, including a proposal to classify *all* FBI records, making them exempt as "national security" information. Another recommendation came from the heads of FBI field offices who suggested that whenever the FBI processed an FOIA request for an individual's file, the bureau should release the same information to the news media. This would discourage individuals from requesting their FBI files because of the embarrassment it might cause them. The FBI's legal counsel rejected this deterrence strategy as a violation of the FOIA's privacy requirement and a reduction of the FBI's ability to use the privacy exemption to avoid disclosure.

In 1979 Director William Webster ordered all special agents to review their office's operations and to document all instances of the FOIA's harmful effect on FBI investigations. Despite the efforts of agents to highlight cases where potential informers refused to cooperate out of fear that they would be publicly exposed, the bureau was unable to document a credible case for nondisclosure. Ultimately, the bureau's agents were directed to ascertain whether the original custodians of FBI information (local police, banks, credit unions, and other federal agencies) would be willing to take the position that all records disseminated to the FBI were to remain confidential.[29]

Despite the bureau's efforts to evade the requirements of the 1974 FOIA amendments, much of the FBI's history was now revealed for the first time. Until 1974 it was virtually impossible to conduct research on the FBI because no FBI record had ever been deposited at the National Archives. The few FBI records that were discovered among State Department, Justice Department, and Customs Service records or at presidential libraries were declared closed to research. Only after the passage of the 1974 amendments were historians able to research such subjects as the career of FBI Director J. Edgar Hoover, FBI surveillance practices, and major criminal and internal security cases. FBI records released under the FOIA confirmed that the FBI had monitored prominent Americans, collected derogatory personal and political information and heresay about them, and attempted to subvert their careers.

Though historians and researchers acquired much important information about the FBI through the FOIA, they soon discovered the severe limitations of the statute. Athan Theoharis, a historian specializing in FBI research, explained: "Having failed to exempt FBI records from the FOIA's disclosure requirements, FBI officials interpreted the act's exemption provisions broadly and capriciously. The resultant release of heavily redacted records has either stymied or discouraged research. Uniformly, historians who have used the FOIA to obtain FBI records have complained . . . that released FBI files are often 'so bowdlerized as to be useless.' "[30]

Theoharis recently concluded that the FBI's poor responsiveness derives from "a bureaucratic culture hostile to the principle of public access to any FBI records. . . . The result has been a sanitized record, and a process that effectively delays or discourages research involving important issues, movements, and personalities."[31]

FBI filing procedures, devised by Director Hoover during the 1940s, were intended to ensure that the bureau's more questionable practices would not be discovered. These procedures included a "Do Not File" designation, a "JUNE Mail" designation, and an "administrative pages" category. Such procedures were used for information on the bureau's "clearly illegal" activities or information that would cause embarrassment to the bureau if distributed. Particularly sensitive documents, such as letters illegally obtained by the FBI or CIA, were stored in a "separate file room." During the 1970s, the FBI prepared various records disposition plans designed to destroy closed field office and headquarters files, including the massive files on homosexuals and "Sex Deviates."[32]

In the preface to his 1981 book *The FBI and Martin Luther King, Jr.*, David Garrow provides a glimpse of the problems faced by researchers who attempt to pry information out of FBI files using the FOIA. FBI headquarters files actually contain only a small part of the paperwork generated by a bureau investigation. Most of the associated information is contained in the FBI's field offices around the country, and, according to Garrow, "The Bureau is very reluctant to process these voluminous field-office files for release under the Freedom of Information Act."

Garrow also complains that the FBI makes unjustified deletions in the files that it does release, particularly under exemption (b)(1), which protects national security information, and (b)(7), which protects the identities of confidential sources. According to Garrow, "The Bureau makes liberal use of these two major exemptions, especially (b)(1), and much information that has no possible relationship to 'national defense' or even the most inclusive conceptions of the widely abused idea of 'national security' is deleted. While the FOIA is seen as a dangerous and even 'un-American' weapon by some, few would view the FOIA as any threat to the country if they had an opportunity to witness firsthand the way the Bureau and other agencies employ it."[33]

One prominent example of the FBI's arbitrary FOIA denials concerned popular singer and composer John Lennon of Beatles fame. Several months after Lennon was murdered in 1980, historian Jon Wiener filed an FOIA request with the FBI for Lennon's files. After lengthy delays and a suit filed with the help of the American Civil Liberties Union (ACLU), Wiener finally received some of Lennon's files in 1997. Most of the records had been withheld on national security and law enforcement claims, yet they consisted of little more than copies of Lennon's song lyrics, descriptions of a friend's apartment, and the story of a parrot trained to say, "Right on."

Wiener wondered about the FBI's motivation in battling for years to keep such trivial information secret. According to Harry Hammitt, editor of *Access Reports*, "When the FBI, constantly fighting to keep its head above water in the battle for public trust, spends precious resources fighting disclosure of publicly available song lyrics or descriptions of eccentric parrots, public confidence in the FBI's ability to perform its job ebbs a bit more. Such incidents are a two-fold public relations disaster—the public astonishment at why the FBI collected such information is compounded by further incredulity over why it fought so hard to protect it."[34]

Similarly absurd examples of the bureau's compulsion for secrecy may have obscured the fact that many of the FBI's records are truly sensitive; almost all of them require review under the FOIA's law enforcement exemptions. In response to requests for such records, the FBI has claimed that its never-ending backlogs and lack of resources constitute "exceptional circumstances" under the FOIA, which would allow it to take all the time it needs to process requests so long as it acts with due diligence and good faith.

The FBI's FOIA backlogs were in excess of 15,000 pending requests in 1996, and they continue to grow. Congress has recently appropriated $3.3 million to be used specifically for FOIA processing at the FBI, but despite the new staff flowing into the bureau's FOIA office, already the largest of any federal agency, few in the requester community anticipate improvement. Meanwhile, other heavily burdened federal agencies that have exemplary records of responsiveness have had their budgets cut, suggesting that Congress has little inclination to reward excellence in the FOIA realm.

Tom Blanton, executive director of the National Security Archive, the nation's most prominent FOIA organization, recently expressed some sympathy for the FBI's position. "The FBI has had a resource problem dating from 1986 until the recent congressional appropriations to the Bureau," said Blanton. "The FBI FOIA people had been pointing to a very real set of clerical vacancies that they were not allowed to fill. They were denied those positions every year, either by the Justice Department, the OMB, the Judiciary Committee or the Appropriations Committee. They were never given the money to fill what eventually amounted to over 200 vacant slots for which they had authority but no funds. Meanwhile, a backlog of 17,000 to 20,000 requests had accumulated. So they were recently given the money to hire these people and get some processing done. Now we'll find out if inadequate resources really was the problem."[35]

The FBI's response to its backlog of requests has not been encouraging. It has sent mass mailings to requesters who have been waiting years for a response, asking those requesters to reconfirm their interest in the original requests. The bureau's form letter warns requesters that if they do not contact the agency within thirty days, their requests will be administratively closed. The requester community has responded with outrage to this policy, pointing out that no agency has the legal right to close a request without the explicit permission of the requester.

The FBI has also claimed "categorical exemptions" to allow them to withhold whole categories of requested records without reviewing them individually. For example, the FBI refuses even to process a request for records concerning an individual unless the request is accompanied by a Privacy Act waiver. Though several courts criticized this policy, it ultimately came to be accepted. A limited categorical exemption for witness statements has also been claimed. The bureau had also been claiming a blanket application of Exemption 7(D) (confidential sources) after convincing a number of appellate courts that any source that spoke to a law enforcement agent did so with the understanding that the communication would be held in confidence. Fortunately, the Supreme Court rejected that practice, saying that confidentiality must be decided on a case-by-case basis.

Ironically, the FOIA itself has recently revealed the unique nature of the FBI's immunity to the FOIA and to public scrutiny in general. In July 1998, a FOIA request made by the *Washington Post* acquired a 1995 memo from FBI Director Louis Freeh, reviewed and concurred in by President Clinton's then national security adviser, Anthony Lake, which secretly established a blanket exemption for the FBI from the automatic declassification requirements of Clinton's Executive Order 12958. The centerpiece of the order was the automatic declassification of any records twenty-five years old or older, to be accomplished by the year 2000, at which time they would be available through the FOIA. The Freeh memo states that the FBI's blanket exemption was based on a determination that the Privacy Act would preclude the automatic release of declassified information in the bureau's main record systems. Freeh claimed that "it is impractical to review all such records within the five-year time period specified in the order; and that substantial harm to the national security could result from the inadvertent automatic declassification of certain information contained in those systems."[36]

No other government agency, not even the CIA or NSA, was given a blanket exemption from that requirement. "It sounds like we pulled a real coup," said one FBI agent, and the bureau's attitude toward FOIA requests demonstrates it. In June 1998, when FOIA lawyer James Lesar attempted to acquire FBI records dating back to the 1930s, the Justice Department confronted him with a 1995 "Memorandum for the President" from Attorney General Reno stating that the automatic release of records in the bureau's Central Records System and Electronic Surveillance Indices would violate the Privacy Act of 1974. "Accordingly," said Reno, "these two records systems are exempt from the automatic declassification provisions of Executive Order 12958." "This is preposterous," says Lesar. "This covers hundreds of millions of pages that have nothing to do with national security at all—every piece of paper they've got, except maybe payroll records."[37]

Steven Garfinkel, director of the government's Information Security Oversight Office and one of the signatories to the Freeh agreement, is uneasy about the results. "We knew it was somewhat risky," he admitted, "but at the same time we were very anxious to get the executive order signed by the president." According to Garfinkel, the FBI received "a very broad exemption in return for a very broad commitment" to declassify its old records on a document-by-document basis. Unfortunately, admitted Garfinkel, the bureau has declassified only a "very minuscule" amount of their older records.[38]

Assistant FBI Director John E. Collingwood declared, "We don't know precisely how many classified documents we have. . . . Whatever the count, no one knows how many are more than 25 years old and no one can tell how much older they'll be before they see the light of day."[39]

An article in the FOIA journal *Access Reports* concludes: "The FBI is probably the most troubled FOIA operation in government. . . . Many in the FOIA community feel that the FBI has responded in bad faith for years in the seemingly inconsistent and inappropriate treatment it has given requesters. The FBI has a long way to go to repair its credibility and to show requesters that it wants to act responsibly."[40]

Harry Hammitt, editor of *Access Reports*, offers sound advice to the bureau. "The FBI desperately needs to regain the public's trust. One way in which to repair its image would be for the agency to make a serious commitment to the disclosure dictates of the FOIA. The FBI has many important secrets that it is obligated to keep to itself. But the agency must also understand that it has many important historic and social stories to tell and it may well be possible to tell those stories without harming legitimate interests."[41]

THE CENTRAL INTELLIGENCE AGENCY

The Central Intelligence Agency is the principal intelligence, counter-intelligence, and secret operations arm of the U.S. government. It was created in 1947, along with the National Security Council, which directs its activities. Its predecessor, the Office of Strategic Services (OSS), was created in 1942 to handle spying and subversion during World War II. The OSS was disbanded at the end of the war, and most of its functions were assumed by the State Department and War Department; however, in 1947, Congress passed the National Security Act which established both the National Security Council and the Central Intelligence Agency.

The CIA was given responsibility for collecting and evaluating national security data and for carrying out a broad range of covert operations. Under the Central Intelligence Agency Act of 1949, the CIA director became the president's chief adviser on national security intelligence from foreign sources, and in 1978, under a presidential executive order, the director was also made coordinator of the broader intelligence community. Despite the fact that the 1947 founding statute had prohibited the

CIA from engaging in domestic security operations, congressional investigations during the 1970s revealed that the CIA had been illegally spying on journalists and political dissenters in the United States; planting informers; engaging in domestic burglaries, buggings, and mail openings; and collecting secret files on more than 10,000 Americans.

Senator Daniel Patrick Moynihan (D-N.Y.), who has recommended that the CIA be disbanded, recently wrote, "A half century ago, in 1947, Dean Acheson warned President Truman that he had the 'gravest forbodings' about the CIA and that in time neither the president, 'the National Security Council, nor anyone else would be in a position to know what it was doing or to control it.' He was right, but by 1948 it was too late."[42]

From its very origin, the CIA has been the epitome of secrecy. Acquiring information from the CIA about controversial or trivial matters is a formidable task, and the FOIA usually provides little help. Indeed, the agency's FOIA process is itself a virtual secret, precluding any interviews of the sort presented earlier in this chapter. For example, when I called the CIA's Information and Privacy office for a brief description of how they handled FOIA requests, I was told that I would need to submit a FOIA request for that information. When I asked if there was anyone I could speak to "for thirty seconds or less" about their administrative structure, I was connected with a nameless man who told me only that FOIA requests were handled through the CIA's Office of Information Management. I asked if the CIA had any FOIA policies or guidelines and was told there was nothing other than the boilerplate entry in the Code of Federal Regulations. When I asked if, in a sentence or two, he could characterize the CIA's FOIA process, the spokesperson replied tersely, "We process requests as required by the Freedom of Information Act." This nifty bit of public relations may explain why the CIA's FOIA operation can be revealed only in the words of its critics.

Like the FBI, the CIA has always sought a blanket exemption from the FOIA, despite the clear congressional intent to the contrary. Indeed, since the passage of the FOIA in 1966, Congress has repeatedly rejected legislative proposals to exempt intelligence agencies from the FOIA disclosure provisions. In 1984 Congress reaffirmed its intention to subject the CIA to the FOIA, rejecting a Reagan administration proposal to exempt the CIA entirely from the mandatory review and disclosure requirements of the FOIA. Congress did, however, pass the CIA Information Act, reaffirming the application of the FOIA to the CIA but exempting from search and review what Congress thought would be only a small category of CIA "operational" files.

CIA officials had assured Congress that such a restriction was modest, since all useful information in the operational files was already exempted from release. The CIA further argued that exempting CIA operational files would free up agency resources, resulting in swifter responses to other

FOIA requests. Congress accepted these claims, but it is now clear that the CIA Information Act has had broader and more disturbing consequences.

According to James X. Dempsey, FOIA scholar and former congressional staffer, the attitude of CIA officials toward the FOIA became markedly more negative after the CIA Information Act passed. The CIA's FOIA office appeared to interpret the act as exempting all information relating to the Directorate of Operations. "Since 1984," stated Dempsey, "it has become much more difficult, if not impossible, for FOIA requesters to obtain anything involving a program that was once in this directorate. Meanwhile, although the agency has been freed of the burden to search for and review operational files, its processing of FOIA requests has not become more efficient; in many cases it is far less responsive to public requests than before."[43]

Making matters worse, the federal judiciary has been reluctant from the outset to enforce the FOIA against the CIA. Despite congressional insistence that the FOIA apply to the CIA, the courts have refused to exercise their review powers and have created broad exemptions contrary to the intent of the statute. In a series of cases heard betwen 1976 and 1981, the U.S. Court of Appeals for the District of Columbia granted the CIA the extraordinary power to avoid even confirming or denying whether it had records responsive to a request. Now known as a *"Glomar* response"* (see Chapter 2), this exemption came about after FOIA requests had been submitted for contract and budget documents related to the *Glomar Explorer*, a secret underwater vessel. CIA officials responded that they would neither confirm nor deny the existence of relevant records, and the appeals court confirmed this new CIA power, effectively allowing the government to treat the mere existence of the records as classified. Today the courts routinely accept a *Glomar* response from the CIA, and subsequent rulings have extended this exemption far beyond its original scope.

For example, FOIA requests seeking CIA records pertaining to a specific foreign national or a specific event abroad frequently produce the boilerplate CIA response that "in all requests such as yours, the CIA can neither confirm nor deny the existence or nonexistence of any CIA records responsive to your request." The CIA has given the Glomar response to requests for records relating to attempted coups in foreign countries and the political leaders of major foreign countries. CIA officials claim that merely disclosing that the agency has such records would harm the national security. In some cases, CIA officials withhold requested records without claiming that disclosure would either harm the national security or disclose sources and methods. They simply deny that the agency has any records at all, on the grounds that the responsive records would be exempt from search and review under the CIA Information Act.

"Such a position makes a mockery of the concept of legitimate secrecy," declared James Dempsey, who believes that the *Glomar* response should not apply to requests about noted public figures in whom the CIA has an obvious interest. As for CIA concerns about how much information to withhold to protect secret sources, Dempsey believes that can be dealt with adequately after the CIA accepts an FOIA request, conducts a search and review of the documents, and acknowledges the existence of the documents.[44]

Many legal scholars believe that the CIA's abominable record with respect to the FOIA is the result of compliant courts which almost uniformly defer to the agency's claims. According to Amy Rees, "By claiming that even meritorious disclosures could unwittingly compromise sensitive intelligence information, the CIA nearly always succeeds in withholding data under the claimed exemption. Thus, with this near-blanket protection from compelled disclosure, the Agency is effectively removed from the ambit of FIOA's authority. The consequence of this judicially created, or at minimum judicially sanctioned, removal of CIA information from the Act's scope is that, as far as the CIA is concerned, the purpose of FIOA is thwarted."

Rees complains that CIA documents are a prime example of the kind of information that is essential to a genuine understanding of the workings of the government, yet they are withheld from popular knowledge. In deferring to the agency's needs, the courts fail to balance those needs against the public's need for access. "Because the exemption is nearly absolute," stated Rees, "it has become impossible to verify the Agency's need for secrecy in individual cases; instead, extreme judicial deference to CIA conclusions of exemption has suppressed almost all data, whether or not its disclosure poses legitimate national security dangers. . . . The purpose of FOIA's access mechanisms has been slowly and subtly marginalized, and now without public notice, FOIA no longer applies in any meaningful way to information held by the CIA."[45]

The CIA exploited this widespread judicial deference during the cover-up of its psychological experimentation programs of the 1950s and 1960s, code-named MKULTRA. In 1973 Director of Central Intelligence Richard Helms ordered the MKULTRA records destroyed. The cover-up was challenged in court, but the unsuccessful lawsuit resulted in what James Dempsey called "the most serious evisceration of the FOIA as it applies to the CIA."[46]

The Public Citizen Health Research Group had filed an FOIA request for the names of the institutions and individuals that had performed MKULTRA research, but the CIA denied the request. Because the names of the researchers had been declassified, the CIA could not rely on FOIA Exempton 1, which protects only information classified on national security grounds. Instead, CIA officials cited Exemption 3 of the FOIA, which allows the government to withold information "specifically exempted from disclosure by [another] statute." In this unusual application of Exemption 3, the CIA relied on section 102 (d)(3) of the National Security Act, a boilerplate statement that "the Director of Central Intelligence shall be responsible for protecting intelligence sources and methods from unauthorized disclosure."

Public Citizen's suit challenging the CIA's withholding claim was decided in 1985 by the Supreme Court. In *CIA v. Sims*, the Court held that the "sources and methods" language of the National Security Act permitted the CIA to withhold the unclassified names of the MKULTRA researchers. In a disasterous blow to the FOIA, the Court ruled that the National Security Act did not simply protect sources of secret intelligence information, but also authorized the CIA to withold even the identity of nonsecret sources. The Court went so far as to note that even the CIA's subscription to an obscure journal was a "source" to be protected.

The opinion in *CIA v. Sims* went beyond the particulars of the case to say that the meaning of the National Security Act's "sources and methods" provision may not be limited "beyond the requirement that the information fall within the Agency's mandate to conduct foreign intelligence." It stated that in addition to simply witholding the names of intelligence sources, "the Director, in exercising his authority under section 102 (d)(3), has power to withold superficially innocuous information on the ground that it might enable an observer to discover the identity of an intelligence source."[47]

Justice Thurgood Marshall objected to the breadth of the Court's opinion, saying its interpretation of the sources and methods exemption was "neither mandated by the language or the legislative history of any congressional Act, nor by the legitimate policy considerations, and it in fact thwarts congressional efforts to balance the public's interest in information and the Government's need for secrecy." Marshall complained that the Court's rationale thwarted the statutory limits on agency discretion. "By choosing to litigate under Exemption 3 and by receiving this Court's blessing," said Marshall, "the Agency has cleverly evaded all these carefully imposed Congressional requirements."

Marshall warned that the Court's interpretation of the sources and methods language would exempt all CIA information because there is virtually nothing the CIA "might have within its many files that might not disclose or enable an observer to discover something about where the agency gathers information."[48]

In responding to FOIA requests, the CIA now routinely claims that the "sources and methods" exemption covers all CIA activites, intelligence procedures, staffing, and funding. Unfortunately, the courts have largely accepted these claims; one court held that CIA information was exempt

so long as "it is at the very least *'arguable'* that the requested paragraph
. . . *could* reveal intelligence methods."[49] An article in *Access Reports*
points out, "[T]he Supreme Court's interpretation of the National Security Act in *CIA v. Sims* has apparently nailed the door shut on access
to records which the agency does not believe should be disclosed. In a
society where intelligence agencies are popularly viewed as untrustwor-
thy and underhanded, the intelligence community misses an opportunity
to gain the trust of citizens when it falls back on such broad exemption
claims."[50] Another article concluded, "As a practical matter, the decision
leaves a gaping hole in the public availability of national security and
foreign policy records."[51]

According to James Dempsey, "After *Sims*, the sources and methods
exemption has become a virtual blanket exemption for all CIA files, even
when disclosure of information would not cause harm to the national
security. . . . As a result of the *Sims* case, the phrase 'sources and methods' has attained talismanic significance as grounds for withholding from
the public information about the CIA. Protecting sources and methods
trumps other values."[52]

Dempsey says the overbreadth of the CIA's uses of the sources and
methods exemption could be remedied by legislation restricting its application to properly classified information. In 1992 the U.S. Court of
Appeals for the Ninth Circuit actually called on Congress to remedy the
constricting effect that *Sims* has had on the FOIA, but Congress failed to
take any action. During that same year, congressional intelligence committees had a perfect opportunity to reconsider the sources and methods
provision when they undertook a reworking of the National Security Act,
but they chose to reenact the provision without change.

An executive solution to this problem is also readily available, but un-
exploited. Because there is no statutory definition of the phrase sources
and methods, the president could require Directors of Central Intelligence (DCIs) to adopt a less restrictive interpretation of the provision.
In addition, because the National Security Act requires only that sources
and methods be protected from "unauthorized disclosure," presidents
or DCIs could authorize or require disclosure of such information when
the public interest outweighs the harm to national security. Unfortunately, no president or DCI has chosen to take any of these steps.

President Clinton passed up an opportunity to address this problem
in 1995 when he issued his executive order on national security information. Clinton's order may be largely irrelevant to the FOIA's application to the CIA because it addresses only the standards for classification
and declassification of information, which relate only to Exemption 1 of
the FOIA. The CIA's expansive interpretation of the sources and methods
exemption, which comes into play under Exemption 3, remains con-

trolled by the *Sims* decision. The Clinton order effectively ratified this approach, authorizing the DCI to establish his own rules for sources and methods.

Thus, armed with the *Sims* decision and the CIA Information Act, the agency has succeeded in cloaking two large categories of information: sources and methods and operational files. As if that were not enough, the CIA discourages FOIA requests through routine bureaucratic irresponsibility. Bill Schaap, a New York attorney who handles FOIA cases, recently declared, "The CIA is by far the most difficult agency to get information from, perhaps with the exception of some of the quasi-secret organizations like the National Security Agency or the National Reconnaissance Organization. Of all the agencies that are likely to maintain files on American citizens, the CIA is far and away the toughest to get anything from. If you file a FOIA request with the CIA today, you'll get a letter back from them saying, 'We understand that the law says we have to respond in 20 days, but this is to inform you that we will respond in approximately four and a half years.' That's what they do. I got a letter in the mail yesterday on behalf of a client who had submitted a request in 1993 or 1994. It was about somebody long dead and did not deal with anything controversial, but it took three or four years before they responded. They plead inadequate resources and overwhelming backlogs, and the courts let them get away with it."[53]

According to James Dempsey, "In addition to excessive delays, CIA officials have employed a variety of obstacles to frustrate FOIA requesters." Though it is true that agencies are not required to examine unreasonable quantities of material to locate records relevant to a request, Dempsey declares that CIA officials have taken this concept to "preposterous lengths." He describes one case in which the CIA said they could not search for an October 10, 1992, CIA *press statement*. In another case, they claimed that they could not even search for the text of a public statement quoted in the *New York Times*, even though the requester gave the subject matter and date of the statement. When requesters ask for records on a general subject, CIA officials are likely to reject the request on the ground that it would produce a vast quantity of material, imposing an excessive burden on the agency.

Dempsey concluded, "A sort of triple Catch-22 is at work here. A request might be rejected as burdensome if it is too general, unsearchable if it lacks specificty, or Glomarized if it specifies the name of a foreign national or a foreign event."[54]

Author David Corn has described the personal obstacles he faced when writing his book on the CIA, titled *Blond Ghost: Ted Shackley and the CIA's Crusades* (1994). "Like many researchers, I turned toward the Freedom of Information Act for assistance and found that when it comes to the CIA it is almost worthless," he said. "There are numerous exceptions to what the government has to release, and amendments to the act in 1984 made it easier for the CIA to withhold some records. Still, the FOIA could be of some small and important value to those seeking to understand what the CIA does, were it not for the way the agency handles FOIA requests. Agency responses to FOIA requests are routinely discouraging, marked by long delays and puzzling answers."

Corn complained that operational material detailing the ins and outs of the CIA's programs was now exempt from disclosure, and even requests for clearly nonsensitive material are met with years of delay. "Such delays dilute the power of the FOIA," he said. "Few book authors or journalists have the luxury of waiting so long. . . . The agency's FOIA office has acted in a fashion that to outsiders appears capricious and spiteful."[55]

In 1994 Corn was one of the ten historians and advocates of freedom of information who were invited to the CIA headquarters in Langley, Virginia, as part of the mandatory ten-year review of the CIA Information Act. Corn recalled the polite but unproductive discussions around the agency's conference table. The assembled members of the requester community explained that the exempted operational files often contained the material most desired by historians and journalists. They also noted that the CIA's general FOIA response time had shown little improvement. Steven Aftergood of the Federation of American Scientists complained that the CIA continued to respond "glacially" to many requests. Historian Stanley Goldberg charged that the agency could not find a set of documents from the 1950s that he knew it had. Historian Nancy Tucker assailed the agency's piecemeal release of historical documents as "of little use to serious history." Sheryl Walter, general counsel for the National Security Archive, displayed examples of silly CIA responses to requests. Corn asked the CIA to scrap the exemption for operational files, pointing out that voluntary releases like the JFK assassination files disclosed thousands of operational files with the most sensitive portions deleted. Why not do the same with FOIA requests?

"This was cross-cultural communication," said Corn. "The congenial C.I.A. officials explained their mentality: Err on the side of silence. We tried to encourage more openness. There was little give from Langley."

The CIA attributed their poor FOIA record to their office staff, low-level GS-8s who supposedly knew little about the subjects they were searching. These staff, claimed the CIA, were not always able to find what they should. "The overall spin: Incompetence, not meanspiritedness, explains the frustrating responses from the F.O.I.A. office," concluded Corn.[56]

Even if the CIA's FOIA office were properly staffed and professionalized, the agency's practice of destroying their sensitive files would render the FOIA ultimately ineffective. In 1994 journalist Tim Weiner was told by a CIA historian that the agency had destroyed most of its files on covert actions, such as the coup in Iran, in the 1950s and 1960s. Only an FOIA lawsuit by author Stephen Schlesinger prevented 180,000 pages of files on the CIA's bloody actions in Guatemala from disappearing into the same black hole.

CIA officials also ignore the intent of Congress when they reject fee waiver requests. They repeatedly claim that the release of documents would not contribute to the public understanding of the operations or activities of the U.S. government, even when the documents concern events central to CIA history or the history of U.S. foreign relations.

The CIA has insisted on keeping its historical records classified, often in contravention of presidential executive orders. The Clinton order requires that records more than twenty-five years old be automatically declassified over a five-year period, but the CIA has accumulated 165 million pages of documents more than twenty-five years old, with more maturing every day. As of January 1997, they had declassified less than twenty thousand of those pages, about 0.0001 of the total covered by the order.[57]

The CIA has made a number of abortive gestures to spruce up its image, but they have proven to be empty public relations ploys. In 1992, when CIA Director Robert M. Gates promised "a greater openness and sense of public responsibility" at the agency, he said he was acting on the recommendations of a special task force on making the CIA more visible, credible, and responsive to the outside world. But when the ACLU submitted an FOIA request for the fifteen-page "Task Force Report on Greater CIA Openness," it was informed that the report was classified Secret. An agency spokesperson said the report was "an internal document" that must be "withheld in its entirety."

Only after a public scolding at a House hearing did Gates approve declassification of most of the report, which turned out to be something of a disappointment to those who had requested it through the FOIA. "It reads like an internal discussion of how we [the CIA] can get people to like us," said the ACLU. "It doesn't call for a serious look at what secrecy is really necessary now that the Cold War is over."[58]

Another abortive public relations move by the CIA was the much heralded creation of a Historical Review Panel to oversee major new declassification projects. Both DCI Gates and his successor, R. James Woolsey, pledged to massively declassify records on significant Cold War covert actions, including CIA activities in Indonesia and Iran, making such records available through direct release or the FOIA. In 1998 CIA Director George Tenet cancelled all historical declassification projects, claiming that "under current budgeting limitations," the CIA could not meet the demands for declassification. Tenet also announced that it was treating 90 million pages of information from its covert action directorate as exempt from President Clinton's executive order calling for declassification of records 25 years old or older.[59]

THE NATIONAL SECURITY AGENCY

The National Security Agency was created in secret on December 29, 1952, when President Harry S. Truman signed a series of recommendations intended to increase the power and secrecy of the Armed Forces Security Agency (AFSA), the NSA's predecessor. There was none of the fanfare that usually accompanies the creation of a major government agency. There was no news coverage, no congressional debate, not even the whisper of a rumor. No statute established the NSA or defined the scope of its responsibility and authority. Even today, President Truman's authorizing memorandum remains a closely guarded secret, though it is the foundation of all subsequent U.S. communications intelligence activities.

The NSA's massive headquarters is located on the grounds of Fort Meade, Maryland. Its workforce is greater than that of all the other intelligence agencies combined. It has been estimated at over 20,000, but the number is closer to 45,000 if one includes the NSA satellite offices nearby. The Office of Signals Intelligence is the centerpiece of the NSA's organization. The Office of Communications Security protects the entire range of American telecommunications. The Office of Research and Engineering develops the technology of spying.

The NSA's system of classifying information goes far beyond the usual Confidential, Secret, and Top Secret designations. Few messages, letters, or reports leave the NSA without the warning "COMINT CHANNELS ONLY," a classification status higher than Top Secret. The category TOP SECRET UMBRA designates the highest signals intelligence sensitivity; SECRET SPOKE is just one step below.

The Government Accounting Office has reported that the NSA classifies between 50 million and 100 million documents a year, probably exceeding the combined classification activity of all other components and agencies of the government. The NSA produces about 40 tons of classified *waste* each day, necessitating elaborate disposal techniques. The NSA even claims the right to classify information already in the public domain, and it has imposed prior restraint on books dealing with the history of the agency. Before David Kahn's book *The Codebreakers* (1967) was published by Macmillan, the NSA persuaded the publisher to submit the entire manuscript to the Pentagon and NSA for review. The NSA took action against another author, James Bamford, *after* the publication of his 1982 book *The Puzzle Palace*. Bamford had used an FOIA request to acquire documents dealing with illegal NSA activities, but the Reagan administration demanded that Bamford return the documents and threatened to use the Espionage Act against him if necessary. Using the footnotes in Bamford's book, government agents went to libraries containing many of his publicly available sources, removed them from the shelves, and stamped them SECRET. In an FOIA case, the NSA deleted material that had been published in the *Pentagon Papers* and rejected an FOIA appeal claiming that the information had been improperly declassified.

Historians, political scientists, and journalists face such heavy secrecy surrounding the NSA's signals intelligence (SIGINT) activities that they find it extremely difficult to understand the subject and its political significance. There is a good deal of primary source material concerning the NSA at the National Archives, at presidential libraries, and at military history centers, but all of these records have been heavily culled by the NSA. President Clinton's 1995 executive order on national security information contains a cryptologic exemption that makes it highly unlikely that the NSA will review these files and declassify the documents in question. In fact, NSA officials have made it clear that they have no intention of declassifying any documents relating to post–World War II SIGINT before the year 2001. As a result, researchers will have little choice but to use the Freedom of Information Act to get these documents declassified, but trying to pry information out of the NSA through the use of the FOIA is usually unavailing. Virtually every document held by the NSA is marked "Exempt from the General Declassification Schedule," ensuring that they remain classified as long as NSA officials believe it necessary. Some documents are marked for classification in perpetuity.

Matthew Aid, a historian specializing in the NSA, found that, when he began researching a history of the NSA ten years ago, submitting an FOIA request to the NSA almost guaranteed an immediate rejection, and an appeal was assured of a similar fate. The grounds for rejection almost uniformly cited two legal provisions: Title 18 U.S.C. Section 798 and Public Law 86-36. These laws date from World War II, when army and navy intelligence officers began pressing for legislation to punish newspapers for publishing information on American cryptologic activities. On May 1, 1950, under considerable pressure from the Defense Department and the Armed Forces Security Agency, the predecessor to the NSA, Congress passed Title 18 U.S.C. Section 798, commonly known as the "COMINT Law," making it a criminal offense for anyone to communcate to any "unauthorized person" any "classified" information regarding the communications intelligence activities of the United States or any foreign government or information obtained by such processes. The bill was signed into law by President Truman on October 31, 1951. Violation of any section of the law was punishable by a fine of $10,000, ten years in prison, or both.[60]

Federal prosecutors have used the COMINT Law a number of times, including during the espionage trials of Joseph S. Peterson, Jr., in 1954, Christopher Boyce in 1977, and Ronald W. Pelton in 1986. During the Pelton trial, CIA Director William Casey threatened to prosecute any newspaper reporter who published information about the NSA's intelligence operations.

Despite the effective use of the COMINT Law, NSA officials lobbied Congress for further protections. On May 29, 1959, Congress passed Public Law 86–36, usually referred to as the National Security Agency Act of 1959. Among its provisions, the act stipulates that "no law shall be construed to require the disclosure of any information concerning the organization, functions or activities of the National Security Agency, or of any information regarding the names, titles, salaries, or number of persons employed by NSA." NSA officials have interpreted this phrase to mean that the agency may prevent the disclosure of any *unclassified* information about the NSA or its operations that they consider "sensitive." This interpretation exempts NSA records from the mandatory disclosure provisions of the FOIA.[61]

FOIA suits challenging the COMINT Law and Public Law 86–36 have invariably failed. Federal district and appellate courts have ruled that the release of requested documents under the FOIA would violate the law, either by disclosing a function of the NSA or disclosing information about the agency's activities.

In addition to these legal obstacles, FOIA requesters are faced with the inability of the small and overworked NSA FOIA staff to keep up with the ever-increasing number of requests. The growing backlog of unprocessed FOIA requests has been exacerbated by recent budget cuts which have reduced the FOIA staff, resulting in an appreciable slowdown in the NSA's processing of requests. FOIA requesters often wait five years or more before receiving any NSA reply, substantive or otherwise. Even then, the reply is usually disappointing and frustrating.

Ironically, some of this denied information is innocuous and can be obtained by FOIA requests to other agencies. For example, the NSA has often deleted from released documents any mention of SIGINT, COMINT (communications intelligence), ELINT (electronics intelligence), or intercepts, even when the context confirmed what had been excised. NSA officials also frequently deny FOIA fee waiver requests, demanding that requesters pay prohibitive processing fees, even when there is no likelihood that the requester will get any substantive response. Such policies cause many of those submitting FOIA requests for NSA documents to give up.

A few hardy researchers who have persevered with FOIA suits have found limited success. In 1992 computer scientist John Gilmore succeeded in getting the NSA to declassify two fifty-year-old texts on cryptanalysis, but only after Gilmore revealed that the books had been available for years at a number of public libraries. Before settling the case, the NSA tried to reclassify the books and threatened to prosecute Gilmore for violating the COMINT Law if he distributed any copies of the two public library books. In another successful FOIA appeal, historian Gar Alperovitz of the Institute for Policy Studies acquired World War II diplomatic decryptions from the NSA. After years of stonewalling, the NSA released the formerly top secret documents to Alperovitz in 1993. In both the Alperovitz and Gilmore suits, the NSA gave in because attorneys for both men had filed legal briefs questioning the constitutionality of the COMINT Law and Public Law 86–36, something the NSA wishes to avoid contesting in a court of law.

The fear that one day the courts may strike down the protection provided by Public Law 86–36 has increased the NSA's concern about the FOIA. In 1980 NSA Director Bobby R. Inman, Jr., tried to convince the Reagan administration to support amendments to the FOIA to exempt all NSA records. Inman warned that some courts did not accept the NSA's view that Public Law 86–36 exempted the agency from the FOIA and that such an interpretation was under systematic attack by groups seeking access to the NSA's records. When Inman failed to organize support for his proposed blanket FOIA exemption for the NSA, he suggested an FOIA amendment that would exempt all intelligence information and revise exemption (b)(3) to make cryptologic records less subject to judicial action. Inman also recommended that President Reagan amend his executive order on national security information to provide greater protection for cryptologic information.

The continuing NSA influence on presidential executive orders is also evident in President Clinton's Executive Order 12958. The Clinton order is a significant improvement over its predecessor, but it is unlikely to result in the declassification of any significant records relating to the NSA since it exempts from automatic declassification any documents that "reveal information which would impair U.S. cryptologic systems or activities." NSA officials have predictably interpreted this provision to mean that NSA records are generally exempt from the order's provisions. The NSA currently holds approximately 129.3 million pages of documents twenty-five years old or older that are subject to the Clinton executive order, but the agency has exempted most of them from the order's mandatory review.

Due in part to the impotence of the FOIA, there has been virtually no media coverage of NSA operations. Historian John Ferris has noted that "we know more about the CIA than the NSA, even though the latter probably had more influence on American diplomacy and strategy."[62] Matthew Aid maintained, "The NSA's equally important contribution to American intelligence history remains unknown, still hidden behind a curtain of secrecy that only becomes more transparent as time goes by."[63]

NOTES

1. Comments by Anthony Lake at a panel discussion, "Secrets: the CIA's War at Home," held on December 2, 1977 in Washington, D.C. Approval given to reproduce his comments.

2. Russell Roberts, telephone interview with author, January 17, 1998.

3. Will Ferroggiaro, telephone interview with author, April 22, 1998.

4. "Report from the FOIA Front," *Newsletter on Intellectual Freedom*, March 1990, pp. 43–44.

5. Ibid.

6. Ibid.

7. Ibid.

8. Ibid.

9. Ibid.

10. Ibid.

11. Terry Anderson, "My Paper Prison," *New York Times Magazine*, April 4, 1993, pp. 35–36.

12. Steve Weinberg, statement in *The Freedom of Information Act: A 25th Anniversary Retrospective* (Lynchberg, Va.: Access Reports, 1991), pp. 30–31.

13. Richard Kleeman, "The View of Access Professionals," *Newsletter on Intellectual Freedom*, March 1990, p. 66.

14. Roberts, telephone interview with author.

15. Carl Coleman, telephone interview with author, January 14, 1993.

16. Ross Cirrincione, telephone interview with author, January 6, 1998.

17. Ibid.

18. Les Weinstein, telephone interview with author, January 9, 1998.

19. John P. Swann, telephone interview with author, January 4, 1998.

20. Charlie Talbott, telephone interview with author, January 4, 1998.

21. Peggy Irving, telephone interview with author, January 13, 1998.

22. Charlene Thomas, telephone interview with author, January 13, 1998.

23. Harry Hammitt, "All We Are Saying, Is Give Peace a Chance," *Access Reports*, October 1, 1997, p. 6.

24. Memo, FBI Director J. Edgar Hoover to Attorney General S. A. Andretta, August 20, 1946, and undated Attachment, in FBI file 62–81830–2, Library of Congress.

25. Memo, FBI Director J. Edgar Hoover to William Rogers, June 13, 1957, FBI file 62–81830–Not Recorded, Library of Congress.

26. Memo, FBI Director J. Edgar Hoover to Frank Wozencroft, April 29, 1966, FBI file 62–81830–52, Library of Congress.

27. Memo, FBI Director L. Patrick Gray to Assistant Attorney General, Office of Legal Counsel, April 20, 1973, FBI file 62–81830–183, Library of Congress.

28. Memo, Jenkins to Mintz, May 31, 1973, FBI file 81830–188, Library of Congress.

29. Athan G. Theoharis, "The Freedom of Information Act versus the FBI," in *A Culture of Secrecy: The Government versus the People's Right to Know*, ed. Athan G. Theoharis (Lawrence: University Press of Kansas, 1998), p. 25.

30. Ibid.

31. Ibid., pp. 22, 33.

32. Theoharis, *A Culture of Secrecy*, p. 10.

33. David J. Garrow, *The FBI and Martin Luther King, Jr.: From 'Solo' to Memphis* (New York: Norton, 1981), p. 11.

34. Harry Hammitt, "All We Are Saying," p. 6.

35. Tom Blanton, telephone interview with author, January 4, 1998.

36. George Lardner, Jr., "FBI Won Exception to Presidential Order Declassifying Secrets," *Washington Post*, June 19, 1998, p. A3.

37. Ibid.

38. Ibid.

39. Ibid.

40. "The FBI Story: Balancing Sensitivity against Openness," *Access Reports*, August 16, 1996, p. 3.

41. Ibid., p. 7.

42. Daniel Patrick Moynihan, "Our Stupid but Permanent CIA," *Washington Post*, July 24, 1994, p. C3.

43. James X. Dempsey, "The CIA and Secrecy," in *A Culture of Secrecy: The Government versus the People's Right to Know*, ed. Athan G. Theoharis (Lawrence: University Press of Kansas, 1998), p. 48.

44. Ibid., pp. 47–48.

45. Amy E. Rees, "Recent Developments Regarding the Freedom of Information Act: A 'Prologue to a Farce or a Tragedy; or Perhaps Both,' " *Duke Law Journal* 44 (1985): 1185–86, 1191.

46. Dempsey, "The CIA and Secrecy," p. 42.

47. *CIA v. Sims*, 471 U.S. 159 (1985).

48. Ibid.

49. *Maynard v. CIA*, 986 U.S. 159 (1985).

50. "Cases Highlight Differences in Obtaining Classified Records," *Access Reports*, April 10, 1996, p. 4.

51. "D.C. Circuit Rules NSC Not an Agency," *Access Reports*, July 31, 1996, p. 6.

52. Dempsey, "The CIA and Secrecy," p. 44.

53. William Schaap and Ellen Ray, telephone interview with author, July 2, 1998.

54. Dempsey, "The CIA and Secrecy," pp. 49–50.

55. David Corn, "Freedom of Information? Not from the CIA," *Washington Post*, May 7, 1992, p. A25.

56. David Corn, "CIA vs FOIA," *The Nation*, October 10, 1994, p. 370.

57. Dempsey, "The CIA and Secrecy," p. 51.

58. "CIA Report on Openness Classified Secret," *Washington Post*, April 23, 1992, p. A1.

59. "CIA Won't Declassify Files, Blames Budget," *Washington Post*, July 16, 1998, p. A5.

60. Matthew M. Aid, " 'Not So Anonymous': Parting the Veil of Secrecy about the National Security Agency," in *A Culture of Secrecy: The Government versus the People's Right to Know*, ed. Athan G. Theoharis (Lawrence: University Press of Kansas, 1998), p. 70.

61. Public Law 86–36, 73 Stat. 63 (codified as amended at 50 U.S.C. 402), 1988.

62. John Ferris, "Coming in from the Cold War: The Historiography of American Intelligence, 1945–1990," *Diplomatic History* 19, no. 1 (Winter 1995): 92.

63. Aid, " 'Not So Anonymous,' " p. 77.

CHAPTER 4

The Effective Use of the FOIA

SUBMITTING A REQUEST

There are a number of helpful books describing how to use the Freedom of Information Act (FOIA), including Congress's own *Citizen's Guide on Using the Freedom of Information Act and the Privacy Act of 1974 to Request Government Records*.[1] In addition, assistance in the preparation of FOIA requests is provided by various public interest organizations, including the National Security Archive and Public Citizen. These sources are recommended for full information and assistance in the use of the FOIA; here we provide a brief outline of the FOIA request process.

Under the FOIA, any person of any nationality may seek access to records from any agency of the U.S. government, including departments, regulatory commissions, and other establishments in the executive branch. The FOIA also applies to the Office of Management and Budget and the Executive Office of the president, but not to the president himself or his advisers within the Executive Office. The FOIA does not apply to Congress, the federal courts, private corporations, tax-exempt organizations, or federally funded state agencies, but documents filed with federal agencies by these groups are subject to disclosure.

All "records" of an agency may be requested under the FOIA. Any information controlled by an agency is usually considered to be a record under the FOIA. The form in which a record is maintained, such as a printed document, tape recording, or computer disk, does not affect its availability. This broad definition of "record" was made explicit in the 1996 Electronic FOIA amendments.

Note that "records," not "information," may be requested under the FOIA. This means that an agency is not required to research or analyze data for a requester. It is required only to look for an existing record or document as described in an FOIA request.

Sometimes, an informal phone call to the FOIA officer at the agency is sufficient to acquire the information needed; only a written request, however, will place the agency under a legal obligation to respond. Since there is no central government office that services FOIA requests, the first step in preparing a request is to identify the agency holding the records of interest. For help in identifying the appropriate agency, a requester may consult a directory such as the *United States Government Manual*, which contains a complete list of all government agencies, including their addresses and major functions.[2]

The request letter should be addressed to the agency's FOIA officer or the agency head, and the envelope should be marked "Freedom of Information Act Request." The name and address of the requester must be included. The letter should state that the request is being made under the FOIA, and it should identify the records being sought as specifically as possible. A requester who cannot identify specific records should explain clearly the kind of information needed.

Several optional items are often included in a request letter. One is the telephone number of the requester. Another is an indication of the amount of fees that the requester is willing to pay. A third optional item is a request for a waiver or reduction of fees.

FOIA requesters may have to pay fees to cover some or all of the costs of processing their requests, but under the 1986 amendments to the FOIA, fees may vary with the status or purpose of the requester. Representatives of the news media and educational or noncommercial scientific institutions who are not seeking records for commercial use can be billed only for reasonable document duplication costs. A commercial FOIA requester can be charged for document duplication, search, and review. All other requesters, including public interest groups and nonprofit organizations, are charged only for document duplication and search. Fees must be waived or reduced if the information is not primarily in the commercial interest of the requester and if disclosure of the information is likely to contribute to the public understanding of the activities of the government.

The 1996 Electronic FOIA amendments extended the time limit for an agency to provide an initial response to an FOIA request from ten working days to twenty working days. Agencies are also allowed to authorize expedited processing of requests if the requester demonstrates a "compelling need for a speedy response."

As we have seen, the disclosure of requested information is subject to nine exemptions and the three exclusions added in the 1986 amendments (see Chapter 2). If a request is wholly or partially denied, the agency must inform the requester of the reasons for denial and of the requester's right to appeal. Such an appeal can be filed with a single letter to the head of the agency in question, but it may be useful to try to negotiate the release of at least some of the denied material before initiating a formal appeal. An FOIA officer may be persuaded to release many of the requested documents if the scope of the request is narrowed.

An agency is required to make a decision on an appeal within twenty working days. Once the time period has elapsed on an administrative appeal, the requester may proceed with a judicial appeal. Such an appeal may be filed in the U.S. District Court in the district in which the requester lives, in the district in which the documents are located, or in the District of Columbia. Most requesters require the assistance of an attorney to file a judicial appeal.

REQUESTS BY PRIVATE CITIZENS

The Freedom of Information Act and the Privacy Act are often used by individual citizens to acquire information about themselves that is maintained in the files of federal agencies. Though such requests do not usually produce historical information of interest to the general public, requests for nothing more than one's personal file can occasionally have broader social significance. One example may be instructive.

In 1976 a married couple, William Schaap and Ellen Ray, submitted identical FOIA requests to the CIA, each requesting "a copy of any file you may have on me." The denial of their requests led to an important court case that affected the legal rights of all FOIA users. In *Ray v. Turner* (1978), the U.S Appeals Court for the District of Columbia applied the strengthening language of the 1974 and 1976 FOIA amendments to encourage in camera inspection of withheld documents and the segregation of exempted from unexempted portions of such documents. The 1974 amendment had, among other things, sought to prevent the arbitrary application of Exemption 1 by requiring that materials stamped SECRET by executive order "are in fact properly classified pursuant to such Executive order." This change in the FOIA was in large part a congressional reaction to a Supreme Court decision, *EPA v. Mink* (1973), discussed later in this chapter.

In *Turner*, the Court ruled that "an agency may not rely on the 'exemption by document' approach even in a national security context." In his concurring opinion, Chief Judge J. Skelly Wright wrote that "the federal bureaucracy has been extremely reluctant to embrace the principle of public disclosure on which the FOIA is founded and, with significant help from the federal courts interpreting the exemptions broadly, not narrowly, has succeeded in frustrating much of its implementation—so much so that Congress has repeatedly overruled court decisions restricting disclosure by amending the Act."

Wright concluded, "My opinion in this case is an effort to consolidate some of the wisdom of prior cases and the legislative history regarding what courts must do to make *de novo* review a reality. The evolution of the review process must continue; additional creative innovations by counsel, the courts, and Congress are necessary to solve the problems that persist. For the time being, however, the courts can at least see to it that the progress that has already been made is not lost."[3]

In early 1998, in an interview with William Schaap and Ellen Ray, I asked them to recall their FOIA request and the subsequent litigation. Ellen Ray responded, "We submitted FOIA requests to the FBI [Federal Bureau of Investigation], the CIA [Central Intelligence Agency], and the military. We had worked in Southeast Asia and elsewhere around the world, and we had just started our magazine, *Covert Action*. Bill was a lawyer for the National Lawyers Guild and the Pacific Counseling Services. During the early 1970s we were learning a lot about the CIA, and we were always submitting FOIA requests for the magazine.

"The suit requesting our files started out as *Ray v. Bush*. George Bush was head of the CIA at the time we sued, but by the time it came to court he had been replaced by Stansfield Turner, and it became *Ray v. Turner*. The CIA said that they didn't have to show us anything because of national security. Though we never received our files, the CIA was required to turn them over to a judge for a final determination. Unfortunately, the judge looked at our files and concluded that they could not be divulged on national security grounds, but the precedent was established that the CIA cannot arbitrarily claim national security. It must go before a judge. We got a bad judge."

Though the CIA refused to reveal their files, Schaap and Ray received a good deal of material from the FBI and from military intelligence, some of which helped them recognize the political surveillance that had been imposed on them. "They gave us material that allowed us to pinpoint the agents in our little social group," said Ray. "They had blacked out much of the documents, but isolated words like 'Jane Fonda' and 'coffee house,' etc., allowed us to surmise that one navy guy who used to hang around was from naval intelligence. Of course, we didn't receive that material until years later, but it was useful after the fact to know who the agent was."

Schaap also recalled the case as a pyhrric victory, in the sense that the requested material was never released, though good legal precedent was established. "The most significant result was that, even if you're the CIA, you can't just say, 'No.' The decision required agencies to explain their reasons for withholding requested material, and if their explanation is inadequate, the court may need to examine the material. The CIA, in particular, had previously taken the position that they didn't have to justify themselves to anyone. They had virtually assumed that there was a CIA exception to the FOIA, that the FOIA applied differently to the CIA than to other agencies."

The case arose around the time that Ray and Schaap began work on a book, *Dirty Work*, about the CIA. Also during this period, the couple launched their magazine, *Covert Action*. Schaap explained, "By that time we had been back for a year or two from working abroad during the Vietnam War, defending GIs and so on. We were interested in learning more about the CIA and decided to find out what they had on us. We were somewhat skeptical about whether we could get anything under the FOIA, because it still depended on the honesty of officials in the agency. We also submitted requests to the FBI, military intelligence and the Defense Department. They had large files on us because we had been doing military defense work for three or four years prior to submitting our letters.

"It was something more than idle curiosity, because we were journalists working in that field. We didn't anticipate that our suit was going to establish any major principle, but when we got such a terrible response from them and decided to go to court, we thought something more might come out of it. We hoped it might establish some broad legal principles, while helping us as journalists."

Schaap recognized that the positive judgments in *Ray v. Turner* were made possible by the FOIA amendments passed by Congress in 1974 and 1976. "Before 1974, the FOIA was not a very effective tool," he said. "Even after the amendments, agencies like the CIA and FBI developed practical ways to make it very, very difficult to get information."

Schaap currently practices law in Manhattan, New York, and he often does FOIA work on behalf of clients. "Most of the FOIA work I've provided has been for journalists," said Schapp. "Sometimes they're looking for background information on particular events, and sometimes they just want their own files. I remember someone who worked at the Center for Constitutional Rights who received a response identifying her as the daughter of blank and blank. There was a note saying that to protect their privacy, the names of her mother and father had been blacked out. That's how ludicrous it gets.

"I'm currently doing a series of FOIA requests for a journalist-client who did a lot of exposé journalism during the Vietnam War. She wants to find out what kind of files were kept on her. The first thing I told her was, 'Look, the State Department is going to be relatively quick, the FBI will be relatively quick, military intelligence will be fairly quick, but the CIA is another matter. If we send off the letter next week, we won't hear from them for years.' "

Despite his difficulties with the FOIA, Schaap has high regard for the act. "I think it's incredibly important, and it should be expanded if it's at all possible. In every country where freedom of information legislation has been enacted, it has contributed to society and government. The problem is, of course, that it's impossible to get more out of an agency than their budget allows. There's no question that the government does not allocate enough to federal agencies to serve the information needs of the public."[4]

AUTHORS AND REPORTERS

Members of the media have long been criticized for their infrequent use of the FOIA, a criticism that is particularly embarrassing given the popular impression that the law was passed primarily for the media's benefit. It is certainly true that daily newspaper reporters with short deadlines will never be able to surmount the routine delays in agency responses to FOIA requests, but investigative journalists and authors, both print and broadcast, vigorously exploit the FOIA.

Early uses of the FOIA by reporters included requests to reveal waste and corruption in government contracting, FBI abuses, and the atrocities of the 1968 U.S. military massacre at My Lai, Vietnam. Will Ferroggiaro, the FOIA coordinator at the National Security Archive, gave me a more recent example of a significant use of the FOIA by a journalist. "There's a reporter named Beth Marcak at the *Cleveland Plain Dealer* who wrote an amazing series of articles on the FAA [Federal Aviation Administration] and airline safety which appeared right before the 1996 ValuJet crash," said Ferroggiaro. "A phenomenal piece of work. She won a Polk award for it. Her information came largely from FOIA. She had to bat the FAA around the head a bit to get the documents, but the end result was positive. She really knew how to work the system, and she had her newspaper backing her too. She was given the time to work on the story and the resources to pursue it."[5]

Because their publications have longer deadlines, authors and scholars have made more effective use of the FOIA than reporters. Harold Weisberg, a journalist and author, has used the FOIA heavily for three decades in his continuing research and reporting on the assassination of President John F. Kennedy. Beginning with his series of Whitewash books in the 1960s and 1970s, which examined the Warren Commission Report and the official cover-up, through his 1994 book, *Case Open: The Unanswered Questions*, Weisberg has provided a scholarly basis for questioning the government's account of the assassination. By building his case on official documents acquired through the FOIA, Weisberg has laid a credible foundation that has been exploited by a host of subsequent conspiracy theorists.

Author David Garrow has used the FOIA to support his acclaimed series of books on the Reverend Martin Luther King, Jr. In *Bearing the Cross*, Garrow acknowledges, "This book has been greatly strengthened by thousands of previously unavailable documents, particularly hundreds of transcripts of Dr. King's wire-tapped phone conversations, that have been released to me by the FBI, thanks to the FOIA."[6]

Garrow also thanks Clarence Jones and Bayard Ruston, two of King's closest advisors, for allowing him unrestricted access to their wiretapped conversations, also acquired through the FOIA. "The conversations, including King's, overheard by those surveillances are still within reach of the FOIA," said Garrow, "and neither [exemptions] (b)(1) nor (b)(7)(D) have blocked release of Bureau memoranda concerning that material."

In the preface to his 1981 book, *The FBI and Martin Luther King, Jr.*, Garrow describes how he acquired two major Justice Department studies of the FBI's pursuit of King throughout the 1960s. "While the latter of these, which reviewed both the FBI 'security' probe of King and the Bureau's assassination investigation, was publicly available, the earlier, more detailed one was classified 'Top Secret' and was obtained only by a Freedom of Information (FOIA) request."[7]

Steven Schlesinger, an author and journalist, used the FOIA to expose an embarrassing episode in American history: the 1954 CIA-instigated coup in Guatemala that ousted a democratically elected government and installed a brutal military dictatorship. In the preface to his 1982 book *Bitter Fruit:The Untold Story of the American Coup in Guatemala*, Schlesinger cites one FOIA request to the State Department that produced over 1,000 pages of material. "We would like to thank the congressional authors of the Freedom of Information Act (FOIA), who provided us with an indispensable tool to review the inner workings of United States foreign policy. The FOIA enabled us to obtain documents from the State Department, the National Archives, the Naval Department and the Federal Bureau of Investigation which described many details of American policy and conduct in Guatemala."[8]

In 1996, while serving as a visiting scholar at New York University, Schlesinger wrote an article in the *Washington Post* describing his ongoing use of the FOIA to break through the CIA's cover-up. Complaining that disclosure of the 1954 files was long overdue, Schlesinger said, "Even after my book [*Bitter Fruit*] was published, I spent years of effort in a campaign to unlock the secret CIA repositories. From the beginning, the agency stalled at every juncture. . . . Eventually, I went into federal court, where, after interminable legal wrangling, the agency admitted that 'by accident' one of its officers had discovered 180,000 pages of records on the operation. But, the agency added, it could not release a single page because of 'national security' considerations."[9]

A federal judge accepted the CIA's national security claim and dismissed Schlesinger's suit, but he has continued to press for the release of the documents.

My own first book, *Surveillance in the Stacks: The FBI's Library Awareness Program* (1991), was heavily supported by FOIA material acquired by a public service organization, the National Security Archive. As a library administrator, I became aware of the FBI's notorious intrusion on libraries in 1988 when an agent visited my library at the University of Maryland, asking our staff to report on the library habits of anyone with a "foreign sounding name or foreign accent." I had some anecdotal evidence that this was not an isolated act by the FBI, and I wrote several articles in the Maryland Library Association's newsletter about what appeared to be a pattern of surveillance. But only through the FOIA was I able to document the FBI's formal program of library surveillance. By using a personal request for my own file and FOIA requests by organizations like the American Library Association, I also discovered that the FBI had initiated investigations of librarians like myself who opposed its Library Awareness Program.

One of the more recent books that represents the effective use of the FOIA is Angus Mackenzie's 1997 exposé *Secrets: The CIA's War at Home*. As the editor of the underground newspaper *Dreadnaught*, Mackenzie had become aware of the government's attempts to suppress the alternative press.

"I soon realized the FOIA might provide a way for me to learn more about the attempts to sabotage not only the *Dreadnaught* but all the underground papers," wrote Mackenzie in the book's introduction. "In short order I filed FOIA requests for documents from the CIA, the FBI, and various other agencies. . . . [T]he book itself began with those FOIA requests. Federal government lawyers contested the requests through more than a decade of litigation, but the information that I eventually obtained is the underpinning for much of this text. The harassing, delaying, and stonewalling tactics of the government were also instructive. . . . [T]he lengths to which CIA and FBI lawyers went to impede my requests were so beyond the pale as to constitute of themselves a form of suppression."[10]

Mackenzie was told that he had to pay an advance deposit of $30,000 to the CIA and $1,100 to the FBI for FOIA search fees. The treatment of his requests merely convinced Mackenzie that the government had something to hide. In 1979, while investigating the disruption of the dissident press during the Vietnam War, he used the FOIA to request documents from the CIA on its operations against some 500 antiwar newspapers. When the request was denied, he sued. A judge subsequently ordered the CIA to follow the "Vaughan procedure," which requires an agency to provide an outline of the withheld materials. In oral sessions, the CIA's information officer read aloud or paraphrased a stack of unexpurgated CIA reports in the presence of Mackenzie and other witnesses. In this way, the FOIA produced a substantial amount of information without the actual release of documents.

Not only the text of Mackenzie's book is based on FOIA-acquired material. Its appendix, an annotated list of domestic political groups under surveillance by the FBI, includes a description of the FBI's response, or lack of same, to FOIA requests concerning each of the groups.

Shortly before finishing his book, Angus Mackenzie died of brain cancer at the age of forty-three. His family assembled the work in progress and prepared it for publication. In June 1998, I interviewed Angus's brother, James Mackenzie, who played a major role in completing the manuscript.

"About 15 years ago Angus discovered that the CIA, FBI, and Army and Navy intelligence had been involved in counterintelligence operations that targeted, among others, America's alternative press," said James Mackenzie. "He proceeded on a number of fronts, including the FOIA, but before the agencies would even process his requests, they demanded huge search fees, despite the provisions for journalists in the FOIA statute. The agencies were generally unresponsive, even though Angus gave them specific detail, including dates and document numbers. It very quickly descended into a fight in federal court between Angus and the CIA.

"We considered it a victory in court, but technically it wasn't, because there was no verdict. Though we were denied direct access to the requested documents, we got a lot of information out of the CIA. They were happy to avoid a court decision with implications for the future. Angus and his attorney spent the larger part of a month on the top floor of the CIA Headquarters in Langley, Virginia, and after a while he developed a working relationship with the Agency people assembled there. Instead of receiving a lot of blacked-out pages, Angus was allowed to take shorthand notes as Agency people read selectively to him from the uncensored documents. It not only revealed a lot of information, but it helped tremendously to demystify the Agency for Angus, allowing him to understand the CIA's bureaucratic interests."[11]

As the result of the FOIA process and subsequent litigation, the public has access to Angus Mackenzie's book, and negotiations are under way to transfer all of Mackenzie's papers and supporting documents to the National Security Archive, where they will be available to scholars and researchers.

CONGRESS

The U.S. Congress normally does not require the FOIA to gain access to executive information. Congressional requests for such material are usually initiated by a congressional committee or subcommittee, and the specified documents are, more often than not, acquired without recourse to the FOIA. Indeed, the FOIA explicitly states that none of its provisions or exemptions confer the authority to withhold information from Congress. Even classified material, exempt from disclosure under the FOIA, is frequently shared with appropriate committees on a need-to-know basis. When the executive refuses to share information with Congress, however, its members have sometimes invoked the FOIA as *individuals*. Congress has an interesting history in this regard.

An important FOIA suit was initiated by "members of Congress, in both their official and private capacities" in 1971, after Representative Patsy Mink (D-Hawaii) read a newspaper article indicating that President Richard Nixon had received conflicting recommendations on the advisability of conducting the underground nuclear test scheduled for that fall at Amchitka Island, Alaska. The article indicated that the latest recommendations were the product of "a departmental under-secretary committee named to investigate the controversy." Two days later, Representative Mink sent a telegram to President Nixon urgently requesting the "immediate release of [the] recommendations and report by interdepartmental committee."[12]

When the request was denied, an action under the Freedom of Information Act was initiated by Representative Mink and twenty-three of her colleagues in the House in an effort to acquire nine withheld documents. In district court, the government claimed that the materials sought were specifically exempted from disclosure under exemptions (b)(1) (national security) and (b)(5) (inter- or intra-agency communications) of the FOIA. In particular, eight of the nine requested documents were described as having been classified Top Secret or Secret pursuant to Executive Order 10501. The district court granted summary judgment on the grounds that all nine documents were exempt from disclosure under the FOIA.

The court of appeals reversed that decision, claiming that the documents had been too broadly classified. Even for the legitimately classified documents the court concluded, "If the nonsecret components are separable from the secret remainder and may be read separately without distortion of meaning, they too should be disclosed." The court instructed the district judge to examine the classified documents "looking toward their possible separation for purposes of disclosure or nondisclosure." Even the material withheld under exemption (b)(5) was to be examined in camera to determine whether "factual data" could be separated from "decisional processes."[13]

The case then went to the Supreme Court, which reversed the appeals court ruling. Justice Byron White delivered the opinion of the Court: "We do not believe that Exemption 1 permits compelled disclosure of documents . . . that were classified pursuant to this Executive Order. Nor does the Exemption permit *in camera* inspection of such documents to sift out so-called 'nonsecret' components."[14]

In his concurring opinion, Justice Potter Stewart reluctantly agreed that "the language of the exemption, confirmed by its legislative history, plainly withholds from disclosure matters 'specifically required by Executive Order to be kept secret. . . . ' In short, once a federal court has determined that the Executive has imposed that requirement, it may go no further under the Act." Nonetheless, Stewart was emotional in his criticism of the government for withholding the requested information and of Congress for leaving such a loophole in the FOIA.

"One would suppose that a nuclear test that engendered fierce controversy within the Executive Branch of our Government would be precisely the kind of event that should be opened to the fullest possible disclosure consistent with legitimate interests of national defense," wrote Stewart. "Without such disclosure, factual information available to the concerned Executive agencies cannot be considered by the people or evaluated by the Congress. And with the people and their representatives reduced to a state of ignorance, the democratic process is paralyzed."

Stewart concluded that Congress "has built into the Freedom of Information Act an exemption that provides no means to question an Executive decision to stamp a document 'secret,' however cynical, myopic, or even corrupt that decision might have been."[15]

In his dissent, Justice William O. Douglas was even more forceful in complaining that "the much-advertised Freedom of Information Act is on its way to becoming a shambles." He concluded, "The Executive Branch now has *carte blanche* to insulate information from public scrutiny whether or not that information bears any discernible relation to the interests sought to be protected by subsection (b)(1) of the Act."[16]

Because both the majority and dissenting opinions complained about a fatal flaw in the FOIA, the government won only a pyrrhic victory over Representative Mink and her congressional colleagues. In direct response to *EPA v. Mink*, Congress immediately set about correcting the loopholes in the FOIA, and a strengthening amendment was passed in 1974 (see Chapter 2).

In a recent interview with Representative Mink, the veteran congresswoman recalled her momentous FOIA action. "We were seeking legislation trying to stop the underwater nuclear test in Amchitka in the Aleutian Islands," said Mink, "and we found an obscure newspaper article saying that five government agencies had written to the White House protesting the tests. We then wrote to the White House. John Dean of Watergate fame was the counsel, and he said no. He claimed that all of these reports were confidential and could not be released for national security reasons. Preposterous!

"About twenty-three members of Congress filed suit," she said. "Our

original effort was not successful, and by the time the lawsuit had concluded, the atomic tests had already been conducted. Nonetheless, it
started the whole idea of *in camera* examination of withheld documents.
As the result of this case, those of us who worked on the lawsuit then
began work on an amendment to the FOIA, which was enacted in 1974.
We were the ones that moved it. John Moss and I."

I asked Representative Mink whether she had used the FOIA subsequent to her 1973 lawsuit. "Absolutely," she said emphatically. "The ability of any citizen to acquire documents through the FOIA has increased
dramatically as the result of the changes that were made following our
Amchitka case. Some of our subsequent requests had to do with government testing, the Provo Utah testing of sheep, and things like that."

In recent years, however, Representative Mink's use of the FOIA has
been primarily in support of constituent requests. "There are dozens that
come through my office every year," she said, "constituents who are seeking information and come up against a stone wall and ask for help. Then
I submit the FOIA request on their behalf. I'm sure other members do
the same. It's part of our constituent services. We assist people who are
anxious to get their records or background information, or those who
run into problems while writing a book or doing research."

When I asked Representative Mink for her personal assessment of the
importance of the FOIA, she responded without hesitation: "As I state in
every report or inquiry that is made about my career, that lawsuit and
the subsequent changes we made in the Freedom of Information Act were
the most significant accomplishments that I could ever claim during my
time in Congress. I think it's absolutely paramount that people have the
right to know. The struggle to break through excessive government secrecy continues to this day."[17]

Though Mink's FOIA litigation may be the most significant ever initiated by a member of Congress, others after her have made good use of
the statute. Indeed, a spate of congressional FOIA requests followed immediately after Mink's suit. In March 1972, Representative John Ashbrook
(R-Ohio) sued the Defense Department under the FOIA to make public
secret documents on Soviet military strength. The documents in question
were the so-called Penkovsky Papers, a statistical analysis of Soviet nuclear
weaponry compiled by Colonel Oleg Penkovsky, a Soviet intelligence officer who had been executed for espionage in 1962. Ashbrook, a conservative challenger to President Nixon during the 1972 presidential
primary, said the documents were essential to the debate on a SALT (Strategic Arms Limitation Talks) treaty with the Soviet Union.

In April 1972, Representative Les Aspin (D-Wis.) filed suit under the
FOIA to force disclosure of the Peers Commission report on the My Lai
massacre. The Peers Commission, headed by Lieutenant General William
R. Peers, had been appointed to investigate the circumstances surround-

ing the U.S. Army's massacre of South Vietnamese civilians at My Lai in 1968. "The military is guilty of a double coverup—first with the massacre and now with the investigation," said Aspin.[18]

A subsequent FOIA request made by Aspin produced a Pentagon list of blacklisted contractors. In a 1973 letter to Aspin, acting Assistant Defense Secretary Hugh McCullough wrote that he had concluded that no useful purpose would be served by continuing to withhold the list, which had previously been considered For Official Use Only. Aspin congratulated the Pentagon for releasing the information, but said, "I only wonder why they made it such a deep, dark secret."[19]

In December 1973, three New York congressmen filed suit under the FOIA asking the Justice Department to show them any FBI files that had been kept on their activities. The congressmen, Representatives Edward I. Koch (D-N.Y.), Benjamin S. Rosenthal (D-N.Y.), and Jonathan B. Bingham (D-N.Y.), had been told by former acting FBI Director L. Patrick Gray III that the FBI had collected information about them. Nonetheless, the FBI refused to release their files.

In 1974 Senator Jacob Javits (R-N.Y.) used the FOIA to acquire a tape recording from the CIA containing interviews given by former Attorney General Ramsey Clark while he was in North Vietnam. In 1975 an FOIA request to the State Department from Representative Aspin acquired a list of foreign aid recipients approved by the United States since 1950. Also in 1975 Representative Charles O. Porter (D-Ore.) used the FOIA to discover that a profile of him prepared by the CIA described his "acute hunger for higher office." That same year, Representative Bella Abzug (D-N.Y.) acquired portions of her CIA dossier through the FOIA, including the fact that the CIA had opened and copied correspondence sent to her.

A prominent congressional use of the FOIA during this period came from then Senator Bob Dole (R-Kans.) who was attempting to acquire information on the drug-running activities of Panamanian dictator Omar Torrijos. Dole wanted to use the information as ammunition against President Jimmy Carter's Panama Canal proposals. According to the journal *Human Events*, Dole's requests to the Drug Enforcement Agency (DEA) on December 16, 1978, netted him seventy-eight pages of documents "that had more deletions than an X-rated movie in Dublin." The Torrijos name had been struck from virtually all of the files received by Dole.

According to one Dole staffer, "Of the 78 pages we received, I would say deletions accounted for about 50 percent. Some pages were totally blank except for one or two sentences. . . . We do not believe that much of what was censored is vital to the national security. It appears without a doubt that they are stonewalling on this."[20]

In a subsequent article published in *Human Events*, M. Stanton Evans characterized the FOIA denials to Senator Dole and CBS News as a massive cover-up. "The 78 pages of files unearthed by DEA are so heavily censored as to be unreadable," wrote Evans, "but it is clear that a major object of the censorship was to block out mention of Gen. Torrijos and other Panama officials, including his brothers, and their alleged connections with narcotics."[21]

Some members of Congress have been inveterate FOIA users; others believe that Congress should seek to enforce its *institutional* right of access to executive information. James X. Dempsey, who served as assistant counsel for Representative Don Edwards's (D-Calif.) Subcommittee on Civil and Constitutional Rights from 1985 until 1994, recently stated that the members of the subcommittee believed that congressional reliance on the FOIA might be viewed as an admission of institutional weakness that could actually encourage executive secrecy.

"We tended to feel that members of Congress should not have to use the FOIA, that their constitutional prerogatives entitled them to any and all information within their jurisdiction," said Dempsey. "This is particularly true for congressional committees, where the notion of oversight as a co-equal branch of government should carry with it the right to all pertinent information. We never encouraged, and probably discouraged, the use of the FOIA by members. We felt that all requests for information should be through the oversight process."

The one circumstance in which members of Congress exploit the FOIA consistently occurs when they desire information about themselves held in government files. "Members of Congress do still request their own files," according to Dempsey. "That would be the one case where the whole presumption of avoiding the FOIA would flip. A member would be advised to request personal files through the FOIA in order to avoid the appearance of using his constitutional prerogatives for private purposes. Indeed, Chairman Edwards used the FOIA to get his own file from the FBI."[22]

Despite his preference for congressional oversight as a means of revealing the workings of the government, Representative Edwards, who retired from Congress in 1995, regarded the FOIA as an essential part of open government. Dubbed "Mr. Constitution" by his colleagues because of his lifelong commitment to constitutional rights, Edwards recognized the limits of the oversight process. "The subcommittee has never sought to substitute itself for an informed public or an alert press," stated Edwards. "Nor does the subcommittee see its access to executive branch information as a substitute for the rights of access established by the Freedom of Information Act. . . . The congressional oversight process thus depends on the FOIA to an important degree."

Edwards concluded, "[T]he FOIA and the congressional oversight are sometimes complementary, but the principle of public accountability does not depend solely on the Congress. The public is entitled to direct access to information about its Government and the actions of the Government's agents."[23]

CORPORATIONS

Contrary to the popular image of the FOIA as a statute designed to inform the public about the workings of their government, the statistics reveal that a preponderance of requests come from corporations seeking business information about their rivals. When businesses discovered that the FOIA could be used to obtain government information about themselves and their competitors, information previously unavailable under the old need-to-know standard, they quickly exploited the FOIA's new concept of the right to know.

Even today, the commercial use of the FOIA dominates statistically. "Businesses and lawyers working for businesses make the lion's share of requests—probably close to 75 percent," according to Harry Hammitt, editor of the FOIA newsletter *Access Reports*.[24] For example, Ronald Draughon, vice president of a small contracting company in North Carolina, admits he submits twenty-five FOIA requests a week. "I think anyone doing business with the government has got to use FOIA," he stated. "If they're not, they're operating blind."[25]

In support of the heavy business use of the act, FOIA service companies have blossomed around the country. Jeff Stachewicz, president of FOIA Group, Inc., calls his five-employee firm "McFOIA, the McDonald's of this business." He files 400 FOIA requests a month, charging $75 per request. Almost all of his clients are businesses.[26]

FOIA Exemption 4 was designed to prevent the release of trade secrets and privileged or confidential information of a commercial or financial nature, but the limits of the exemption were inititially unclear. A 1983 study, *Entrepreneurship, Productivity and the Freedom of Information Act*, expressed the business community's view that too much proprietary information was available through the FOIA. Historically, freedom-of-information legislation was intended to open government files to scholars, public-interest groups, and members of the press. The study concluded that FOIA requests from such individuals or groups "are relatively rare compared to those emanating from business firms and their legal representatives or from market intermediaries."

Although the study acknowledges that "the prevention of political corruption may be worth a billion dollars of released business information," it claimed that "the lion's share of information disclosures to past and present FOIA requesters has little to do with preventing the abuse of political power."[27]

The surge of FOIA requests for competitive business information in the early 1980s produced an oxymoronic legal response: the reverse-FOIA lawsuit (see Chapter 2). These suits were brought by businesses attempting to *prevent* the release of government-held commercial information to FOIA requesters.

The Reagan administration, bowing to business pressure to protect a very broad definition of trade secrets, proposed legislation to exempt the disclosure of *all* commercial or financial information if its release might "impair . . . the legitimate business interests" of the firm. The bill was headed off by critics, including consumer advocate Ralph Nader, who pointed out, "Exempting such information from disclosure under the FOIA could allow the government to suppress evidence of unsafe consumer goods, affirmative action violations, deceptive advertising, dangerous food and drugs, and environmental hazards."[28]

In 1987 President Reagan issued an executive order that required companies to be notified in advance of an FOIA release of their information. Subsequent court decisions placed further limits on the use of the FOIA for competitive business purposes.

Thomas Susman, a Washington attorney who lobbied for a business coalition in the mid-1980s, recently declared, "There aren't very many reverse FOIA cases anymore. For at least a decade, perhaps since the Reagan Executive Order on consultation with submitters, agencies have, by and large, been very protective of commercial information. Agencies have been generally sympathetic to claims of confidentiality, and businesses have become a lot more realistic in the claims they make. There are fewer spurious claims and a lot less litigation, reverse actions or straight FOIA claims, on commercial information."[29]

Within these more practical guidelines, the FOIA continues to serve the public interest in the commercial and consumer areas. *Former Secrets: Government Records Made Public Through the Freedom of Information Act* documents examples of FOIA revelations in such areas as consumer product safety, the environment, government fraud, and business: "Critics of the FOIA, primarily within the business community itself, charge that commercial entities are using the FOIA to pry loose trade secrets and other confidential information from their competitors in a form of 'industrial espionage.' . . . [H]owever, professional FOIA personnel say that agencies are very careful to avoid disclosing confidential business information that has been submitted to the agency."[30]

Former Secrets reveals a variety of legitimate purposes for which businesses use the FOIA, such as acquiring information necessary to submit competitive bids on government contracts, inspection reports to monitor their status with federal regulators, and information about health, safety, and employment regulations, administrative opinions, and agency manuals that could help them avoid problems in complying with the law.

Even greater public interest has been served by FOIA requests for consumer information. *Former Secrets* concludes, "The battle to get information on potentially dangerous consumer goods often pits public interest against business claims of confidentiality, and agencies at times are caught in the middle. If the FOIA were not at work, it would be the consumer who would suffer."[31]

THE NATIONAL SECURITY ARCHIVE

Within the FOIA community, perhaps the most socially significant use of the statute is by the numerous public service organizations that specialize in the FOIA. Prominent among these organizations is the National Security Archive, a nonprofit research institute on international affairs which includes a library and archive of declassified U.S. documents obtained through the Freedom of Information Act. It is also an indexing and publishing house and a public interest law firm that defends and expands public access to government information through the FOIA.

The archive was founded in 1985 by a group of journalists and scholars, led by Scott Armstrong, who had obtained extensive materials from the U.S. government under the FOIA and sought a centralized repository for them. Under current Executive Director Tom Blanton, the archive has become the world's largest nongovernmental library of declassified documents. Currently located within George Washington University's Gelman Library in Washington, D.C., the archive applies the latest in computer indexing technology to the massive amount of material already released by the U.S. government on international affairs, makes it accessible to researchers and the public, and builds comprehensive collections of documents on topics of greatest interest to scholars and the public.

The archive's mainframe computer system hosts major databases of released documents, authority files of individuals and organizations in international affairs, and FOIA requests filed by archive staff members and outside requesters. Its reading room, open to the public without charge, has welcomed visitors from across the United States and around the world. Archive staff are frequently called on to testify before Congress, lecture at universities, and appear on national broadcasts and media interviews on the subject of FOIA, free access to government information, and international affairs generally.

Using material acquired through the FOIA, the archive has published a sizable number of scholarly works, including *The Cuban Missile Crisis* (1992), *Presidential Directives on National Security: From Truman to Clinton* (1994), *White House E-mail* (1995), *U.S. Espionage and Intelligence, 1947–1996* (1997), and *U.S. Nuclear History: Nuclear Arms and Politics in the Missile Age, 1955–1968* (1998).

In the process of developing its extensive collections and publications, the archive has become the leading nonprofit user of the FOIA, inheriting more than 2,000 requests from outside scholars who donated their documents and pending requests to the archive, and initiating more than 10,000 other FOIA requests over the past decade. The archive's work has set new precedents under the FOIA, including more efficient procedures for document processing at the State Department, less burden on requesters to qualify for fee waivers, and the archival preservation of electronic information held by the government. Their expertise in the use of the FOIA, as well as in archival and library practices, has brought delegations from countries around the world to learn from the archive's innovative model of nongovernmental institutional memory for formerly secret documents.

In 1995 the archive established a close administrative connection with the Center for National Security Studies (CNSS), a relationship which the archive's executive director, Tom Blanton, recently explained.

"It can best be characterized as a partnership," said Blanton. "We have a long history of cooperation during which the Archive's FOI projects have often been represented by the Center and their lawyers, particularly Kate Martin. At the point that the Center left the ACLU's Washington Office, where it had been until 1995, I proposed to Kate that she become the general counsel of the Archive. We had a vacancy and they were leaving the ACLU [American Civil Liberties Union], so we essentially merged their FOIA litigation project with ours by hiring Kate. It should be noted, however, that the bulk of our legal work is done by outside pro bono counsel."

One of the current FOIA cases being handled by the archive is that of former Lebanon hostage Terry Anderson. According to Blanton, Anderson filed FOIA requests when he returned to the United States after being held as a hostage in Lebanon. "The requests were filed in 1992 when he was writing a book which came out in late 1993," said Blanton. "He first looked through our Iran-Contra material in an attempt to find how much our government knew about his kidnappers, the Hezbollah and similar groups in Lebanon. After submitting his FOIA requests he received two strange responses. First, he received press clippings of his own articles filed from the Middle East. Second, he was informed by some nameless bureaucrat that the U.S. government could not release information on Anderson's terrorist captors unless he first acquired a waiver of privacy rights from the terrorists. It was clearly a boilerplate response, but it really set him off. He came to us and we helped him find a lawyer and put together a complaint. He still hasn't had a full response to his requests, but the lawsuit is forcing folks in the intelligence agencies to process some information."[32]

Will Ferroggiaro, the archive's FOIA coordinator, also recalls the origins of Anderson's connection with the archive. "He was here researching through our Iran-Contra era material for his book, *Den of Lions*," said

Ferroggiaro, "and he decided to file a FOIA request. He had heard of us and wanted to make use of our expertise. He was interested in determining to what degree the government had relations with various players during the captivity, to what degree his captivity and negotiations were involved in Iran-Contra, and other aspects of the government's involvement at that time. In the fall of 1993, Anderson asked us to monitor all of his requests, and now all the agencies send his requested documents here. He turned over all of his documents to us, and I've processed them and sent him copies. In the fall of 1994, he filed suit with our aid, so the litigation is also coming through us. Kate Martin, our general counsel, is assisting the pro bono representation provided by Crowell and Moring."

Ferroggiaro says Anderson is disturbed by the embarrassing degree to which the government has prevented him from having access to information that relates very uniquely to himself and his case. "The government's rationale for withholding the information is, on the face of it, asinine. In additon to pursuing his personal information needs, Anderson is guided by the principle that all citizens have a right of access to information that the government controls on behalf of the public."

The archive's aggressive FOIA litigation in the Anderson case is typical of its continuing struggle to open up the federal government, yet, surprisingly, the archive maintains a cordial working relationship with federal agencies. "I think there are some neanderthals within the government who still consider us a thorn and a problem," said Ferroggiaro, "but it has become much more collegial because we've been around for a while and they know we're not going away. We're an established research institute now, and we use a little more finesse. We're civil, we too wear blue blazers at meetings, and we get along well with government officials. We try to give credit where credit is due.

"Occasionally you still come across the mind set that we shouldn't have access to this material, but if you're adversarial, you tend to back people into a corner. At the same time, I think there is a danger, and we've all experienced it at conferences and seminars, that this collegiality may lead government officials to assume that you have the same interest in secrecy that they do. But if they have the chance to talk to us, they will see that we're really on a different wavelength. If we're a little less aggressive, it's not because our views have changed."[33]

Blanton feels that maintaining good relations with the agencies and avoiding advocacy on issues other than information policy have made it easier for the archive to obtain government records. "It helps us a great deal," said Blanton, "because we're not in an adversarial position with the government, except on the issue of information access. It also makes it easier for us to recruit pro bono counsel, because we're not arguing for or against any policy, and it adds to our credibility when we interpret the acquired documents. We certainly don't shrink from a candid inter-

pretation of those documents, but we don't use them to attack a particular policy, other than secrecy. We have found that it is far more
productive to seek out people within the agencies who are true access
professionals, to work with that portion of the bureaucracy whose interests are served by greater public debate. We use those interests to
increase the net sum of openness. It's a much more sophisticated approach.''

When asked to compare the mission of the archive to that of similar
public interest organizations like Public Citizen, Blanton stated, "The
heart of what we're about is getting government documents out to the
public, and that is key to a whole series of purposes we share with organizations like Public Citizen. Those common purposes include government accountability and the use of the FOIA toward that end, but we
have more to do with scholarly and historical research and journalistic
support than than does Public Citizen. Also, Public Citizen is a forceful
advocate on a wide range of policy issues, but we are an advocate only
for information policies related to the FOIA and government openness.
We don't take positions on government regulation of businesses or foreign policy issues. We simply define ourselves in terms of using the rules
of openness, primarily the FOIA, to enrich the public debate, hold government accountable, and build a more transparent international information system, particularly in the area of national security, which is the
most conflict-prone and most shrouded from public view."

Blanton described the evolution of the archive into an effective voice
for the right to know and an important publishing house as well. "Things
have really changed in the last decade," he said. "The major transition
for the Archive has occurred in the last five or six years when we grew
from being a watchdog on the national security state during the Cold
War into a new arena which offers more opportunity for multinational
and international openness and cooperative investigation. We have developed partnerships in 14 different countries, through which we work
with historians, journalists, archivists and public interest advocates. They
use declassified American files as leverage on their host countries to open
up important but sometimes tragic histories, such as in Guatemala. One
of our partnerships was with a group of Solidarity intellectuals in Poland
who were trying to unearth their hidden history.

"This is the post–Cold War era, and we have taken our methodologies,
capacities and materials to a multitude of other countries. At the same
time, we've learned an enormous amount from these people that we can
bring back here. We have a wonderful dialog that works both ways. We
take released American documents, say on the Cuban Missile Crisis, to
Moscow and challenge the Russian archivists to release their documents.
Similarly, we take Soviet documents on, say, Eastern Europe back to the
U.S. State Department and challenge them and the CIA to release their

secret materials. Each new advance anywhere in the world thus exercises leverage to move the entire international system to a higher plane of openness."

When asked whether the FOIA would always remain the basis for building the archive's collections, Blanton responded, "Not necessarily. I can envision an optimal future in an electronic age of routine openness of government functions. I can envision it, but I didn't say it was going to happen in your lifetime or mine. In the current world of routine government secrecy, the Archive does, of course, acquire most of its collections through the FOIA, although a significant amount of material comes from mandatory review. Even if the President's executive order on classification really works, we are likely to continue to rely heavily on the FOIA."

Blanton believes that President Clinton's executive order has had some positive effects on agency compliance with the FOIA. "There are several agencies, the State Department and Air Force in particular, that are doing a good job in meeting the executive order requirement to declassify 25-year-old documents. They are actually ahead of schedule in getting them out. Then there are agencies like the CIA that have exempted 60 percent of their files from even being reviewed under the executive order. It's a real scofflaw. Even if there is a virtual Niagara Falls of 25-year-old and older documents being pushed out of the secrecy system, some of those materials are going to remain classified and will require outside pressure through the FOIA to acquire them. The less than 25-year-old documents will all require FOIA because there's no automatic review for documents of that age. So FOIA will remain the heart of our operation for the forseeable future."

I asked Blanton why agencies continued to receive poor marks, overall, from the FOIA requester community. "When you talk to agency people, which we do all the time, these folks say that they have been whipsawed by competing demands and statutes," he said. "In a period of declining resources, this has meant that FOIA has been short-changed, even though the net overall openness is arguably far greater. For example, the agency people talk about the JFK assassination records bill, the net effect of which has been to release millions of pages of documents which should have been released long ago. But Congress gave no additional resources to the agencies to do the processing. These and other demands on agencies, like the Gulf War syndrome investigation, the radiation experiments project or the POW/MIA effort, have taken scarce resources away from FOIA and declassification."

Though Blanton acknowledges that some agencies have rationalized their poor FOIA compliance with claims of inadequate resources, he believes the problem is real and requires creative solutions. He referred to the imaginative approach used by Senator Patrick Leahy (D-Vt.) in 1989 when he sat on both the Appropriations subcommittee and the FOIA subcommittee of the Judiciary. During hearings, said Blanton, Leahy chided Secretary of State James Baker for having one of the worst FOIA records in government and pointedly declared that he was sitting in a position of authority on Baker's overseas budget. According to Blanton, "Baker then went back to the State Department and 'found' $900,000 in his administrative kitty to hire a bunch of retired foreign service officers to process FOIA requests. They actually got their average turnaround down from about two years to about eleven months. So where there's a will there's a way."

Blanton says a little extra agency money can make a dramatic difference in agency response time. "We see it every summer in the State Department," he said. "During the two-month period near the end of the summer, after they've brought in a bunch of those summer interns, we get fifty percent of our year's FOIA requests answered. The documents had already been reviewed by agency personnel, but they hadn't been xeroxed, put in envelopes, stamped and mailed. Our argument is simply that the government is spending its resources on the wrong things."[34]

The National Security Archive has its own problems in applying scarce resources to the heavy FOIA workload. Will Ferroggiaro, the FOIA coordinator at the archive, described the archive's internal procedures for generating FOIA requests and organizing the received material. The archive files more than a thousand FOIA requests each year, many of which are still pending. All of these requests are monitored on the archive's computer database. "The analysts decide what they want to pursue, generally working from a chronology of important events and then inputting those requests into the database," said Ferroggiaro. "I give the requests a final review and a tracking number, and the analysts send them out to the agencies. When an agency responds, we track their correspondence on the database, constantly updating the records. We can check the database at any moment to determine the status of any request, whether documents have been received, whether they were redacted, appealed, and so on."

When asked how priorities were assigned on possible requests, Ferroggiaro responded, "During the lifetime of a project, FOIA requesting will ebb and flow. We're constantly filing requests, and the priority in terms of subject matter is determined by the analyst. There are currently nine analysts who initiate the requests, representing the major documentation projects underway. The requests originate from the background research, where important information is identified that may require the use of FOIA. If I see a request that isn't clear or specific, I'll suggest revisions to the analyst.

"When requested documents arrive, I do a review of them to monitor agency behavior, how they process the documents, the amount of excisions made, whether they are asserting exemptions not allowed under the law, or if they're not identifying their withholdings. That sort of thing. Then the documents go to the analyst who requested them. Any decision to appeal is made by the analyst. I may suggest an appeal if I observe an egregious pattern of withholding on the part of the agency."

The determination of which FOIA documents make the final cut for a published set is accomplished through a similarly decentralized process. "It's really the editorial judgements of the analysts and the director of analysis," said Ferroggiaro. "It depends on what your request yields. You may know that the State Department has the documents and you may write the best request in the world, but if they don't release them you have nothing to work with. Sometimes you get something interesting from an agency you wouldn't have expected."

As the archive has grown into a publishing house, realistic business judgments have become necessary, but Ferroggiaro says this does not mean that FOIA requests are crafted simply on the basis of their likely value for subsequent publication. "I really don't think it directs the decision to request," said Ferroggiaro, "because you never know what you're going to get. You can't assume you're going to get anything, especially in the foreign policy and defense areas. Still, we don't undertake any project of interest to the public without the assumption that it could result in a publication."

The majority of the acquired documents go unpublished, but even these materials are heavily used by the public. "We probably have a couple of researchers scheduled each day to use our collections," said Ferroggiaro. "They may have become acquainted with the collections through our Web site, which lists the subjects contained and brief descriptions of what is available. Or they may have simply called and asked about our collections. One of our librarians can search the database and see what we have in their area of interest."

The archive has a growing interest in the official documents becoming available from former Communist countries. I asked if that indicates a flagging interest in American secrecy. "I think it's more subtle than that," said Ferroggiaro. "Foreign policy is the predominant interest of the Archive, but there's a considerable overlap with civil liberties at home that may be compromised because of a perceived national security threat abroad. We write op ed pieces and letters to the editor on this subject. We've provided evidence and testimony to the Moynihan Commission on Protecting and Reducing Government Secrecy, and we met with congressional staff on openness issues. We also provided testimony when the Clinton Administration began their review of the Executive Order on national security information. So our interest and advocacy on issues related to American secrecy is substantial, but it's often behind the scenes."

Ferroggiaro said virtually all of the archive's collections, including those donated or transferred to the archive, were acquired through the FOIA. "Our research is very much FOIA related," he said, "except for the few issues like Iran-Contra or Iraqgate where there was Congressional or independent counsel release of material. Occasionally there is actual affirmative government disclosure, like the material from the UN Truth Commission or El Salvador, but otherwise it's almost all FOIA material."

With the exception of a few videotapes, maps, and similar materials, almost all of the archive's collection is on paper. Given the massive amount of documents acquired through the FOIA, I wondered how the archive decided what to keep and what to dispose of. "I don't think we dispose of anything," said Ferroggiaro. "During the early years of the Archive we were approaching a space crisis as we solicited donations of FOIA collections accumulated by reporters, authors and researchers. But here at George Washington University, we have access to off-site storage capability from which we can recall materials within twenty-four hours. So we have no need to throw away anything documentary. Perhaps we've disposed of some reference materials, but not documents."

Ferroggiaro spends much of his time advising the general public about the FOIA process. "As a public service I help individuals draft requests, advise them on whether they have a case or not and whether to file an appeal," he said. "I also assist them in deciphering the language in the government's correspondence. Most people are completely confused by the government's responses, by some of the jargon. We can offer assistance in person, by mail, or by phone. I also have an e-mail address, through which I receive an increasing number of requests for assistance from around the world."[35]

THE CENTER FOR NATIONAL SECURITY STUDIES

The Center for National Security Studies is a nongovernmental advocacy and research organization, founded in 1974 to work for control of the FBI and CIA and to prevent violations of civil liberties in the United States. From 1978 to 1994, the CNSS was a joint project of the ACLU and the Fund for Peace. It now works in partnership with the National Security Archive at George Washington University, sharing projects and cooperating on FOIA requests. The CNSS and the National Security Archive are currently involved in several freedom of information lawsuits against the intelligence agencies. Kate Martin, director of the CNSS, also serves as general counsel for the National Security Archive.

In its publicity handout, the CNSS states, "In order to participate effectively in the political process, citizens need not only the rights to assemble, to speak, and to write; they also need the information that makes effective participation possible. The Center's long-standing project on access to government information works to secure this information and eliminate excessive government secrecy. In the aftermath of the abuses of power associated with the Vietnam War and Watergate, the United States established a system of oversight and accountability of its intelligence, national security and federal law enforcement agencies. Yet much remains to be done: Too much information is still classified secret and withheld from public debate in the name of national security. The FBI still operates without a legislative charter and continues to claim broad authority to spy on Americans engaged in political activity. . . . Defense of human rights and constitutional procedures in the face of claims of national security is a never-ending task that requires constant vigilance and public awareness. The Center for National Security Studies plays that role."[36]

The CNSS has a long history of effective FOIA use. Indeed, during the 1970s and early 1980s, the center probably initiated more politically significant FOIA requests than any other organization. Most of their requests were to the CIA, FBI, Department of Defense (DOD), Department of State, and Defense Intelligence Agency.

CNSS's CIA requests alone have produced records revealing such things as CIA attempts to kill undesirables through apparent natural causes; CIA confinement of a foreign leader in a mental institution after he had assisted the agency; CIA proposals to use drugs, shock treatment, and brain surgery to silence "blown" agents and defectors; Project Bluebird, in which the CIA conducted top secret behavior-control experiments and tested LSD and other drugs on prisoners at the U.S. Public Service Hospital; mind control experiments, including CIA techniques to induce unwitting subjects to commit assassinations; CIA destabilization activities in Allende's Chile; CIA plots to assassinate Fidel Castro and other leaders; information on the capture and execution of Che Guevara in Bolivia; CIA assessment of the Soviet buildup in Cuba; CIA attempts to acquire poisonous viscera from an African witch doctor; CIA training of seals and fish for new espionage methods; CIA-FBI agreements on domestic operations; activities outside the CIA charter, including domestic surveillance; CIA surveillance of college students; and CIA use of academics.

CNSS's early FOIA requests to the FBI acquired information on wiretap authorization during the Franklin Roosevelt administration; surveillance documents on President John F. Kennedy; FBI "black bag jobs"; FBI surveillance of the civil rights movement, Black nationalist leaders, the Weather Underground, antiwar activists, and such individuals as Julian Bond and Martin Luther King, Jr.; FBI harassment of Martin Luther King, Jr., Muhammad Kenyatta, and Adlai Stevenson; FBI infiltration of Black political organizations; FBI investigations of the sexual behavior of politicians and other prominent people; and FBI agents posing as reporters at the 1964 Democratic convention.

The fruits of these FOIA requests were made public through a variety of publications, including such newspapers as the *New York Times, New York Post, Boston Globe, Dallas Morning News*, and *Washington Post*; such magazines as the *Chronicle of Higher Education, Facts on File, Newsweek, Federal Times*, and CNSS's *From Official Files*; such books as David Garrow's *The FBI and Martin Luther King, Jr.* (1981) and Susan Kaplan's *Documents* (1980); and such television shows as *ABC News Close-up, CBS Morning News*, and the CBS-News documentary *1968*; and the film *The Private Files of J. Edgar Hoover*.

Since 1995 the CNSS has worked on freedom of information and government secrecy issues in partnership with the National Security Archive, with which it shares office space. When asked about their FOIA work, Duncan Levin, public policy analyst at the center, responded, "We believe that a reasonable balancing of national security and civil liberties concerns can be reached only if the princple of openness is also respected. The ideal embodied in the First Amendment—that wise policy will result from free, robust, and unfettered public debate—applies to national security issues in the same way it applies to all other types of issues. This does not preclude the government from keeping truly sensitive information secret, but it does mean that meaningful debate requires the greatest possible amount of information, with the presumption in favor of openness."[37]

Levin explained that efforts to stifle public debate can take two forms. One is the traditional effort to outlaw, disrupt, or chill public expressions of opposition to government policies. The other is to classify and withhold information that is necessary for informed political debate. The Center for National Security Studies, he said, resists both.

One of CNSS's most successful recent projects resulted in the unprecedented disclosure of the U.S. intelligence budget. Kate Martin, the center's director, declared, "I think our lawsuit for the CIA budget is the quintessential story about the importance of the FOIA. After President Clinton and then-CIA Director John M. Deutch publicly stated in April 1996 that revealing the CIA's budget would do no harm to the national security, Steven Aftergood of the American Federation of Scientists submitted a FOIA request for that budget. The CIA denied the request, citing FOIA exemption (b)(1), the national security exemption. On appeal, we pointed out to the CIA that exemption (b)(1) only applies when release of the information would cause national security harm. In this case, the President and the CIA Director have admitted that there would be no harm. I wrote the CIA's General Counsel, saying, in effect, 'Look, you can't be serious, and if you are, we're going to sue.' Still, they refused to release the figure. We had to actually sue under the FOIA. I told the Justice Department lawyers, 'You don't have a defense here.' "

I asked Martin whether the Justice Department acknowledged the weakness of their case. "Only after four months," she said, "and only when they were required to present their case to a judge. Without the ability to sue under the FOIA, we could never have forced the CIA to comply with the law. They knew they were violating the law by denying our request, and it was only because we took them to court that they finally released the figure. Even then, the number they released is only the aggregate amount for all the intelligence agencies, so we still don't have the amount spent by each agency. That request is pending. We have also asked for next year's requested appropriation. The agency has not yet agreed to release the budget for past or future years, but in the end I believe they will have to disclose both. I am hopeful, because I think it is required under the law."[38]

I asked Duncan Levin whether the CNSS suit had convinced the CIA to deliver future budget figures without argument. "We certainly hope that's the case," said Levin. "The CIA was forthcoming this past year in voluntarily releasing the FY1998 figure, and we hope it continues to be that way. The release of the FY1997 budget was the first of its kind since the founding of the CIA during World War II. When Director of Central Intelligence George Tenet released the first number, he said he would have to examine the consequences of revealing 'trends' in the successive data figures. With this last release, though, he said the disclosure of a second number posed no threat to the national security. So we are hopeful that, with outside pressure, the CIA will continue to release this critical budget information."[39]

PUBLIC CITIZEN

Ralph Nader's Public Citizen Foundation is a venerable and influential public interest organization that includes extensive FOIA advocacy and litigation among its activities. Founded by Nader in 1971, Public Citizen describes itself as "the consumer's eyes and ears in Washington," fighting for safer drugs and medical devices, cleaner and safer energy sources, a cleaner environment, fair trade, and a more open and democratic government.[40]

Located in Washington, D.C., Public Citizen has six divisions: Congress Watch, the Health Research Group, the Critical Mass Energy Project, Global Trade Watch, Buyers Up, and the Litigation Group, which includes the Freedom of Information Clearinghouse. For the purposes of this book, the last division is the most significant.

The Litigation Group, a ten-lawyer public interest law firm, was co-founded by Ralph Nader and Alan Morrison in 1972. From its origin, it has focused a significant part of its efforts on fighting government secrecy. The Freedom of Information Clearinghouse is a project of Nader's Center for Study of Responsive Law. Housed at the Litigation Group offices and directed by Lucinda Sikes, one of their lawyers, the Freedom of Information Clearinghouse has provided technical and legal assistance on the FOIA since 1972 to individuals, public interest groups, and the media who seek access to government information. Together, the Litigation Group and the FOI Clearinghouse seek to enhance public access to government-held information under the FOIA and other access laws through litigation, public education, and congressional and administrative advocacy.

Since 1972 Litigation Group lawyers have litigated more cases under the FOIA than any other organization, representing FOIA requesters in approximately 300 lawsuits challenging government secrecy. Early procedural victories include the precedent-setting *Vaughan v. Rosen* (1974) and *Phillippi v. CIA* (D.C. Cir. 1976).

Among the many recent FOIA suits initiated by Public Citizen was the path-breaking *Armstrong v. Executive Office of the President* (1993), which established that electronic records generated by the executive branch are subject to federal open-records laws. As a result of this litigation, the government released over 3,000 e-mail records from the Reagan White House. The *Armstrong* litigation led to *Public Citizen v. Carlin* (1997), a successful effort to prevent the arbitrary destruction of electronic records (see Chapter 5).

The FOI Clearinghouse has assisted thousands of people in placing FOIA requests and has published the widely distributed *Freedom of Information Act User's Guide*. The FOI Clearinghouse and Litigation Group have also led workshops at the ACLU's annual conference and training seminars held for the American Society of Access Professionals (ASAP).

David Vladek, the director of the Public Litigation Group, supervises the Freedom of Information Clearinghouse. He has been with Public Citizen for twenty years. "We are litigators and we've been doing this now for twenty-five years and over 300 FOIA cases. If you look back, much of the prominent early FOIA litigation was handled by this office. We were the principal lobbyists for the 1974 amendments to the Act. We go way back. It wasn't really until the early 1980s that other organizations started to do any FOIA work at all.

"The ACLU started to do some national security litigation in the 1980s when one of our lawyers, Mark Lynch, went over there to work with Mort Halperin and their National Security Project. The ACLU has dropped that now, but they did some of the early pioneering litigation under Exemption 1. Of course they lost all of those cases. I don't think they ever won any of them. We don't have a much better record either, because national security cases are always hard to win. We've done very well in other areas, but not national security."

As the director of the FOI Clearinghouse, Vladek approves all the litigation and handles some of the cases himself. He described three sources for his FOIA cases. "One is internal, where we represent components of

Public Citizen. Our organization generates a very substantial volume of FOIA work. For example, we've done an enormous amount of health and safety litigation, trying to pry loose documents out of FDA [the Food and Drug Administration], NIH [the National Institutes of Health], the Occupational Safety and Health Administration [OSHA] and the EPA [Environmental Protection Agency], typically on behalf of our Public Citizens Health Research Group [PCHRG], which is why there are a lot of *Health Research Group versus FDA* cases."

Indeed, the Health Research Group may be the most prominent section of Public Citizen because of its highly publicized battles with the government over public health and safety. For example, in January 1985, the Health Research Group used the FOIA to publicize 249 workplaces where some 250,000 workers faced increased risk of cancer, heart disease, and other illnesses because of working conditions.

Vladek explained, "The PCHRG is part of the Public Citizen Foundation, like the Public Citizen Litigation Group. PCHRG is headed by Dr. Sidney Wolfe, a very prominent physician. They publish and do a lot of work on drug safety, occupational safety and food safety. We've probably litigated 75 or 80 cases on their behalf against FDA, OSHA and EPA, trying to pry loose health and safety data. For example, we just won a case in the district court here involving a big diabetes drug that was pulled from the U.S. market a few years ago. We had been asked by our colleagues at Health Research Group to bring this suit because they wanted access to that data and the FDA refused to release it."

In addition to internally generated FOIA cases, Public Citizen frequently handles litigation for other public service organizations. "We've acted as counsel for many of the cases that the National Security Archive has participated in," said Vladek. "We've done a lot of their legal work. They are one of our many, many client groups."

Authors and journalists also frequently rely on Public Citizen for their FOIA litigation. Vladec said, "Our clients include Stanley Kutler, whose book *Abuse of Power* is based on tapes of the Nixon presidency that we managed to compel disclosure of through litigation. Taylor Branch, Pulitzer Prize–winner for *Parting the Water*, is another client. The introduction to that book has a lovely acknowledgement of all the work we did. Scott Armstrong is another client. We represent Scott in lots of his litigation. I would say twenty percent of our clients are journalists or historians. We recently helped a researcher who is writing about a man named Morris "two-gun" Cohen, the Canadian who ended up being a close adviser to Sun Yat Sen. We provided some FOIA work related to his manuscript. We're currently representing the Yale art historian in a case against the FBI to get some biographical information on an artist who had communist ties."

I asked Vladeck to name some of the tougher agencies to deal with.

"There are different ways to be 'tough,' " he said. "The CIA and NSA [National Security Agency] are tough because they make very inflexible, very rigid and very broad claims on exemption status and they litigate fiercely. On the other hand, they are quite responsive, they talk to you, you talk to them, they don't ignore you. We have very cordial relations with the general counsels of the offices of those agencies. We disagree about the law, but I don't think there's an effort by those agencies to evade their responsibilities under the FOIA. They just see those responsibilities very differently than we do. In that sense they are very tough.

"There are other agencies like the Justice Department and the Department of State that, in our experience, are unresponsive and will try to game you. In that sense, dealing with those agencies is tough. Not necessarily because their positions on FOIA are going to be so extreme, but just because they don't like FOIA, they're hostile to it, and they try to thwart your use of it."

Vladeck said there were two different variables at work in determining the effectiveness of the FOIA. "One is the administration of the Act, who's there, who's implementing it. And the second variable is what's going on in the courts. In my view, there have been major swings in the way the FOIA is administered, the way it is managed, but since the Reagan Administration the courts have been predominantly hostile."

Despite these concerns, Vladeck remains a dedicated FOIA supporter. "We use it every day," he said, "and by and large we get a lot of what we ask for. That doesn't mean that it's a problem-free system. It doesn't mean that the government is releasing everything it should. It doesn't mean that the courts are not grudging in the way they apply the FOIA. But we're far better off with it than we would be without it."

Vladeck and the Public Citizen staff are not members of the ASAP, and they do not think that membership would be useful for their organization. "If you're in the business of processing FOIA requests it might be useful, but frankly we are steeped in FOIA law. Our mission is not to apply the FOIA the way the Justice Department wants to apply it, but rather to push the envelope and use the courts to enhance access. We participate in ASAP's forums, but we try to use their meetings as a platform to proselytize, for want of a better word."[41]

THE AMERICAN CIVIL LIBERTIES UNION

The ACLU is a nonprofit, nonpartisan public interest organization devoted to protecting the civil liberties of all Americans. Its mission is to preserve the Bill of Rights for each new generation of Americans. Today, the ACLU continues to urge free expression as the best way to address our society's long-standing social problems, including racism, sexism, homophobia, and religious intolerance.

Although the ACLU maintains its national office in New York and a legislative office in Washington, D.C., it has a fifty-state network of affiliate offices in most major cities, more than 300 chapters in smaller towns, and regional offices in Denver and Atlanta. It is governed by an eighty-four-member board of directors that has one representative from each state affiliate and thirty at-large members elected by all ACLU members within a state. The ACLU's national office is located at 132 West 43rd Street, New York, New York 10036.

The ACLU has a number of national projects devoted to specific issues: AIDS, arts censorship, capital punishment, children's rights, education reform, lesbian and gay rights, immigrants' rights, national security, privacy and technology, religious freedom, voting rights, women's rights, and workplace rights. The ACLU's more than sixty staff attorneys collaborate with more than 2,000 volunteer attorneys in handling almost 6,000 cases annually, making it the largest public interest law firm in the nation. Indeed, the ACLU appears before the U.S. Supreme Court more than any other organization except the Department of Justice.

During the 1950s, when the press first brought the issue of a citizen's right to know before the public, the ACLU commissioned a report by journalist Allen Raymond entitled *The People's Right to Know: A Report on Government News Suppression* (1955). The report cited the complaints of numerous journalists about government secrecy. In the decades that followed, the ACLU has continued to make government secrecy one of its primary targets. In 1971 it submitted an amicus brief in support of the right of the *New York Times* and *Washington Post* to publish the Pentagon Papers. It published two important reports documenting restraints on the press, "The Engineering of Restraint" (1971), describing the Nixon administration's attacks on the press, and "A Question of Survival" (1972), reporting on the deliberate underfunding of public television to prevent it from serving as an independent source of public affairs programming.

During this same period, the ACLU brought numerous suits in support of democratic access to the media. It also made effective use of the FOIA, including two large releases of FBI documents related to the bureau's surveillance of the ACLU itself. The first release covered the period from 1920 to 1943 and the second, containing about 10,000 documents, covered the period from 1943 to 1976.

Unlike the National Security Archive and Public Citizen, the ACLU does not make the FOIA a major focus; it uses the FOIA instead as a selective tool to accomplish its broad objectives. Nonetheless, the ACLU has a long history of significant FOIA use, and, indeed, from 1978 to 1994 the CNSS functioned as a project of the ACLU. It was during this period that the CNSS accomplished much of the groundbreaking FOIA work described above.

Morton Halperin, who headed the ACLU's National Security Project during that period, recently recalled the ACLU's early FOIA activities. "We were more involved in the policy issues relating to the preservation and expansion of the Freedom of Information Act than we were in directly using it," he said. "We did both, of course. Most of our direct use of the FOIA came through the Center for National Security Studies (CNSS), which used it to acquire documents relating primarily to intelligence operations. We published what we acquired in our periodical, *From Official Files*. CNSS also published a book titled *Documents*, a collection of abstracts of documents we had acquired relating to intelligence agencies."

Halperin described the ACLU's crucial lobbying efforts on behalf of the FOIA. "We played a supportive role in the 1974 amendments and everything that came after that," he said. "We attempted to broaden the Act and also to fight off efforts to narrow the Act. There was a concerted effort by the Reagan Administration to weaken the FOIA, and we tried to prevent this. It was a major priority of the Republicans to destroy the FOIA, and we managed to moderate the 1986 amendments. I did a lot of the negotiating myself, and Mark Lynch, who was a FOIA litigator for us, did a great deal of it. Allan Adler was also an important lobbyist for us during that period."

Though Halperin is no longer actively involved with the FOIA, he maintains an undiminished respect for it. "I think it's enormously important," he said. "Obviously it could be strengthened and there are those who would like to weaken it, but, by and large, it's been very successful. The Electronic FOIA amendments are certainly an advance as well."[42]

Arthur Spitzer, the legal director of the ACLU of the National Capital Area, described current ACLU use of the FOIA. "The FOIA is certainly a much larger part of what organizations like Public Citizen and the National Security Archive do than it is for the ACLU's current operations," he said. "We lobbied in favor of the FOIA when it was first debated and passed in Congress. We think it's a very important law giving citizens access to government information, which belongs to the public in the first place. We still use the FOIA as part of our fight to defend people's civil rights and civil liberties, but we don't tend to do a lot of stand-alone FOIA litigation. We are more likely to use the FOIA in connection with our other projects. For example, we may be using FOIA requests as part of a case or project concerning police brutality."

Spitzer emphasized the decentralized nature of ACLU operations in pointing out the difficulty in itemizing current FOIA use. "Every ACLU office around the country, of which there are about 50, does its own litigation," he said, "so no one would have any way to tell you how many FOIA cases the ACLU has done nationwide over the past several years. The FOIA is used locally with local needs in mind."[43]

THE REPORTERS COMMITTEE FOR FREEDOM OF THE PRESS

The Reporters Committee for Freedom of the Press, located in Arlington, Virginia, describes itself as "a voluntary association of journalists dedicated to protecting a free press." It claims to be "the only nonprofit legal defense and research organization in the country that provides round-the-clock, cost-free services to the media,"[44] including legal advice and assistance and amicus briefs. The committee undertakes legal defense and research projects in all areas of media law, including libel, freedom of information, prior restraint, secret courts, privacy, broadcasting, confidential sources and national security.

The Reporters Committee was created in 1970 at a time when the news media faced a wave of government subpoenas asking reporters to reveal confidential sources. After *New York Times* reporter Earl Caldwell was ordered to reveal his sources in the Black Panther party to a federal grand jury, a meeting of prominent newsmen was convened at Georgetown University to organize legal assistance for reporters. Among those involved in this effort were J. Anthony Lukas, Murray Fromson, Fred Graham, Jack Nelson, Ben Bradlee, Eileen Shanahan, Mike Wallace, Robert Maynard, and Tom Wicker. Out of this meeting came a committee and staff that began recruiting attorneys to donate their services, and with the support of foundations and news organizations that committee has developed into the media's most important legal support organization.

Jane Kirtley, executive director of the Reporters Committee, is a strong advocate for open government. She acknowledges that "there's a tiny, tiny, tiny, tiny percentage" of government information that can appropriately be kept secret, but "it's a much smaller percentage . . . than our government would have us think it is. That's where the battle is always going to be."[45]

The Reporters Committee operates a Freedom of Information Center and publishes the quarterly *News Media & the Law*, the newsletter *News Media Update*, and a number of guidebooks, including *How to Use the Federal FOI Act*. The FOI Service Center, directed by Rebecca Daugherty, maintains an FOI Hotline (800–336–4243) which handles amost 2,000 calls each year. It is part of a larger Reporters Committee hotline which serves reporters facing problems in gathering and covering the news.

In an August 1998 interview, Rebecca Daugherty explained that the FOI Center primarily serves the needs of reporters, although they do occasionally assist other FOIA requesters on issues that are important to journalists. "I will frequently help FOIA requesters who are facing the kinds of problems that reporters will face," said Daugherty. "We don't assist commercial requesters, but where the issues are similar to those faced by reporters, we will help."

The committee's status as a tax exempt organization prevents them from lobbying Congress on particular legislative issues, but they have an important role in keeping Congress informed. For example, in the spring of 1998, Jane Kirtley testified before Congress on federal agency compliance with the 1996 Electronic FOIA.

"We track legislative proposals," said Daugherty, "and try to describe them in our newsletter and our magazine so that others who are in a position to lobby can do so knowledgeably. We will not usually take a public position on legislation. We did not do so with the E-FOIA for example. We don't directly lobby Congress, but, of course, we are often contacted by congressional staff who are working on access issues. In addition, we have probably been more active than any other group in commenting on the proposed FOIA regulations that each federal agency submits for review. When an agency proposes such regulations, we let them know if there are provisions that reporters or other requesters might have trouble with. We've actually had some success in this regard. For example, the E-FOIA statute has a requirement that anyone seeking expedited review must certify that their stated reasons are true. We envisioned fairly complicated back and forth negotiation on this matter which would take more time than the expedited review system would save. We therefore asked agencies to waive that requirement, and a number of them have done that."

The FOI Center maintains a hot line for journalists, at which reporters can get advice and assistance on a broad range of freedom of information issues. "Usually they call us when they have tried to get information without the use of the FOIA and failed," said Daugherty. "They might ask about what should be included in the initial request. Often they don't know what's covered by the Act, and sometimes they want to discuss whether they should even bother with a FOIA request, given the routine delays and exemptions. We don't have any crystal ball here, but sometimes we can advise on the likely agency response. We can be helpful in avoiding some of the knee-jerk denials that agencies use. We will tell them how to file a request, and sometimes we will actually fax them the language that they need. Frequently I will send them information from other FOIA cases that will help in framing their request or appeal. We may also refer them to our Web site (www.rcfp.org), which contains a FOIA letter generator that reporters have been enthusiastic about. If the inquiry concerns a federal issue, I will usually handle it. If it's a state issue, they may talk to a legal fellow assigned to that issue."

Given the routine agency delays, I asked whether reporters on short deadlines had much use for the FOIA. "Hopefully the expedited review provisions of the E-FOIA are going to ease that burden somewhat for reporters," said Daugherty. "We have an expedited review section in our

FOIA handbook. The agency FOIA people tell me that almost no one is asking for expedited review, so it's not been tested very much yet."

The FOI Center rarely submits FOIA requests under its own name or on behalf of a reporter. "We will submit FOIA requests to find out what the government is doing as part of our FOIA tracking process," said Daugherty. "For example, before the E-FOIA was passed, when agencies were reporting on their response to FOIA requests for electronic records, we filed a request for such records because we wanted to monitor their processing.

"We also assist the FOIA community by maintaining subject files at our office on a variety of helpful topics. For example, we would have files on access to hospital information, access to medical information, access to autopsies, and so on. Occasionally, in our magazine *The News Media and the Law*, we will do a roundup of how the various states have treated these access issues. We don't maintain an archive of material acquired under the FOIA. Our interest is in seeing that requesters get what they want."

The Reporters Committee's publications are an important part of its service. "We're in the 8th edition of *How to Use the Federal FOI Act*," said Daugherty. "It's an inexpensive and very useful book for reporters and others who use the Act. Each edition updates the FOIA regulations and the changes effected by the courts. One of the best-sellers among our various guides is called *Access to Electronic Records in the States*. It goes through the statutes and court cases in each state involving electronic records. It's been very useful to reporters and news organizations in states where they were facing legislation to raise the prices or reduce access to electronic records."

The FOI Center often works with other FOIA organizations, including ASAP, in which Daugherty has been active. "I think ASAP has been very good at bringing a professional demeanor to the enforcement of the FOIA," said Daugherty. "Until its creation, FOIA people were really floundering. I joined ASAP during the second year of its existence, back in the Dark Ages. Russ Roberts, an ASAP founder, did some wonderful things within his agency [HEW, later to become HHS] that became models for other agencies. He made the FOIA regulations readable by getting rid of the legalese."

The staff of the Reporters Committee includes three attorneys and three legal fellows. "We try to help reporters before and after they've gone to court, though we do not litigate cases for them," said Daugherty. "If they do not already have a lawyer, we'll help them find one, and we may discuss the case with the lawyers. We frequently file *amicus* briefs at the state Supreme Court level or with the U.S. Appeals Court if the case involves an issue of importance to the press."

The last FOIA case litigated by the committee was *Department of Justice v. Reporters Committee for a Free Press* (1989), an important Supreme Court case that seemed to limit the scope of the FOIA to information directly related to the operation of government (see Chapter 5). "A CBS reporter had filed a FOIA request for the criminal records on a defense contractor who had ties to a congressman who had been censured for corruption," recalled Daugherty. "We filed our own FOIA request for the same information and ultimately became a party to the case. The Court produced an unfortunate decision, and, coincidentally, we have not directly litigated on the FOIA since then."[46]

PEOPLE FOR THE AMERICAN WAY

People for the American Way (PAW) is a Washington, D.C.–based organization that promotes pluralism, freedom of expression, and religious diversity as fundamental American values. The organization was founded in 1980 by television producer Norman Lear to counter the growing political influence of the Moral Majority and its leader, Jerry Falwell. Its 300,000 members include religious, business, media, and labor figures. It provides support to groups and individuals facing challenges to their First Amendment rights and produces educational materials and seminars on related issues. It maintains a speakers bureau, conducts research, and distributes information on such issues as censorship, school prayer, and abortion.

People for the American Way, like the ACLU, is one of the many public interest groups that uses the FOIA very selectively to serve its broader purposes. Elliot Mincberg, general counsel for PAW, said, "We have filed lots of FOIA requests in our time with the various agencies and received useful information, though perhaps not as much as some other public interest groups. We did more in this regard a few years ago, perhaps because of the relative openness of the Clinton Administration and the reduced need to file lawsuits. It may also reflect our growing emphasis on legislative, rather than executive, information and on state and local matters rather than federal agency matters. We make a lot of use of the state equivalents of the FOIA in our work, for example, with school boards."

According to Mincberg, PAW has done some FOIA litigation as well. "We filed a FOIA request with the Equal Employment Opportunity Commission (EEOC) during the Clarence Thomas hearings," he said. "It produced a short-lived piece of litigation and we managed to get hold of some information relating to his tenure at the EEOC that we wanted to get into the public record. We have also litigated on behalf of private citizens. Some years ago we filed a FOIA lawsuit on behalf a gentleman who was having some difficulty with the Department of the Air Force. We thought he had a meritorious claim that raised important issues. We litigated it and won the case here in D.C. We've filed a number of routine FOIA requests with various agencies ranging from the National Endowment for the Arts [NEA], when we were concerned about censorship at the NEA, to national security agencies back in the 80s."

In recent years, PAW's use of the FOIA has diminished considerably. "During my tenure at People for the American Way," said Mincberg, "which began in 1989, we've probably averaged only two or three FOIA requests a year, some generated within our organization and some in response to problems brought to us by private citizens. Sometimes one of our projects requires a FOIA request to acquire information on an issue. If an individual calls for a little routine help with the FOIA, we usually just send them some materials and have them submit the request on their own. But if a citizen, particularly a member, calls us about about an important issue that we have the time to spend on, we'll do a FOIA request in our own name."

When asked whether he had noticed any change in agency compliance with the FOIA over the years, Mincberg replied, "I think compliance has varied with the Administration in power. There were more problems during the Bush and Reagan administrations in a number of areas, some of which the Clinton Administration early on indicated that they were going to change. I believe things have improved in some ways, but there remain areas where further improvements are called for. There is a need to apply the FOIA to electronic information in a more explicit way. The issue of how to deal with agency backlogs of FOIA requests has also been difficult to resolve. Some agency backlogs seem intractable. For example, just this year I received a response from one national security agency for a request that was filed before I came to this organization, back in the mid- to late 1980s. This was their first acknowledgement of our request. At many agencies it is a question of scarce resources, but the problem of how to ensure a timely response hasn't been worked out to everyone's satisfaction."

Mincberg has not lost his enthusiasm for the Freedom of Information Act. "Despite all its flaws, he said, "there's absolutely no question that the Act has been tremendously beneficial in terms of getting citizen access to government information, not only at the federal level, but at the state and local level [*sic*] as well."[47]

CONCLUSION

This chapter has chosen selectively among the many institutions and public service organizations that effectively exploit the FOIA. Space constraints may have forced us to overlook some organizations well known for their FOIA support, not to mention those who use the FOIA significantly but infrequently. There are also a number of FOIA service companies that make a good living providing legal advice and support to FOIA users, with an emphasis on corporate customers. Another vital source of support for freedom of information are the publications specializing in the FOIA. The most prominent of them, *Access Reports*, has been frequently quoted throughout this book. These unheralded groups, together with the organizations described in this chapter, form the most significant force for open government in the United States—the FOIA community.

NOTES

1. U.S. House of Representatives, First Report by the Committee on Government Reform and Oversight, *A Citizen's Guide on Using the Freedom of Information Act and the Privacy Act of 1974 to Request Government Records* (Washington, D.C.: U.S. Government Printing Office, 1995).

2. *United States Government Manual, 1997/98* (Washington, D.C.: U.S. Government Printing Office, 1998).

3. *Ray v. Turner*, 587 F.2d 1187 (1978), at 1200, 1223.

4. William Schaap and Ellen Ray, telephone interview with author, July 2, 1998.

5. Will Ferroggiaro, telephone interview with author, May 19, 1998.

6. David J. Garrow, *Bearing the Cross: Martin Luther King, Jr., and the Southern Christian Leadership Conference* (New York: Morrow, 1986), p. 627.

7. David J. Garrow, *The FBI and Martin Luther King, Jr.: From 'Solo' to Memphis* (New York: Norton, 1981), pp. 10–12.

8. Stephen Schlesinger and Stephen Kinzer, *Bitter Fruit: The Untold Story of the American Coup in Guatemala* (Garden City, N.Y.: Doubleday, 1982), p. viii.

9. Stephen Schlesinger, "The CIA's legacy in Guatemala," *Washington Post*, September 25, 1996, p. A23.

10. Angus Mackenzie, *Secrets: The CIA's War at Home* (Berkeley: University of California Press, 1997), pp. 3–4.

11. James Mackenzie, telephone interview with author, June 8, 1998.

12. *Environmental Protection Agency v. Mink*, 93 S.Ct 827 (1973), at 830.

13. Ibid., at 831–32.

14. Ibid., at 833.

15. Ibid., at 839–40.

16. Ibid., at 847.

17. Patsy Mink, telephone interview with author, May 14, 1998.

18. "Aspin Plans to Sue for My Lai Report," *Washington Post*, April 4, 1972, p. A6.

19. "Contractors in Pentagon Ban Listed," *Washington Post*, April 5, 1973, p. A16.

20. "DEA Stonewalling Dole on Torrijos Drug Files," *Human Events*, January 7, 1978, p. 3.

21. M. Stanton Evans, "Torrijos' Drug-Trafficking: Cover-up Confirmed," *Human Events*, January 28, 1978, p. 7.

22. James X. Dempsey, telephone interview with author, July 8, 1998.

23. *Congressional Record*, House, Proceedings and Debates of the 101st Congress, 1st session, January 27, 1989, H108.

24. "Panning for Gold in Government Files," *Baltimore Sun*, July 28, 1997, p. A1.

25. Ibid.

26. Ibid.

27. William L. Casey, Jr., John E. Marthinsen, and Laurence S. Moss, *Entrepreneurship, Productivity, and the Freedom of Information Act: Protecting Circumstantially Relevant Business Information* (Lexington, Mass.: D. C. Heath, 1983), pp. 189–90.

28. Ralph Nader, "Reagan's Reign of Secrecy: Shortchanging the Public on Information," *Multinational Monitor*, August 1986, p. 3.

29. Thomas M. Susman, telephone interview with author, May 5, 1998.

30. Evan Hendricks, *Former Secrets: Government Records Made Public through the Freedom of Information Act* (Washington, D.C.: Campaign for Political Rights, 1988), p. 89.

31. Ibid., p. 49.

32. Tom Blanton, telephone interview with author, January 4, 1998.

33. Ferroggiaro, telephone interview with author.

34. Blanton, telephone interview with author.

35. Ferroggiaro, telephone interview with author.

36. Center for National Security Studies, publicity material, 1998.

37. Duncan Levin, telephone interview with author, June 2, 1998.

38. Kate Martin, telephone interview with author, June 28, 1998.

39. Levin, telephone interview with author.

40. Public Citizen Web page, www.citizen.org.

41. David Vladek, telephone interview with author, January 7, 1998.

42. Morton Halperin, telephone interview with author, May 17, 1998.

43. Arthur Spitzer, telephone interview with author, May 2, 1998.

44. Reporters Committee for Freedom of the Press, publicity material, 1998.

45. Jon Cohen, "Guarded Speech," *City Paper*, August 7–13, 1987, p. 18.

46. Rebecca Daugherty, telephone interview with author, August 20, 1998.

47. Elliot Mincberg, telephone interview with author, May 25, 1998.

CHAPTER 5

Freedom of Information in the New Millennium

IMPEDIMENTS TO THE RIGHT TO KNOW

In 1986, on the twentieth anniversary of the signing of the Freedom of Information Act (FOIA), former Representative John Moss (D-Calif.), regarded by many as the father of the act stated, "I am repeatedly asked today, as I have been since 1966, if the law has worked as I would like it to work. The answer must be: Of course not! . . . At the time the legislation was debated on the House floor, I characterized it as a timid first step. The fact is, much must be done on a continuing basis if we are to truly ensure that information is available to the people of this nation and that no withholding will be tolerated except that small part that truly touches upon the real security of this nation. . . . Were I in Congress today, I would commence hearings to follow up every instance alleged to have occurred in which the Act has caused any damage to our national security. I would provide a forum for each person in a responsible position, who has made such allegations, to support them. Under oath . . . I doubt that they could show such harm."[1]

As we enter the twenty-first century, the status of the people's right to know and the legislative embodiment of that right, the Freedom of Information Act, has changed little since Moss's comments made on its twentieth anniversary. There have been promising government initiatives, but fundamental problems remain.

In a 1998 interview, Ralph Nader described the most daunting obstacle facing the Freedom of Information Act. "The implementation of the FOIA is the problem," he said. "Freedom of information today is almost entirely to be evaluated in terms of its implementation, which has received minimal scrutiny by the major media. For years I've been trying to get the *New York Times* to do a series on the inadequate FOIA implementation.

"First of all, the agencies delay you. Most of the agencies, like the Justice Department, are underfunded, and this allows them to say they can't fully implement the FOIA because they don't have enough full-time people processing requests. The agencies also overuse the FOIA exemptions and have unbridled discretion to black out material in released documents. For example, I just acquired a copy of a $7 billion contract that NASA let out to Rockwell and Lockheed Martin to run the space agency at Kennedy. Most of it was blacked out, because anything the company claims to be proprietary is excised by the agency without question. This sort of thing bleeds the value out of the FOIA, and the same thing is done with the other exemptions."

Nader also decried the absence of meaningful congressional oversight. "You don't have John Moss to do investigative hearings," he said, "so no one in Congress examines the failure to implement the FOIA. Instead, Congress is interested in curtailing public access to its own routine government information by overpricing its cost and reducing the availability of print materials. There are rumors that they want to get rid of the Government Printing Office altogether and privatize the whole thing. Shades of Lincoln!"

Nader maintains that historians need to organize and demand access to government information. "A lot of the important investigations by government agencies have been suppressed in the past," he said. "For example, the anti-trust division was investigating the auto industry in the late 1950s in order to break up companies like GM [General Motors]. They were unsuccessful, of course, but by the time they gave up they had accumulated all kinds of subpoenaed material, including grand jury proceedings. Just days before Jimmy Carter took office, the Ford Administration called in General Motors' shredders and collectors and told them, 'We're giving all of this to you.' So they took it all back and destroyed most of it. You can imagine the enormous history that goes down the drain routinely.

"A lot of this approach comes from the agency's own bureaucratic culture, but some of it comes from how they read the White House. I suspect that under Reagan a lot of material was destroyed out in the warehouses, but it no longer matters so much who controls the White House. The abuses are now transcending the parties."[2]

Thomas Susman, a former Senate staffer and architect of the 1974 amendments, pointed out, "One of the interesting things about the poor administration of the FOIA is that in the early 1970s the government bureaucrat was the problem. Today, there is such a core of highly qual-ified and competent access professionals that the problem now resides with the policy makers. Today's FOIA personnel throughout the bureauc-racy are quite supportive of the statute, but, at the policy level, agencies have found that if they starve these offices they can slow down the release of information. And it works. I had a client who was going to submit a FOIA request to the Justice Department on an antitrust investigation, but I said forget about it. By the time we get the information, it's going to be so stale that it'll be absolutely useless.''[3]

Sam Archibald, former staff director for the House subcommittee that shepherded the FOIA into existence, warned that no legislative tool can ever guarantee federal compliance without the cooperation and support of the entire government. Archibald, who later ran the University of Mis-souri Freedom of Information Center, stated, "In the final analysis, the effectiveness of laws on access to government information depends upon the governors, whether the law is the Freedom of Information Act or the First Amendment. . . . [T]he sharpness of the tool depends substantially upon the will of the government—the will of the executive branch to honor the open-records provisions of the law, the will of the judicial branch to enforce the access-to-information provisions of the law, and the will of the legislative branch to stand up for the people's right to know if the other two branches emasculate the freedom of expression necessary to make participatory democracy work in the Information Age.''[4]

As we approach the new millenium, it is not clear that all branches of the American government have the will to support the public's right to know. We conclude this chapter with an examination of the opportunities and impediments posed by a cautious Executive Branch, a hostile Judi-ciary, and a conservative Congress.

A CAUTIOUS CLINTON ADMINISTRATION

After the dark secrecy of the Reagan and Bush administrations, Presi-dent Bill Clinton's election was seen by FOIA advocates as the dawn of opportunity. Indeed, during the first term of the Clinton administration, the rhetoric out of the White House was uniformly supportive of open government, and the performance, for the most part, matched the rhet-oric.

On October 4, 1993, in a pair of reinforcing memos to all departments and agency heads, President Clinton and Attorney General Janet Reno announced their "openness initiative." The president's memo affirmed that the FOIA was "a vital part of the participatory system of government . . . based on the fundamental principle that an informed citizenry is es-sential to the democratic process." Clinton asked all agency personnel "to renew their commitment" to the FOIA, "to its underlying principles of government openness, and to its sound administration." Clinton also asked all agencies "to take a fresh look at their administration of the Act, to reduce backlogs . . . and to conform agency practice to the new litigation guidance issued by the Attorney General."[5]

Attorney General Reno's attached memorandum began, "First and foremost, we must ensure that the principle of openness in government is applied in each and every disclosure and nondisclosure decision that is required under the Act. Therefore, I hereby rescind the Department of Justice's 1981 guidelines for the defense of agency action in Freedom of Information Act litigation. The Department will no longer defend an agency's withholding of information merely because there is a 'substantial legal basis' for doing so. Rather, in determining whether or not to defend a nondisclosure decision, we will apply a presumption of disclosure."

Reno declared that the department would henceforth defend the assertion of an FOIA exemption only when there is foreseeable harm that could result from disclosure. She concluded, "I strongly encourage your FOIA officers to make 'discretionary disclosures' whenever possible under the Act. Such disclosures are possible under a number of FOIA exemptions, especially when only a governmental interest would be affected."[6]

In early 1994, Reno authorized new procedures to expedite the handling of FOIA requests in cases of extraordinary interest to the news media. In September 1995, she issued an order requiring all Justice Department employees who have any role in FOIA processing to be rated on how quickly, thoroughly, and efficiently they handle requests. Reno's order, the first of its kind in the federal government, made efficient FOIA processing a part of the staffers' job descriptions and an important part of their job evaluations.

Reginald Stuart, president of the Society of Professional Journalists, commented, "This is a major move forward by a key federal agency. It's recognition that FOIA is important to restoring the public's trust in government. I hope other agencies will follow suit and make FOIA compliance one of the yardsticks by which an employee's performance is measured."[7]

After the passage of the 1996 E-FOIA amendments, Attorney General Reno reinforced the openness initiative in a May 1, 1997, memo to all heads of departments and agencies. "I urge you to be sure to continue our strong commitment to the openness-in-government principles that President Clinton and I established on October 4, 1993. These principles include applying customer-service attitudes toward FOIA requesters, following the spirit as well as the letter of the Act, and applying a presumption of disclosure in FOIA decision making. Most significant is that an agency should make a discretionary disclosure of exempt information whenever it is possible to do so without foreseeable harm."[8]

Tom Blanton, the executive director of the National Security Archive, believes that the Clinton-Reno FOIA policies have contributed to improved agency responsiveness. "We see the openness initiative in practice on a fairly regular basis," he said. "There is a different kind of approach than pre-existed the Clinton administration, even with respect to national security secrets and covert operations. Agency releases, particularly for the older documents, don't leave us with huge amounts of blacked out information. In fact, the recently released Bay of Pigs documents probably had fewer than 30 lines deleted out of 400 pages. It was a spectacular release. This kind of thing is definitely influenced by the openness initiative, by the signals sent from the president, and by the fact that the new CIA Director was a member of the staff that produced the president's Executive Order and the initiative."[9]

Like his openness initiative, President Clinton's Executive Order 12958, "Classified National Security Information," made a strong impression because of its dramatic improvement over its predecessor. The introduction to E.O. 12958 began, "In recent years . . . dramatic changes have altered, although not eliminated, the national security threat that we confront. These changes provide a greater opportunity to emphasize our commitment to open Government."

The Clinton order established a ten-year limit on how long newly classified documents could remain classified, *unless* the information fell within eight broad national security categories. Another important provision in the executive order requires that already classified documents twenty-five years old or older be declassified unless they fall within exemptions similar to those specified for newly classified material. Agencies were given until the year 2000 to find and set aside sensitive material that would require the regular declassification review process; everything else twenty-five years old or older was to be automatically declassified.

Unfortunately, the exemptions to the ten- and twenty-five-year limits have been invoked all too often. As a result of the inadequate application of the Clinton executive order, classified government information continues to accumulate, imposing some very practical limits on the administration's openness initiative. For example, if information is properly classified under an executive order, agencies may not exercise discretionary disclosure in contravention of Exemption 1. Similarly, Exemptions 3, 4, 6, and 7(c) do not, for the most part, admit of discretionary disclosures.

Janet Reno has admitted that the openness initiative has not significantly reduced FOIA backlogs: the FBI alone has fallen 5.6 million pages behind in FOIA processing. Thus, despite the attorney general's good intentions, many journalists claim they have seen little improvement in agency responsiveness since the Reno memo. Some in the FOIA community have complained that the Clinton administration left the Justice Department's Office of Information and Privacy in the hands of the co-directors who had served throughout the entire Reagan and Bush administrations.

By the second term of President Clinton's administration, the press was beginning to lose patience with White House information policies. The high expectations set by Clinton's rhetoric may have been part of the problem. Jane Kirtley, executive director of the Reporter's Committee on Freedom of the Press, exclaimed, "I don't doubt Janet Reno's basic commitment to open government. But that still hasn't really reached fruition among the rank and file. . . . There is still the perception that handling FOIA requests is a diversion from an agency's real work and that the allocation of resources to that is inappropriate."[10]

Amid the quibbling over the meager dividends from its openness initiative, the Clinton administration's reputation was further tarnished by a highly publicized FOIA battle over White House e-mail in which Clinton became the third consecutive president to defend the secrecy of White House communications. Given his pronouncements on open government, Clinton's action in this regard has been disappointing, but the public villain has been the National Archives and Records Administration (NARA), an executive agency that most Americans think is just a big library. NARA is the agency responsible for acquiring and maintaining the records of the federal government of the United States. Its statutory mission requires it to make those records available to the general public unless access is restricted by the nine FOIA exemptions; however, in recent years, it has joined the forces of executive secrecy. This is due, in large part, to the fact that NARA's leadership comes from the U.S. archivist, a presidential appointment with a history of partisanship. The spineless complicity of two consecutive archivists in denying access to all electronic communications within the White House may have destroyed NARA's reputation as an independent protector of historical information.

The current dispute over White House e-mail began in early 1989 when the National Security Archive, a prominent FOIA support group, discovered that President Reagan and U.S. archivist Don Wilson intended to purge the entire White House e-mail system on the eve of President-elect George Bush's inaugural. Included among the targeted e-mail was a communications network known as the Professional Office System (PROFS), which was used to store National Security Council (NSC) interagency e-mail. Included within the PROFS system was significant information on the Iran-Contra affair and the personal involvement of Reagan and Bush.

Scott Armstrong, founder of the National Security Archive, called the White House counsel's office to express his concern, but he was told that e-mail was not a record category requiring preservation. When Armstrong argued that this would violate NARA's guidelines on records preservation, he was told that NARA's director of presidential libraries, John Fawcett, had personally approved the deletion of the e-mail. Fawcett was already notorious for taking the side of former presidents in their political management of presidential libraries, leading many of his colleagues to doubt his commitment to the preservation and accessibility of government records.

Fawcett told Armstrong that White House officials would simply print out any e-mail messages that *they* considered to be records, after which they would delete the original electronic data, including all hard disks on which word processing files were stored. Fawcett's criteria would also allow NSC documents arbitrarily to be transformed from NSC records to "presidential" records, removing them from the immediate reach of the FOIA.

Armstrong hurriedly consulted with his staff. "We had only two alternatives: allow the destruction to take place or go to court."[11]

They chose to seek a temporary restraining order (TRO). Armstrong, his staff, and pro bono lawyers had to stay up all night preparing the request for a TRO just hours before the destruction deadline, the January 20 inauguration day for George Bush. When Armstrong appeared before U.S. District Judge Barrington D. Parker, he was opposed by acting attorney general John R. Bolton who argued the government's case for secrecy. Bolton told Judge Parker that Reagan's White House staff were doing what anyone does when leaving a job: taking pictures off the wall and cleaning out their desks.

Judge Parker responded, "They [Armstrong et al.] are not seeking a restraining order against taking pictures off the wall. . . . [W]hat is happening to the material that is the subject of this litigation?"[12]

When Bolton said it was being prepared for deletion, the incredulous judge granted a TRO against President Reagan, President-elect Bush, and the NSC. The case was then assigned to Judge Charles Richey.

Armstrong's suit, joined by various public interest organizations, argued that the Presidential Records Act (PRA) and the Federal Records Act (FRA) limited the power of White House officials to dispose of e-mail and that at least some of that e-mail should be available to the public under the FOIA. On September 15, 1989, Judge Richey ruled that Armstrong had standing to sue to protect White House e-mail. The Bush White House appealed, but two years later, in *Armstrong v. Bush* (1991), the D.C. Circuit Court of Appeals ruled that the FRA permits limited judicial review of White House compliance with record-keeping law.

On November 19, 1992, Judge Richey issued a restraining order preventing the destruction of the Bush White House computer tapes, and on January 6, 1993, he ruled that e-mail tapes from both the Reagan and Bush administrations had to be preserved like any other government records. The electronic versions of these records, said Richey, included unique and valuable information not contained in a paper printout.

Richey also declared that the archivist of the United States, Don Wilson, "had failed to fulfil his statutory duties under the Federal Records Act."[13]

In the *Michigan Law Review*, James D. Lewis described the shameful role of the archivist in the destruction of White House e-mail. "Over a period of several years," wrote Lewis, "the Archivist remained idle while the Executive Office of the President (EOP) and National Security Council (NSC) staff exercised virtually complete discretion in deciding whether to preserve or delete electronic mail messages. The Archivist thus failed to carry out duties required under the FRA, including inspecting agency record management practices and notifying the head of the agency of any FRA violations. In addition, if agency records were indeed being destroyed in contravention of the FRA, the Archivist failed to request that the Attorney General take action. . . . [T]he enforcement and oversight provisions of recordkeeping law remained uninvoked while White House officials deleted whatever e-mail messages they wanted whenever they wanted."[14]

Tom Blanton, current executive director of the National Security Archive, recently recalled the *Armstrong* litigation. "Kate Martin and I stayed up all night writing the original e-mail injunction complaint that saved the Bush/Reagan e-mail from destruction," said Blanton. "Public Citizen handled the discovery and argument part of that case, but Kate won the first victory. What we fought and won was the attempt by the Reagan and Bush administrations to define e-mail as non-records. The four prongs of the test for whether government information qualifies as a record are: does it have historical, legal, administrative or evidentiary value. A series of appeals courts, upheld by the Supreme Court, have ruled that e-mail meets the required standard and may not be denied record status under the FOIA. This means that e-mail is definitely covered by the FOIA, but that doesn't mean that every e-mail will be saved or will be released under the FOIA."[15]

Indeed, although the original litigation won in court on the key issues—(1) electronic information constitutes records under the FRA and the FOIA and (2) the government must process those records—the White House continued to fight against release of the information. Having been prevented by the courts from destroying the e-mail tapes, President Bush resorted to a devious strategy. In the last hours of his presidency, Bush negotiated a secret deal with Archivist Donald Wilson, already cited by Judge Richey for his failure to protect government records. That midnight agreement, signed by Bush and Wilson on January 20, 1993, placed all of the disputed e-mail under Bush's personal control. A National Archives team worked all night at the White House, using rented trucks to cart away 4,852 tapes and 135 hard disk drives just before the Clinton staff arrived. As it turned out, they had nothing to fear from the Clinton administration.

Lawyers for the Justice Department and NARA, now working for President Clinton, supported the Bush-Wilson agreement and continued to resist Judge Richey's authority. On May 21, 1993, Richey cited the Clinton White House and Archivist Wilson for contempt of court for failing to carry out his order to preserve the Reagan-Bush e-mail tapes. Richey warned that should the Clinton administration fail to take appropriate action, he would impose fines of $50,000 per day for a week and double the fines each week thereafter. The Clinton administration again appealed Richey's ruling, and on August 13, 1993, in *Armstrong v. Executive Office of the President* (1993), the U.S. Court of Appeals for the D.C. Circuit ruled that the Federal Records Act required the preservation of e-mail at the White House, and presumably at all other agencies. The appeals court sent the case back to Richey to distinguish between "agency" records, which are controlled by the FRA, and "presidential" records, which are covered by the Presidential Records Act.

As the result of the *Armstrong* litigation, the government released over 3,000 of the originally contested e-mail records used by the Reagan White House and National Security Council. After being recovered from backup tapes preserved by court order, the records were processed under the FOIA. Public Citizen, the organization that handled the litigation, declared, "We believe that this is the first time that e-mail records have been recovered from electronic storage devices to respond to a FOIA request. The e-mail records released by the government contained many new insights concerning the foreign policy activities and internal politics of the Reagan Administration."[16] Tom Blanton of the National Security Archive used the records obtained in the *Armstrong* litigation to compile a book, *White House e-mail* (1995), which revealed the importance of e-mail as a record of government policy and decision making.

On March 25, 1994, in a desperate response to the court-facilitated release of NSC documents, the Clinton White House shocked the FOIA community by submitting a brief to Judge Richey declaring that the National Security Council was not an agency at all, but a group of informal presidential advisers. As such, all documents created by the NSC were "presidential" records and therefore not subject to the FOIA or the Federal Records Act. If upheld, this argument would end many years of established practice under which past administrations acknowledged that the NSC created both presidential and agency records, the latter of which were subject to the FOIA. Presidential records remain secret for up to twelve years after a president leaves office, and the president can decide which of these records to preserve.

It now appeared that Clinton would succeed in doing what Reagan and Bush had failed to do. The FOIA community was outraged, and in an attempt to salvage his fading reputation for open government, Clinton directed that a new disclosure review process be created within the NSC to allow voluntary release of appropriate documents. The procedure, which would not provide the legal review available through the FOIA, was derided by Tom Blanton, executive director of the National Security Archive, as a "trust-me FOIA."[17] Other FOIA advocates puzzled over Clinton's motivation in removing NSC records from the reach of the FOIA, since that statute already protects classified records and those providing advice to the president. "The only category the extra step protects is illegal and improper action," declared Scott Armstrong.[18]

In February 1995, Judge Richey again rejected the Clinton administration's secrecy policies. First, he ruled that the disreputable Bush-Wilson agreement, defended by Clinton, was in violation of the Presidential Records Act and was therefore "null and void." By now, the secret agreement had surfaced publicly, causing the embarrassed Wilson to flee his job as archivist to become head of the George Bush Presidential Library. Clinton would soon appoint his own crony, John Carlin, as NARA's new archivist.

Richey also rejected Clinton's attempt to define the NSC as a non-agency, characterizing the action as "arbitrary and capricious . . . contrary to history, past practice and the law." Richey ruled that the NSC had to comply with FOIA requests for records, so long as they did not deal with advice to the president on sensitive national security matters.[19] The Clinton administration immediately appealed.

On August 2, 1996, the U.S. Court of Appeals for the D.C. Circuit overturned Judge Richey's decision. By a 2 to 1 vote, the appeals panel ruled that, though the NSC looks and sometimes acts like an independent agency, it functions more like a part of the president's staff and is therefore not subject to the FOIA or the FRA. NSC records were now to be considered "presidential" records, governed by the Presidential Records Act. They would not be subject to judicial review, and FOIA requests for them could not even be filed until at least five years after the president had left office, twelve years if the records were classified, which most are.

In a twenty-seven-page dissent, Judge David S. Tatal wrote, "With all due respect, I fear the president's membership on the NSC has obscured from my colleagues the extent to which the NSC actually exercises independent authority."[20]

Kate Martin, director of the Center for National Security Studies, declared, "This is a terrible decision for government accountability. If this remains the law, we will not be able to prevent the destruction of NSC records." Had it been the law in 1989, said Martin, President Reagan would have been free to shred all of the White House e-mail relating to the Iran-Contra investigation.[21]

Armstrong petitioned the Supreme Court to review the appeals court decision on NSC records, and when the Court refused to grant certiorari, Armstrong concluded, "As a practical matter, the Clinton administration has successfully made one of the most—if not the most—sweeping assertions of secrecy of the past twenty-five years."[22]

Having won the fight to hide NSC records from the public, the Clinton administration, with the help of an ally at NARA, sought secrecy for all categories of White House e-mail. Clinton had replaced one weak and compliant archivist, Don Wilson, with another, John W. Carlin. Under Carlin's authority, NARA maintained a policy, known as GRS (General Records Schedule) 20, which authorizes all agencies to wipe out their electronic mail and other computerized records without regard for their content, so long as paper copies are made of any records they deem important. Ignoring Armstrong's hard-won victories in court, these guidelines gave agencies a virtual free hand to destroy electronic information.

In June 1997, a number of public interest groups, led by Ralph Nader's Public Citizen, filed suit seeking to invalidate GRS20. They accused Archivist John Carlin of abdicating his responsibility to appraise the value of electronic records on an agency-by-agency basis. Scott Armstrong, one of the plaintiffs, called GRS20 "the electronic shredder" and "the Fawn Hall statute," referring to Oliver North's secretary, who had helped him shred Iran-Contra documents. Public Citizen lawyer Mike Tankersley declared, "The Archivist has opened the flood gates, allowing agencies to destroy records without regard for their historical value."[23] Undeterred, the Clinton administration continued to defend the policy.

In October 1997, District Court Judge Paul Friedman ruled that Archivist Carlin had failed in his statutory duty to oversee the appropriate retention of federal records. "[T]he Archivist has absolved both himself and the federal agencies he is supposed to oversee of their statutory duties to evaluate specific electronic records as to their values. The Archivist has also given agencies carte blanche to destroy electronic versions without the Archivist's approval when the agency believes they are no longer needed by the agency."

In declaring GRS20 "null and void," Friedman stated that the government's position "not only contradicts the clear intent of Congress, but is irrational on its face." Friedman noted that electronic records often have a number of unique and valuable features not found in paper printouts. Hence, destroying e-mail after selectively printing it out was inappropriate. "Such a method for disposing of records is inconsistent with the responsibility placed on the Archivist to insure the protection and preservation of valuable government records."[24]

Despite the forceful clarity of the court's opinion, Archivist Carlin continued to advise federal agencies to comply with GRS20, and in March 1998 Friedman ordered Carlin and his lawyers to explain "why they should not be sanctioned or held in contempt" for failing to submit a "timely" response to the court's earlier demands.

A *Washington Post* editorial declared: "The Archives has been taken to court repeatedly by outside groups seeking to prevent the destruction of what could be historically significant records—precisely the goal for which the Archives themselves were created."[25]

Public Citizen's Mike Tankersley asked the court for an injunction against Carlin that would prevent him from deleting records on the basis of GRS20, but NARA's lawyers claimed that if an "oppressive, 'no delete' " order were granted, many government computer systems would grind to a halt.[26] On April 9, an exasperated Judge Friedman ruled that Archivist Carlin had for the past five months been "flagrantly" violating his court order.

"The Court's language and conclusion," said Friedman, "could not have been more clear: The Archivist was violating the law in promulgating and implementing GRS20." Friedman promptly issued an order enjoining Carlin from making any more statements in disregard of the court's order and directed him to publish notice in the Federal Register within ten days that GRS20 was "null and void."[27] Indeed, Friedman dictated the precise wording that the notice should contain.

Despite the Clinton administration's disappointing role in supporting GRS20 and appealing the court judgment against the archivist, the FOIA community continues to assume a right of access to White House e-mail. Tom Blanton, whose organization, the National Security Archive, was among the litigants in the series of e-mail cases, recently asserted, "The current dispute with the National Archives concerns their claim that agencies can simply print out the e-mail that they believe has historic value and dispose of the electronic versions. We argued, successfully, that this was self-defeating, that the electronic format was a different and more valuable form of the record, because the printout doesn't have the electronic trail or the relational character. It's been affirmed at a lower court and we're currently awaiting the appeal. We're trying to work out a negotiated settlement, for obvious reasons. At a time when the government is spending tens of millions of dollars digitizing old files, it's stupid for them to spend money to destroy digital versions of new files."[28]

HOSTILE COURTS

From the beginning, the courts have offered timid support for the FOIA, deferring to government demands for secrecy on virtually all matters relating to law enforcement and national security. In the years immediately following the passage of the FOIA, courts justified such deference on the basis of the statute's ambiguity and inadequacy. Supreme Court opinions, such as *EPA v. Mink* (see Chapter 4), gave reluctant support to government claims while openly urging Congress to close the FOIA's loopholes. The 1974 FOIA amendments did just that, but it soon became clear that the courts' compliance with government secrecy had little to do with the language of the statute.

As described in Chapter 4, the courts' deference to the the Federal Bureau of Investigation (FBI), the Central Intelligence Agency (CIA), and the National Security Agency (NSA) has gone beyond expansive interpretations of the FOIA's exemptions to the point of creating new exemptions unsupported by the statute. The CIA has been the greatest beneficiary of this deference; the court-created *Glomar* response is the most prominent example of this (see Chapters 2 and 3). The Supreme Court's decision in *CIA v. Sims* (1985) was another gift to the CIA, providing it with a virtual blanket exemption for all CIA files by way of FOIA Exemption 3.

Another disturbing decision came in *Hunt v. CIA* (9th Cir. 1992), in which the court acknowledged that "with this decision, we are now 'only a short step [from] exempting all CIA records' from FOIA." In recognizing the contradiction between a virtual blanket exemption and the spirit of the FOIA, the court went so far as to concede, "That result may well be contrary to what Congress intended." The court nonetheless threw up its hands and said, "If Congress did not intend to give the CIA a near-blanket FOIA exemption, it can take notice of the court's incremental creation of one, and take the necessary legislative action to rectify the matter."[29]

Like the CIA, the NSA has also found easy going in the courts. According to historian Matthew Aid, "Appeals of the NSA's FOIA denials invariably fail, no matter how well crafted or well justified. . . . Faced with this seemingly insurmountable wall, most researchers choose not to challenge the NSA's FOIA denials in court."[30]

FOIA attorney James Lesar testified before the Senate Committee on Government Affairs in 1992: "Most requesters cannot afford the time or money to litigate their FOIA requests. . . . You might be tempted to conclude from the general absence of litigation that the FOIA is working just fine. The opposite is true. The FOIA has been severely damaged by the 1984 amendments eliminating access to CIA operational files and by the 1986 amendments to Exemption 7 . . . as well as by a string of decisions in the Supreme Court and the U.S. Court of Appeals for the District of Columbia which have greatly expanded the amount of material which can be withheld from the public."[31]

The Supreme Court's hostility toward the FOIA can be seen in the views of such Reagan and Bush appointees as Justice Antonin Scalia. In 1982, while he was a professor of law at the University of Chicago, Scalia wrote a scathing article titled "The Freedom of Information Act Has No Clothes," in which he decried the influence of "public interest law," "consumerism," and "investigative journalism" on the FOIA. Scalia demanded higher fees for the use of the FOIA, the introduction of a "need to know" standard for requesters, increased privacy exemptions, and the removal of court authority to review national security classification.

Offended by even the most limited claims of a citizen's right to know, Scalia declared, "The defects of the Freedom of Information Act cannot be cured as long as we are dominated by the obsession that gave them birth—that the first line of defense against an arbitrary executive is do-it-yourself oversight by the public and its surrogate, the press. On that assumption, the FOIA's excesses are not defects at all, but merely the price for our freedoms. It is a romantic notion, but the facts simply do not bear it out."[32]

Shortly after Scalia's public advocacy of government secrecy over the citizen's right to know, President Ronald Reagan appointed him to the U.S Court of Appeals for the D.C. Circuit. After demonstrating his hostility to the FOIA at the appeals court level, Scalia was elevated to the Supreme Court in 1986 by an appreciative President Reagan.

In his first major speech after joining the Supreme Court, Scalia proposed relegating large categories of cases, including Freedom of Information Act suits, to special tribunals designed to handle such routine and "trivial" cases. Scalia said the specialized courts would relieve the federal courts from the burden of dealing with the explosion of federal rights, "some created by Congress, some by the courts."

Scalia's controversial proposals caused concern among some lawyers and civil libertarians who feared that the federal courts would no longer be available to ordinary people. Reverend Robert F. Drinan, a former member of Congress, criticized the notion of relegating FOIA claims to specialized tribunals, characterizing it as "second class justice." Drinan asserted that the right to acquire government information was "basic constitutional law."[33]

In 1989 Scalia joined a Supreme Court opinion that drastically narrowed the scope of the FOIA by redefining its "core purpose." In *Department of Justice v. Reporters Committee for a Free Press*, the Court denied a reporter's request for an FBI rap sheet (criminal history of an individual), declaring that the "public interest" under the FOIA extended only to information that illuminated government operations. The FOIA's purpose, said the Court, "is not fostered by disclosure of information about private citizens that is accumulated in various governmental files but that reveal little or nothing about an agency's own conduct."[34]

The Court concluded, "FOIA's central purpose is to ensure that the Government's activities be opened to the sharp eye of public scrutiny, not that information about private citizens that happens to be in the warehouse of the Government be so disclosed."[35]

The *Reporters Committee* decision flew in the face of the FOIA's legislative history. While it is true that the origins of the FOIA, as detailed in this book, grew primarily out of the public's demand to know about the workings of their government, those activities and responsibilities are of such breadth and complexity that the original Freedom of Information Act broadly declared "a general philosophy of full agency disclosure."[36]

The sponsors of the 1974 strengthening amendments were even more explicit in endorsing the role of the FOIA in accessing government clearinghouse information, the kinds of information acquired by government but not directly related to the operation of government. During the Senate debates, Senator Edward Kennedy (D-Mass.) declared, "The processes of Government touch every aspect of our lives, everyday. From the food we eat to the cars we drive, to the air we breathe, Federal agencies constantly monitor, regulate, and control. . . . The Freedom of Information Act guarantees citizens access to Government information and provides the key for unlocking the doors to a vast storeroom of information."[37]

In this context, the FOIA has been used by journalists, historians, and individuals as an open-records statute to acquire a broad range of information in the public interest. In *Reporters Committee*, the newly restricted interpretation of what constitutes public interest under the FOIA was made in the context of an Exemption 7(c), or personal privacy, decision, but its language seems applicable to any FOIA case in which the question of public interest arises. In particular, a number of Exemption 6, cases (personnel and medical files) have been decided on the *Reporters Committee* standard.

Even Attorney General Janet Reno, coarchitect of the Clinton administration's openness initiative, has endorsed the *Reporters Committee* opinion, and has chided reporters for seeking information about what the government *stores* rather than what it *does*.

Robert G. Vaughan, writing in the *Administrative Law Journal*, warned, "Recent Supreme Court decisions question the scope of the FOIA and its ability to accommodate a range of information policies and practices. These decisions also pose considerable uncertainty regarding the interpretation and application of the FOIA. The Supreme Court clouded the future of the FOIA as a general information statute by suggesting that the purpose of the FOIA is limited to citizens' discovery of the operations of government. These decisions reflect confusion about FOIA and its place in government information policy."[38]

Cases like *Department of Justice v. Tax Analysts* (1989), *John Doe Agency v. John Doe Corp.* (1990), and *Bibles v. Oregon Natural Desert Association* (1997) have built upon the *Reporters Committee* standard, repeating the theme that the principal function of the FOIA, perhaps the only function of legal significance, is to reveal the operation of the government. Such a view virtually excludes government "clearinghouse information" from FOIA access.

"This narrow conception disregards the history of the FOIA which

shows that Congress was aware of the range of benefits provided by access to government information," declared Vaughan. "Consumer access
to consumer product safety information not only provides the basis for
market decisions by individual consumers, but also provides the information necessary for consumers to act politically to advance their interests. Such information ultimately implicates government policy and the
performance of government agencies. A limitation of the FOIA based on
a narrow concept of purpose or benefit is ill conceived, inaccurate, and
probably unattainable."[39]

The Supreme Court's constricted view of the FOIA has caused concern
among the press. An article published in the *Newspaper Research Journal*
warns, "The new public interest standard bodes ill for journalists and
others who seek government records in any broader context than simply
observing how agencies operate. As Judge Patricia Wald of the D.C. Circuit has pointed out, the *Reporters Committee* view of public interest
'resulted in a ruling that effectively shut out many traditional historical
and reportorial uses of FOIA.' While the text of the FOIA exemptions . . .
does not necessarily lend support to the *Reporters Committee* approach,
the Court's crabbed view of public interest is the law unless and until
Congress acts to clarify its intent."[40]

Tom Blanton is unequivocal in rejecting the *Reporters Committee* approach to the FOIA. "The Supreme Court has said that the 'core purpose'
of the statute is to shed light on the operations of government," said
Blanton, "but that's a very narrow definition, one that the congressional
debate on the original statute would not support. I think the purpose of
the FOIA was to set in stone the principle that the government's information belongs to the people, with only a few specified exceptions.

"The Electronic FOIA statute that passed in 1996 tried to remove any
ambiguity on this point by stating in its preamble that the core purpose
of the FOIA is to make government information available to anyone who
wants it. The FOIA is part of our system of checks and balances used
competitively by businesses. One good example of why the transparency
of business and economic information is part of the FOIA's purpose can
be seen in places like Japan, where such transparency doesn't exist. As a
result, you have cronyism, bid rigging, and extensive corruption in government contracting and in the regulation of health and safety."[41]

Blanton's assumption that the E-FOIA has overcome the crabbed view
of the FOIA expressed in *Reporters Committee* is supported by the legislative history of the 1996 amendment. This is important because the
"core purpose" analysis is not an interpretation of the statute, but of
congressional intent, and such a judicial interpretation can always be
corrected when Congress clarifies its views on the intent of the statute.
The original Senate E-FOIA bill did just that by addressing the core pur-

pose issue directly, and the House report implicitly supported the Senate's view.

The findings section of the Senate report points out that "the purpose of the FOIA is to require agencies of the Federal Government to make records available to the public through public inspection and upon the request of any person for *any public or private use*" (emphasis added). The House findings express the purpose in almost identical language.

Senator Patrick Leahy (D-Vt.) further clarified congressional intent in the Senate report by specifically declaring that the *Reporters Committee* decision "analyzed the purpose of the FOIA too narrowly." Leahy explained, "The purpose of the FOIA is not limited to making agency records and information available to the public only in cases where such material would shed light on the activities and operations of Government. Efforts by the courts to articulate a 'core purpose' for which information should be released imposes a limitation on the FOIA which Congress did not intend and which cannot be found in its language, and distorts the broader import of the Act in effectuating Government openness."[42]

These congressional findings indicate that all records in the custody and control of federal agencies are subject to the FOIA and that the public interest balancing test for privacy exemptions articulated in *Reporters Committee* must be discarded in favor of the previous case-by-case determination process.

Unfortunately, the courts have continued to impose the Supreme Court's narrow core purpose interpretation on the nation, usually acting on the presumption that the FOIA is an information control statute. For example, in *Michael J. O'Kane v. U.S. Customs Service* (1997), a Florida District Court declared that "there is no indication that Congress, in enacting the Electronic FOIA Amendments, intended to effect the dramatic change contemplated by the Plaintiff. Had Congress intended to significantly enlarge the scope of the public interest served by the FOIA, Congress could have taken a more clear and direct approach, most likely by amending the exemptions themselves. This they did not do."[43]

Harry Hammitt, editor of *Access Reports*, has stated that the core purpose theory, which was developed by the Justice Department for litigation purposes, has been largely accepted with little or no thought by the Supreme Court. "The 'core purpose' argument has little support in any legislative history and is just plain wrong," according to Hammitt. "The FOIA is a government accountability tool, but accountability flows from the unchecked right to obtain government information, not from the requester's laudatory purposes for making the request."[44]

Thomas Susman, prominent Washington attorney and self-described "FOIA junkie," maintains, "If Congress had in mind a 'core purpose' analysis, it would never have written the FOIA the way it did. Clearly, the

FOIA contemplates disclosure of information that has no relevance to such an analysis. The legislative history of the FOIA gives an indication of why we want government information to be public, but it gives no indication that there was a 'core purpose' for the Act. No member of Congress said, 'The reason we're passing this Act is to facilitate access to a limited class of government information.' I think it represents revisionist history."

Taking this position does not come easily to Susman, who has a long history of supporting the confidentiality of commercial and contract information. "My attitude toward the release of government contract information is that using the FOIA for competitive disclosure purposes doesn't serve any purpose, core or otherwise," said Susman. "But if you invoke core purpose, you would release zero commercial information. That can't be right. That was not the congressional intent of the statute."[45]

Virtually all of the disturbing cases described here derive from Reagan-Bush court appointees, but there has been little improvement during the Clinton administration. David Vladek, FOIA point man at Ralph Nader's Public Citizen, stated in an interview, "I think, by and large, with the concentration of Reagan and Bush judges in the courts, you've really seen a growing judicial hostility toward the FOIA. So it's become much more difficult to win FOIA cases. Clinton hasn't had the impact on the appointment of judges, particularly at the Circuit Court level, that Bush and Reagan had. Most of the Clinton appointments have been to the district court. The FOIA cases, the FOIA law, is really made at the circuit court level, and that has not been changed under Clinton. As a result, Clinton has not been able to undo the damage that has been done to the Judiciary."[46]

A CONSERVATIVE CONGRESS

Since the passage of the 1974 strengthening amendments to the FOIA, Congress has shown little inclination to improve access to government information. As we have seen, the CIA Information Act, passed in 1984, provided a virtual blanket exemption for the agency's "operational files." The disasterous 1986 FOIA amendments created new "exclusions," giving the FBI broad authority to withhold information relating to foreign intelligence, counterintelligence, and international terrorism. In recent years, the courts have suggested ways for Congress to repair glaring FOIA loopholes, but, despite several opportunities (e.g., the 1992 reworking of the National Security Act), Congress has turned its back on the FOIA.

When asked if he was working for legislative improvement of the act, David Vladek responded, "That's a dumb question. How are we going to get progressive changes in the statute through this Congress? It has been true for quite some time that anything the Congress is likely to do in the FOIA area is bad. Even Senator Leahy's electronic amendments, which I think were well-intentioned, have had mixed effect. It's only been in effect for a short period, and I would say it's too early to tell whether it's succeeded or not."[47]

The weakness of Congress in the face of executive secrecy is particularly striking in the area of national security. Congress, like the FOIA itself, remains captive of the national security system created by the executive branch. As we have seen, the Clinton-Reno initiatives for improving FOIA responsiveness bog down when it comes to classified information, because there is no room for discretionary releases of such material. Only a fundamental change in the way in which information is classified can break the logjam, and the best possibility for reform rests with the legislative recommendations in the 1997 report of the Commission on Protecting and Reducing Government Secrecy, chaired by Senator Patrick Moynihan (D-N.Y.).

In calling for the declassification of America's aging mountain of secret documents, the report noted, "The public does have a right to know. A fair amount of information is eventually declassified, but too often . . . only after years of expensive processing (and sometimes lawsuits) under the Freedom of Information Act." In conclusion, "It is time for legislation. There needs to be some check on the unrestrained discretion to create secrets. There needs to be an effective mode of declassification. Apart from aspects of nuclear energy subject to the Atomic Energy Act, secrets in the Federal Government are whatever anyone with a stamp decides to stamp secret. There is no statutory base and never has been; classification and declassification have been governed for nearly five decades by a series of executive orders, but none has created a stable and reliable system that ensures we protect well what needs protecting but nothing more."[48]

Primary among the Moynihan commission's recommendations was a proposed statute establishing the principles of federal classification and declassification of government information. Bills subsequently introduced in the House and Senate maintained the framework presented in the 1997 Moynihan report, and they have received serious consideration.

Senate bill S. 712, titled the "Government Secrecy Act of 1997," was introduced by its sponsor, Senator Moynihan, on May 7, 1997. The bill's original cosponsor was Senator Jesse Helms (R-N.C.), the powerful and ultraconservative chairman of the Senate Foreign Relations Committee. After S. 712 was referred to the Senate Committee on Governmental Affairs, it acquired three additional cosponsors, Senators William V. Roth (R-Del.), Tom Daschle (D-S.D.), and majority leader Trent Lott (R-Miss.).

An identical House bill, H.R. 1546, was introduced along with the Senate bill and was referred to the House Government Reform and Oversight Committee.

The text of the Government Secrecy Act of 1997 begins: "It is the purpose of this Act to promote the effective protection of classified information and the disclosure of information where there is not a well-founded basis for protection or where the costs of maintaining a secret outweight the benefits."

After referring to the recommendations of the Moynihan commission's report, the bill states: "Enactment of a statute would create an opportunity for greater oversight by Congress of executive branch classification and declassification activities, without impairing the responsibility of executive branch officials for the day to day administration of the system."

Under the proposed statutory classification system, the president would also be authorized to establish resources and procedures for declassifying information. Although the details of the classification and declassification process are left in the hands of executive agency officials, a significant balancing standard is declared: "In determining whether information should be classified or declassified, the agency official making the determination shall weigh the benefit from public disclosure of the information against the need for initial or continued protection of the information. . . . If there is significant doubt as to whether information requires such protection, it shall not be classified."

The Government Secrecy Act would allow information to remain classified for no more than ten years, unless the head of the agency that created the information certifies to the president that, under the balancing standard, it requires continued protection. Information that is kept classified beyond the ten-year period must be declassified within thirty years, unless the appropriate agency head certifies to the president that continued protection of the information is "essential to the national security" or that "demonstrable harm to an individual will result from release."

The Government Secrecy Act would amend the FOIA statute only to the extent of making Exemption (b)(1), the national security exemption, cover information "specifically authorized to be classified under the Government Secrecy Act of 1997" or information authorized before passage of the Act under an executive order.[49] The anticipated effect on the FOIA would be reasonable control, if not reduction, of the use of exemption (b)(1).

As one might guess from the fact that Senator Helms is a cosponsor, the Government Secrecy Act offers no immediate improvement over the provisions of President Clinton's executive order. Its strength is its reliability and its check on the kind of arbitrary and sweeping executive authority that produced President Reagan's outrageous E.O. 12356. According to an article published in the *Washington Post*, the bill "would provide a floor below which a secrecy-obsessed future president could not descend." Still, the *Post* warns, "[T]he main pressure on the legislation is coming from those forces inclined to weaken it, not to make it more robust. The CIA has objected to expanding judicial review. The Justice Department has intimated that the whole idea of Congress's writing classification rules may violate the constitutional separations of powers. The White House has not articulated clearly what sort of secrecy legislation the president would be willing to sign. And some Republicans on Capitol Hill have objected to spending money on declassification."[50]

Indeed, the national security state has become such a mystical icon to congressional Republicans, and many Democrats, that they hesitate to approach its hallowed structure with legislation. Senator Richard C. Shelby, a conservative Republican from Alabama, who has expressed "grave concern" over S. 712, declared before the Senate, "U.S. security has depended and still depends on secrecy to succeed. We must proceed with caution in our commitment to make more classified information available to the public.... I believe sanctions for unauthorized disclosures should be added to the bill. We need to consider new and unique categories of secrecy for our most sensitive intelligence operations, perhaps to include very serious penalties for public discussion of these activities."[51]

Even if it should pass in its present form, the Government Secrecy Act is no panacea for government secrecy. According to Kate Martin, general counsel for the National Security Archive, "As originally written, the bill was very short on specifics, and it's not clear what effect it would have on actual classification. Its most important aspect is that it would require that the public interest be balanced against national security harm in making declassification decisions, and that process would become part of the FOIA. Unfortunately, that is the part of the bill that has drawn the most objections from the Administration. They followed the CIA's lead in opposing judicial review of classification decisions."

Despite congressional pressure to weaken the Government Secrecy Act, Martin has not given up on the bill. "The balancing test in the Moynihan bill, although it's a bit of a longshot at this point, would certainly strengthen the FOIA," said Martin. "The mere fact that it has been introduced in a bill is a hopeful sign. I'm an optimist."[52]

There is indeed some evidence that the FOIA can be strengthened by this indirect legislative approach, through bills that require the expedited declassification of government information or incorporate minor FOIA amendments as a tool to accomplish some specific objective. For example, the JFK Assassination Records Collection Act of 1992 mandates an independent review of all government records relevant to the assassination of President Kennedy. Toward that end, the law empowered a special

Assassination Records Review Board to ensure the centralized collection and "timely disclosure" of all relevant records. The destruction, alteration, or mutilation of any such record was prohibited, and information contained therein was to be withheld "only in the rarest case" and then only if there was a "legitimate need for continued protection."

The blanket FOIA exemptions employed by FBI and CIA officals would not apply here, and disclosure of records could be postponed only "if there is clear and convincing evidence" that disclosure would pose a threat "of such gravity that it outweighs the public interest." FBI and CIA officials would not be allowed to rule on these postponements; that authority is vested in an Assassination Records Review Board, and only the president has the power to override its rulings. Members of the board are appointed by the president, "after considering persons recommended by the American Historical Association, the Organization of American Historians, the Society of American Archivists, and the American Bar Association."[53]

The review board may decide that an assassination record shall be disclosed contrary to the judgment of a federal agency or held in protected status at the National Archives. The president may override the board's decision by imposing a postponement of disclosure, but he must provide the board with a written, unclassified justification for such action.

Two other bills, the Nazi War Crimes Disclosure Act and the Human Rights Information Act affect the FOIA by addressing particular aspects of the public's right to know.

The Nazi War Crimes Disclosure Act (H.R. 4007 and S. 1379) which became law on October 8, 1998, amends the Freedom of Information Act and the National Security Act to require disclosure under the FOIA of Nazi war crime records that do not reveal sensitive intelligence matters or impair any investigation or prosecution conducted by the Justice Department. Under the act, "the president shall establish the Nazi War Crime Records Interagency Working Group," which shall "1) Locate, identify, inventory, recommend for declassification, and make available to the public at the National Archives . . . all classified Nazi war criminal records of the United States; 2) Coordinate with agencies and take such actions as necessary to expedite the release of such records to the public; and 3) Submit a report to Congress . . . describing all such records, the disposition of such records, and the activities of the Interagency Group and agencies under this section."[54]

The Nazi War Crimes Disclosure Act specifies several exemptions to disclosure, the application of which are subject to the same standard of legal review that applies to records withheld under the FOIA. The act concludes by stating that for purposes of expedited processing under the FOIA, "any requester of a Nazi war criminal record shall be deemed to have a compelling need for such record."[55]

A similar bill that is pending in Congress, the Human Rights Information Act (H.R. 2635 and S. 1220), calls for the declassification of records concerning human rights violations in Honduras and Guatemala. What may make this bill more difficult to pass is that the crimes being addressed were committed by U.S.–trained security forces and death squads. The bill begins with an unusual set of complaints: "Members of both Houses of Congress have repeatedly asked the Administration for information on Guatemalan and Honduran human rights cases. . . . Victims and survivors of human rights violations, including United States citizens and their relatives, have also been requesting the information. . . . Survivors and the relatives of victims have a right to know what happened."[56]

Section 4 of the act provides that "each agency shall identify, review, and organize all human rights records regarding activities occurring in Guatemala and Honduras after 1944 for the purpose of declassifying and disclosing the records to the public."[57]

Agencies may postpone declassification of human rights records only if the agency determines that "the threat to military defense operations or conduct of foreign relations of the United States raised by public disclosure . . . is of such gravity that it outweighs the public interest."[58]

As in the Nazi war crimes act, the Human Rights Information Act lists several specific exemptions, such as intelligence sources and methods, but an interagency appeals panel has the authority to review any agency decision to withhold human rights records.

The bill concludes with the statement: "Nothing in this act shall be construed to limit any right to file a request with any executive agency or seek judicial review of a decision pursuant to Section 552 of Title 5, United States Code [Freedom of Information Act]."[59]

The House has referred the bill to the Committee on Government Reform and Oversight, and the Senate has referred it to the Committee on Governmental Affairs. In May 1998, hearings were held by the House Subcommittee on Government Management, Information, and Technology. At those hearings, Leo Valladares, the national commissioner for human rights in Honduras, told the panel that timely access to files documenting U.S. ties to the Honduran death squads was "critical" to his efforts to obtain justice for the families of the "disappeared." Lee Strickland, senior CIA spokesman, urged Congress to reject the Human Rights Information Act, claiming that, under its provisions, "sources will be imperiled and the mission of the CIA . . . will be disadvantaged."[60]

Kate Martin lobbied effectively for the passage of the Nazi war crimes act and she is confident that the Human Rights Information Act will eventually pass, helping the FOIA and the right to know in the process. "The Nazi war crimes bill called for the declassification of all this very old material related to German war crimes," she said. "It's too bad that a bill was even required to address such an overdue need. The material is so old, who's going to object to it? The other bill, the Human Rights Information Act, is one we've been working on. It addresses information in U.S. government files concerning human rights violations in Central America. A few months ago I would have told you that this is a symbolic gesture that wasn't going anywhere, but after the House hearings they seem much more serious about it than I would have expected. Like the Nazi war crimes act, it would set up a kind of independent review to release the material as an adjunct to the FOIA process."[61]

Of all the "indirect" amendments to the FOIA, the most recent and controversial is Public Law 105–227, passed with little debate in November 1998 at the end of a hectic 105th Congress. The law, virtually hidden in a 4,000-page appropriations bill, includes a provision that directs the Office of Management and Budget (OMB) to amend OMB Circular A-110 to allow "all data" produced by researchers receiving federal grants to be obtained through the FOIA.

The law arose from a dispute over a Harvard University study that found a link between air pollution and health. When the Environmental Protection Agency (EPA) cited the study in proposing tougher air standards, industry groups opposed to regulation demanded that Harvard make its research public. The researchers allowed independent scientists to review the data, but refused to release full details. In the floor debate on P.L. 105–277, its author, Senator Richard Shelby (R-Ala.), said, "The lack of public access to research data feeds general public mistrust of the government and undermines support for major regulatory programs. This measure was long overdue and it represents a first step in ensuring that the public has access to all studies used by the Federal Government to develop Federal policy."

Senate majority leader Trent Lott (R-Miss.) said the new law "represents a first step in ensuring that the public has access to all studies used by the Federal Government to develop Federal policy."[62]

Prior to P.L. 105–277, the FOIA did not consider federally funded research data to be "Federal records" unless the data was in the files of a Federal agency. This interpretation had been affirmed by the Supreme Court in *Forsham v. Harris*, 445 U.S. 169 (1980). Now the reach of the FOIA appears to have been extended in ways that frighten some researchers.

As required by P.L. 105–277, OMB proposed the following revision to Circular A-110:

"(c) . . . [I]n response to a Freedom of Information Act (FOIA) request for data relating to published research findings produced under an award that were used by the Federal Government in developing policy or rules, the Federal awarding agency shall, within a reasonable time, obtain the requested data so that they can be made available to the public through the procedures established under the FOIA. If the Federal awarding agency obtains the data solely in response to a FOIA request, the agency may charge the requester a reasonable fee equaling the full incremental cost of obtaining the data. This fee should reflect costs incurred by the agency, the recipient, and applicable subrecipients. This fee is in addition to any fees the agency may assess under the FOIA (5 U.S.C. 552 (a)(4)(A))."

OMB published its proposed revision to Circular A-110 in the *Federal Register* and gave interested parties until April 5, 1999 to submit comments. The response from scientists and scientific organizations was overwhelmingly negative. Among the questions posed by concerned research organizations were: What does the proposed regulation mean by the word "data?" Will only data collected by the government for policy-making purposes be subject to the FOIA? What constitutes "publication" under the new regulation and when would data need to be made publicly accessible? How would the confidentiality and privacy of human subjects of scientific research be protected? Is the FOIA the right framework for ensuring disclosure of federally-funded research?

On January 24, 1999, the Council for the American Association for the Advancement of Science (AAAS) issued a statement of concern about the draft regulations. The following month, Mark Frankel, Director of the AAAS Scientific Freedom, Responsibility and Law Program, recommended that the definition of "data" in the new law "be determined through negotiations between the funding agencies and the institutions covered by Circular A-110." He said any reference to published research findings "should state that 'publication' is acknowledged to mean 'in a scientific journal after formal peer review.' " Frankel also recommended that Circular A-110 "should include a cost-recovery provision for grantees." Finally, he urged Congress to hold hearings on H.R. 88, a pending bill to repeal P.L. 105–277.[63]

Universities and hospitals were particularly disturbed by the new law, which they said could put research notes, confidential material, and incomplete or misleading data in the hands of those who oppose the research for political reasons.

"I see nothing positive in this," said Eugene Braunwald, who oversees 2,000 researchers in Massachusetts hospitals. "It's mischievous."

Kevin Casey, a spokesman for Harvard University, said, "We have grave concerns. This is a large problem, and the more we look into it, the more sirens go off."

"There is no way to implement this law that is tolerable," said Dr. David Korn of the Association of American Medical Colleges.

"Sometimes a company will provide us with confidential information

. . . that they do not want public," said David Lister, vice-president for research at MIT. "This law just seems to cast a very broad net, and nobody knows quite what could be scooped up."[64]

This new wrinkle to the FOIA was hotly debated at the Secrecy in Science conference held at the Massachusetts Institute of Technology (MIT) on March 29, 1999. I was a speaker at that conference, and there was no topic more frequently mentioned, whether in formal presentations or in private conversations over lunch. Claims that the obligation to respond to FOIA requests would be an "undue burden" on researchers were eerily reminiscent of the dire predictions by federal bureaucrats in 1966 when the FOIA was first passed.

Surprisingly, the only speaker to support the goals of P.L. 105–277 was John Deutch, former CIA Director and current Institute Professor at MIT. "In essence," Deutch said, "the comment made by this law . . . is that there is too much secrecy on university campuses with respect to ongoing research. . . . We are not always as open with our own research as both our scientific principles require and the public expects, and we should find manageable, sensible mechanisms to make public research more readily and more rapidly accessible."

Deutch said the research community's rejection of P.L. 105–277 "is not accompanied by any steps to meet the expressed, though imperfectly expressed, public concern that knowledge sponsored by the United States Government belongs to the public and should be made accessible as soon as possible." Rather than continuing the attacks on the new FOIA requirements, Deutch recommended "a response that is more constructive and more positive and meets the public desire to have prompter, more accurate information on ongoing research."

Deutch reminded his MIT audience, "Universities per se are not always enormously willing to share information about themselves—the basic right to know."[65]

Congressional scholar Harold Relyea regards these new applications of the FOIA as evidence that the pursuit of the citizen's right to know may be accomplished through a variety of instruments. "These recent realizations of freedom of information seem to occur when Congress actively pursues its overseer role," stated Relyea, who quoted approvingly the view expressed long ago by a young graduate student, Woodrow Wilson, later to become the twenty-eighth president of the United States. "Unless Congress have and use every means of acquainting itself with the acts and the disposition of the administrative agents of the government," wrote the young Wilson, "the country must be helpless to learn how it is being served."[66]

NOTES

1. Statement by John E. Moss, *Access Reports*, December 17, 1997, pp. 4–5.
2. Ralph Nader, telephone interview with author, March 16, 1998.
3. Thomas M. Susman, telephone interview with author, May 5, 1998.
4. Sam Archibald, "The Early Years of the Freedom of Information Act—1955 to 1974," *PS: Political Science and Politics* (December 1993): 731.
5. "Administration of Freedom of Information Act," Memo from President Bill Clinton to Heads of Departments and Agencies, October 4, 1983, in *Weekly Compilation of Presidential Documents* 29 (October 11, 1993): 1999–2000.
6. Department of Justice, Office of the Attorney General, "Memorandum for Heads of Departments and Agencies: The Freedom of Information Act," October 4, 1993.
7. Debra Hernandez, "Speeding up Response to FOIA Requests," *Editor and Publisher*, September 23, 1995, p. 9.
8. "The Freedom of Information Act," Memo from Attorney General Janet Reno to Heads of Departments and Agencies, May 1, 1997.
9. Tom Blanton, telephone interview with author, January 4, 1998.
10. Gary Blonston, "Reno Says Justice Takes FOIA Seriously Now," *American Editor*, June 1996, p. 22.
11. Scott Armstrong, "The War over Secrecy: Democracy's Most Important Low-Intensity Conflict," in *A Culture of Secrecy: The Government versus the People's Right to Know*, ed. Athan G. Theoharis (Lawrence: University Press of Kansas, 1998), p. 148.
12. Ibid., p. 150. From transcript of Oral Argument, available from Scott Armstrong, p. 150.
13. "Judge Tells White House to Save Computer Tapes," *New York Times*, January 7, 1993, p. A15.
14. James D. Lewis, "White House Electronic Mail and Federal Recordkeeping Law: Press 'D' to Delete History," *Michigan Law Review* 93 (February 1985): 823–24, 848.
15. Blanton, telephone interview with author.
16. *Public Citizen Litigation Group and the Freedom of Information Clearinghouse: Obtaining Access to Government Records since 1972*, Public Citizen Web page, www.citizen.org.
17. "Clinton Tries to Limit Access to NSC Data," *Washington Post*, March 26, 1994, A7.
18. "White House Curbs Access to Security Council's Data," *New York Times*, March 26, 1994, A6.
19. "NSC Not Subject to Information Act, Court Rules," *Washington Post*, August 3, 1996, p. A3.
20. Ibid.
21. Ibid.
22. Scott Armstrong, "The War over Secrecy," p. 140.
23. "Record-Destruction Order Assailed," *Washington Post*, June 28, 1997, p. A8.

24. *Public Citizen v. John Carlin*, Civil Action No. 96-2840 (PLF), U.S. District Court for the District of Columbia, October 22, 1997.

25. "Those Electronic Jottings," *Washington Post*, March 28, 1998, p. A14.

26. "Judge Threatens U.S. Archivist with Injunction," *Washington Post*, March 22, 1998, p. A6.

27. "Judge Finds U.S. Archivist Has 'Flagrantly' Violated Order," *Washington Post*, April 10, 1998, p. A21.

28. Blanton, telephone interview with author.

29. *Hunt v. CIA*, 981 F.2d 1116, 1119 (9th Cir. 1992).

30. Matthew M. Aid, " 'Not So Anonymous': Parting the Veil of Secrecy about the National Security Agency," in *A Culture of Secrecy: The Government versus the People's Right to Know*, ed. Athan G. Theoharis (Lawrence: University Press of Kansas, 1998), p. 72.

31. Senate Committee on Governmental Affairs. *The Assassination Materials Disclosure Act of 1992*. Hearing. 102d Cong. 2d sess., May 12, 1992. (Washington, D.C.: U.S. Government Printing Office, 1992).

32. Antonin Scalia, "The Freedom of Information Act Has No Clothes," *AEI Journal on Government and Society Regulation*, March/April 1982, p. 19.

33. Stuart Taylor, Jr., "Scalia Proposes Major Overhaul of U.S. Courts," *New York Times*, February 16, 1987, p. A1.

34. *Department of Justice v. Reporters Committee for Freedom of the Press*, 489 U.S. 749 (1989) at 764.

35. Ibid., at 773.

36. 5 U.S.C. at 552 (e).

37. House Committee on Government Operations, Senate Committee on the Judiciary, *Freedom of Information Act and Amendments of 1974, Sourcebook*, 94th Cong., 1st sess. (Washington, D.C.: U.S. Government Printing Office, 1975), pp. 284–85.

38. Robert G. Vaughan, "Consumer Access to Product Safety Information and the Future of the Freedom of Information Act," *Administrative Law Journal* 5 (1991): 706.

39. Ibid., pp. 709–10.

40. Matthew Bunker and Stephen Perry, "Privacy Exemptions and the Press under the FOIA," *Newspaper Research Journal* 16, no. 1 (Winter 1995): 93.

41. Blanton, telephone interview with author.

42. "Will EFOIA Amendments Affect Reporters Committee?," *Access Reports*, October 9, 1996, p. 2.

43. *Michael J. O'Kane v. U.S. Customs Service*, Civil Action No. 95-0683-CIV-MORENO, U.S. District Court for the Southern District of Florida.

44. Harry Hammitt, "Reinventing FOIA," *Access Reports*, November 20, 1996, p. 4.

45. Susman, telephone interview with author.

46. David Vladek, telephone interview with author, January 7, 1998.

47. Ibid.

48. *Report of the Commission on Protecting and Reducing Government Secrecy*, S-Doc 105-2 (Washington, D.C.: U.S. Government Printing Office, 1997), p. xxii.

49. *Congressional Record*, Senate, Proceedings and Debates of the 105th Cong., 1st sess., May 7, 1997, S4111–12.

50. "The Secrecy Legislation," *Washington Post*, April 10, 1998, p. A22.

51. *Congressional Record*, Senate, Proceedings and Debates of the 105th Cong., 2d sess., March 3, 1998, S1251–52.

52. Kate Martin, telephone interview with author, June 28, 1998.

53. Harold Relyea, "Freedom of Information Revisited," in *Federal Information Policies in the 1990s: Views and Perspectives*, ed. Peter Hernon, Charles R. McClure, and Harold C. Relyea (Norwood, N.J.: Ablex Publishing, 1996), pp. 197–98.

54. Nazi War Crimes Disclosure Act, Public Law 105-246, full text online in Congressional Universe, Lexis-Nexis, 1998.

55. Ibid.

56. Human Rights Information Act, House Bill H.R. 2635, Senate Bill S. 1220, full text online in Congressional Universe, Lexis-Nexis, 1998.

57. Ibid.

58. Ibid.

59. Ibid.

60. "CIA Opposes Release of Secret Files," *Washington Post*, May 12, 1998, p. A7.

61. Martin, telephone interview with author.

62. *Congressional Record*, Senate, Proceedings and Debates of the 105th Congress, 2nd sess., October 9, 1998, S12134.

63. Mark S. Frankel, "Public Access to Data," *Science*, February 19, 1999, p. 1114.

64. Aaron Zitner, "Disclosure Law Worries Researchers," *Boston Globe*, February 11, 1999, p. A1.

65. "The Cultures of Universities, Industry, and Governments," an address by John M. Deutch at the conference, *Secrecy in Science: Exploring University, Industry, and Government Relationships*, held at the Massachusetts Institute of Technology, March 29, 1999.

66. Relyea, "Freedom of Information Revisited," p. 206.

APPENDIX 1

Text of the FOIA

**TITLE 5, UNITED STATES CODE
PART I—THE AGENCIES GENERALLY
CHAPTER 5—ADMINISTRATIVE
SUBCHAPTER II—ADMINISTRATIVE PROCEDURE**

§552. PUBLIC INFORMATION; AGENCY RULES, OPINIONS, ORDERS, RECORDS, AND PROCEEDINGS

(a) Each agency shall make available to the public information as follows:

(1) Each agency shall separately state and currently publish in the Federal Register for the guidance of the public—

(A) descriptions of its central and field organization and the established places at which, the employees (and in the case of a uniformed service, the members) from whom, and the methods whereby, the public may obtain information, make submittals or requests, or obtain decisions;

(B) statements of the general course and method by which its functions are channeled and determined, including the nature and requirements of all formal and informal procedures available;

(C) rules of procedure, descriptions of forms available or the places at which forms may be obtained, and instructions as to the scope and contents of all papers, reports, or examinations;

(D) substantive rules of general applicability adopted as authorized by law, and statements of general policy or interpretations of general applicability formulated and adopted by the agency; and

(E) each amendment, revision, or repeal of the foregoing.

Except to the extent that a person has actual and timely notice of the terms thereof, a person may not in any manner be required to resort to, or be adversely affected by, a matter required to be published in the Federal Register and not so published. For the purpose of this paragraph, matter reasonably available to the class of persons affected thereby is deemed published in the Federal Register when incorporated by reference therein with the approval of the Director of the Federal Register.

(2) Each agency, in accordance with published rules, shall make available for public inspection and copying—

(A) final opinions, including concurring and dissenting opinions, as well as orders, made in the adjudication of cases;

(B) those statements of policy and interpretations which have been adopted by the agency and are not published in the Federal Register;

(C) administrative staff manuals and instructions to staff that affect a member of the public;

(D) copies of all records, regardless of form or format, which have been released to any person under paragraph (3) and which, because of the nature of their subject matter, the agency determines have become or are likely to become the subject of subsequent requests for substantially the same records; and

(E) a general index of the records referred to under subparagraph (D); unless the materials are promptly published and copies offered for sale. For records created on or after November 1, 1996, within one year after such date, each agency shall make such records available, including by computer telecommunications or, if computer telecommunications means have not been established by the agency, by other electronic means. To the extent required to prevent a clearly unwarranted invasion of personal privacy, an agency may delete identifying details when it makes available or publishes an opinion, statement of policy, interpretation, staff manual, instruction, or copies of records referred to in subparagraph (D). However, in each case the justification for the deletion shall be explained fully in writing, and the extent of such deletion shall be indicated on the portion of the record which is made available or published, unless including that indication would harm an interest protected by the exemption in subsection (b) under which the deletion is made. If technically feasible, the extent of the deletion shall be indicated at the place in the record where the deletion was made. Each agency shall also maintain and make available for public inspection and copying current indexes providing identifying information for the public as to any matter issued, adopted, or promulgated after July 4, 1967, and required by this paragraph to be made available or published. Each agency shall promptly publish, quarterly or more frequently, and distribute (by sale or otherwise) copies of each index or supplements thereto unless it determines by order published in the Federal Register that the publication would be unnecessary and impracticable, in which case the agency shall nonetheless provide copies of such index on request at a cost not to exceed the direct cost of duplication. Each agency shall make the index referred to in subparagraph (E) available by computer telecommunications by December 31, 1999. A final order, opinion, statement of policy, interpretation, or staff manual or instruction that affects a member of the public may be relied on, used, or cited as precedent by an agency against a party other than an agency only if—

(i) it has been indexed and either made available or published as provided by this paragraph; or

(ii) the party has actual and timely notice of the terms thereof.

(3)(A) Except with respect to the records made available under paragraphs (1) and (2) of this subsection, each agency, upon any request for records which (i) reasonably describes such records and (ii) is made in accordance with published rules stating the time, place, fees (if any), and procedures to be followed, shall make the records promptly available to any person.

(B) In making any record available to a person under this paragraph, an agency shall provide the record in any form or format requested by the person if the record is readily reproducible by the agency in that form or format. Each agency shall make reasonable efforts to maintain its records in forms or formats that are reproducible for purposes of this section.

(C) In responding under this paragraph to a request for records, an agency shall make reasonable efforts to search for the records in electronic form or format, except when such efforts would significantly interfere with the operation of the agency's automated information system.

(D) For purposes of this paragraph, the term "search" means to review, manually or by automated means, agency records for the purpose of locating those records which are responsive to a request.

(4)(A)(i) In order to carry out the provisions of this section, each agency shall promulgate regulations, pursuant to notice and receipt of public comment, specifying the schedule of fees applicable to the processing of requests under this section and establishing procedures and guidelines for determining when such fees should be waived or reduced. Such schedule shall conform to the guidelines which shall be promulgated, pursuant to notice and receipt of public comment, by the Director of the Office of Management and Budget and which shall provide for a uniform schedule of fees for all agencies.

(ii) Such agency regulations shall provide that—

(I) fees shall be limited to reasonable standard charges for document search, duplication, and review, when records are requested for commercial use;

(II) fees shall be limited to reasonable standard charges for document duplication when records are not sought for commercial use and the request is made by an educational or non-commercial scientific institution, whose purpose is scholarly or scientific research; or a representative of the news media; and

(III) for any request not described in (I) or (II), fees shall be limited to reasonable standard charges for document search and duplication.

(iii) Documents shall be furnished without any charge or at a charge reduced below the fees established under clause (ii) if disclosure of the information is in the public interest because it is likely to contribute significantly to public understanding of the operations or activities of the government and is not primarily in the commercial interest of the requester.

(iv) Fee schedules shall provide for the recovery of only the direct costs of search, duplication, or review. Review costs shall include only the direct costs incurred during the initial examination of a document for the purposes of determining whether the documents must be disclosed under this section and for the purposes of withholding any portions exempt from disclosure under this section. Review costs may not include any costs incurred in resolving issues of law or policy that may be raised in the course of processing a request under this section. No fee may be charged by any agency under this section—

(I) if the costs of routine collection and processing of the fee are likely to equal or exceed the amount of the fee; or

(II) for any request described in clause (ii) (II) or (III) of this subparagraph for the first two hours of search time or for the first one hundred pages of duplication.

(v) No agency may require advance payment of any fee unless the requester has previously failed to pay fees in a timely fashion, or the agency has determined that the fee will exceed $250.

(vi) Nothing in this subparagraph shall supersede fees chargeable under a statute specifically providing for setting the level of fees for particular types of records.

(vii) In any action by a requester regarding the waiver of fees under this section, the court shall determine the matter de novo: *Provided*, That the court's review of the matter shall be limited to the record before the agency.

(B) On complaint, the district court of the United States in the district in which the complainant resides, or has his principal place of business, or in which the agency records are situated, or in the District of Columbia, has jurisdiction to enjoin the agency from withholding agency records and to order the production of any agency records improperly withheld from the complainant. In such a case the court shall determine the matter de novo, and may examine the contents of such agency records in camera to determine whether such records or any part thereof shall be withheld under any of the exemptions set forth in subsection (b) of this section, and the burden is on the agency to sustain its action. In addition to any other matters to which a court accords substantial weight, a court shall accord substantial weight to an affidavit of an agency concerning the agency's determination as to technical feasibility under paragraph (2)(C) and subsection (b) and reproducibility under paragraph (3)(B).

(C) Notwithstanding any other provision of law, the defendant shall serve an answer or otherwise plead to any complaint made under this subsection within thirty days after service upon the defendant of the pleading in which such complaint is made, unless the court otherwise directs for good cause shown.

(D) [Repealed.]

(E) The court may assess against the United States reasonable attorney fees and other litigation costs reasonably incurred in any case under this section in which the complainant has substantially prevailed.

(F) Whenever the court orders the production of any agency records improperly withheld from the complainant and assesses against the United States reasonable attorney fees and other litigation costs, and the court additionally issues a written finding that the circumstances surrounding the withholding raise questions whether agency personnel acted arbitrarily or capriciously with respect to the withholding, the Special Counsel shall promptly initiate a proceeding to determine whether disciplinary action is warranted against the officer or employee who was primarily responsible for the withholding. The Special Counsel, after investigation and consideration of the evidence submitted, shall submit his findings and recommendations to the administrative authority of the agency concerned and shall send copies of the findings and recommendations to the officer or employee or his representative. The administrative authority shall take the corrective action that the Special Counsel recommends.

(G) In the event of noncompliance with the order of the court, the district court may punish for contempt the responsible employee, and in the case of a uniformed service, the responsible member.

(5) Each agency having more than one member shall maintain and make available for public inspection a record of the final votes of each member in every agency proceeding.

(6)(A) Each agency, upon any request for records made under paragraph (1), (2), or (3) of this subsection, shall—

(i) determine within ten days[1] (excepting Saturdays, Sundays, and legal public holidays) after the receipt of any such request whether to comply with such request and shall immediately notify the person making such request of such determination and the reasons therefor, and of the right of such person to appeal to the head of the agency any adverse determination; and

(ii) make a determination with respect to any appeal within twenty days (excepting Saturdays, Sundays, and legal public holidays) after the receipt of such appeal. If on appeal the denial of the request for records is in whole or in part upheld, the agency shall notify the person making such request of the provisions for judicial review of that determination under paragraph (4) of this subsection.

(B)[2] In unusual circumstances as specified in this subparagraph, the time limits prescribed in either clause (i) or clause (ii) of subparagraph (A) may be extended by written notice to the person making such request setting forth the reasons for such extension and the date on which a determination is expected to be dispatched. No such notice shall specify a date that would result in an extension of more than ten working days. As used in this subparagraph, "unusual circumstances" means, but only to the extent reasonably necessary to the proper processing of the particular request—

(i) the need to search for and collect the requested records from field facilities or other establishments that are separate from the office processing the request;

(ii) the need to search for, collect, and appropriately examine a voluminous amount of separate and distinct records which are demanded in a single request; or

(iii) the need for consultation, which shall be conducted with all practicable speed, with another agency having a substantial interest in the determination of the request or among two or more components of the agency having a substantial subject-matter interest therein.

(C) Any person making a request to any agency for records under paragraph (1), (2), or (3) of this subsection shall be deemed to have exhausted his administrative remedies with respect to such request if the agency fails to comply with the applicable time limit provisions of this paragraph. If the Government can show exceptional circumstances exist and that the agency is exercising due diligence in responding to the request, the court may retain jurisdiction and allow the agency additional time to complete its review of the records. Upon any determination by an agency to comply with a request for records, the records shall be made promptly available to such person making such request. Any notification of denial of any request for records under this subsection shall set forth the names and titles or positions of each person responsible for the denial of such request.[3]

(b) This section does not apply to matters that are—

(1)(A) specifically authorized under criteria established by an Executive order to be kept secret in the interest of national defense or foreign policy and (B) are in fact properly classified pursuant to such Executive order;

(2) related solely to the internal personnel rules and practices of an agency;

(3) specifically exempted from disclosure by statute (other than section 552b of this title), provided that such statute (A) requires that the matters be withheld from the public in such a manner as to leave no discretion on the issue, or (B) establishes particular criteria for withholding or refers to particular types of matters to be withheld;

(4) trade secrets and commercial or financial information obtained from a person and privileged or confidential;

(5) inter-agency or intra-agency memorandums or letters which would not be available by law to a party other than an agency in litigation with the agency;

(6) personnel and medical files and similar files the disclosure of which would constitute a clearly unwarranted invasion of personal privacy;

(7) records or information compiled for law enforcement purposes, but only to the extent that the production of such law enforcement records or information (A) could reasonably be expected to interfere with enforcement proceedings, (B) would deprive a person of a right to a fair trial or an impartial adjudication, (C) could reasonably be expected to constitute an unwarranted invasion of personal privacy, (D) could reasonably be expected to disclose the identity of a confidential source, including a State, local, or foreign agency or authority or any private institution which furnished information on a confidential basis, and, in the case of a record or information compiled by criminal law enforcement authority in the course of a criminal investigation or by an agency conducting a lawful national security intelligence investigation, information furnished by a confidential source, (E) would disclose techniques and procedures for law enforcement investigations

or prosecutions, or would disclose guidelines for law enforcement investigations or prosecutions if such disclosure could reasonably be expected to risk circumvention of the law, or (F) could reasonably be expected to endanger the life or physical safety of any individual;

(8) contained in or related to examination, operating, or condition reports prepared by, on behalf of, or for the use of an agency responsible for the regulation or supervision of financial institutions; or

(9) geological and geophysical information and data, including maps, concerning wells.

Any reasonably segregable portion of a record shall be provided to any person requesting such record after deletion of the portions which are exempt under this subsection. The amount of information deleted shall be indicated on the released portion of the record, unless including that indication would harm an interest protected by the exemption in this subsection under which the deletion is made. If technically feasible, the amount of the information deleted shall be indicated at the place in the record where such deletion is made.

(c)(1) Whenever a request is made which involves access to records described in subsection (b)(7)(A) and—

(A) the investigation or proceeding involves a possible violation of criminal law; and

(B) there is reason to believe that (i) the subject of the investigation or proceeding is not aware of its pendency, and (ii) disclosure of the existence of the records could reasonably be expected to interfere with enforcement proceedings, the agency may, during only such time as that circumstance continues, treat the records as not subject to the requirements of this section.

(2) Whenever informant records maintained by a criminal law enforcement agency under an informant's name or personal identifier are requested by a third party according to the informant's name or personal identifier, the agency may treat the records as not subject to the requirements of this section unless the informant's status as an informant has been officially confirmed.

(3) Whenever a request is made which involves access to records maintained by the Federal Bureau of Investigation pertaining to foreign intelligence or counterintelligence, or international terrorism, and the existence of the records is classified information as provided in subsection (b)(1), the Bureau may, as long as the existence of the records remains classified information, treat the records as not subject to the requirements of this section.

(d) This section does not authorize withholding of information or limit the availability of records to the public except as specifically stated in this section. This section is not authority to withhold information from Congress.

(e)(1) On or before February 1 of each year, each agency shall submit to the Attorney General of the United States a report which shall cover the preceding fiscal year and which shall include—

(A) the number of determinations made by the agency not to comply with requests for records made to such agency under subsection (a) and the reasons for each such determination;

(B)(i) the number of appeals made by persons under subsection (a)(6), the result of such appeals, and the reason for the action upon each appeal that results in a denial of information; and

(ii) a complete list of all statutes that the agency relies upon to authorize the agency to withhold information under subsection (b)(3), a description of whether a court has upheld the decision of the agency to withhold information under each such statute, and a concise description of the scope of any information withheld;

(C) the number of requests for records pending before the agency as of September 30 of the preceding year, and the median number of days that such requests had been pending before the agency as of that date;

(D) the number of requests for records received by the agency and the number of requests which the agency processed;

(E) the median number of days taken by the agency to process different types of requests;

(F) the total amount of fees collected by the agency for processing requests; and

(G) the number of full-time staff of the agency devoted to processing requests for records under this section, and the total amount expended by the agency for processing such requests.

(2) Each agency shall make each such report available to the public including by computer telecommnnunications, or if computer telecommunications means have not been established by the agency, by other electronic means.

(3) The Attorney General of the United States shall make each report which has been made available by electronic means available at a single electronic access point. The Attorney General of the United States shall notify the Chairman and ranking minority member of the Committee on Government Reform and Oversight of the House of Representatives and the Chairman and ranking minority member of the Committees on Governmental Affairs and the Judiciary of the Senate, no later than April 1 of the year in which each such report is issued, that such reports are available by electronic means.

(4) The Attorney General of the United States, in consultation with the Director of the Office of Management and Budget, shall develop reporting and performance guidelines in connection with reports required by this subsection by October 1, 1997, and may establish additional requirements for such reports as the Attorney General determines may be useful.

(5) The Attorney General of the United States shall submit an annual report on or before April 1 of each calendar year which shall include for the prior calendar year a listing of the number of cases arising under this section, the exemption involved in each case, the disposition of such case, and the cost, fees, and penalties assessed under subparagraphs (E), (F), and (G) of subsection (a)(4). Such report shall also include a description of the efforts undertaken by the Department of Justice to encourage agency compliance with this section.

(f) For purposes of this section, the term—

(1) "agency" as defined in section 551(1) of this title includes any executive department, military department, Government corporation, Government controlled corporation, or other establishment in the executive branch of the Government (including the Executive Office of the President), or any independent regulatory agency; and

(2) "record" and any other term used in this section in reference to information includes any information that would be an agency record subject to the requirements of this section when maintained by an agency in any format, including an electronic format.

(g) The head of each agency shall prepare and make publicly available upon request, reference material or a guide for requesting records or information from the agency, subject to the exemptions in subsection (b), including—

(1) an index of all major information systems of the agency;

(2) a description of major information and record locator systems maintained by the agency; and

(3) a handbook for obtaining various types and categories of public information from the agency pursuant to chapter 35 of title 44, and under this section.

NOTES

1. Under section 12(b) of the Electronic Freedom of Information Act Amendments of 1996 (Pub. L. 104–231; 110 Stat. 3054), the amendment made by section 8(b) of such Act striking "ten days" and inserting "20 days" shall take effect on October 3, 1997.

2. Under section 12 (b) of the Electronic Freedom of Information Act Amendments of 1996 (Pub. L. 104–231; 110 Stat. 3054), the amendment made by section 7(b) of such Act striking subparagraph (B) and inserting a new subparagraph (B) shall take effect on October 3, 1997. As a result of the amendment, upon that date subparagrph (B) will read as follows:

(B)(i) In unusual circumstances as specified in this subparagraph the time limits prescribed in either clause (i) or clause (ii) of subparagraph (A) may be extended by written notice to the person making such request setting forth the unusual circumstances for such extension and the date on which a determination is expected to be dispatched. No such notice shall specify a date that would result in an extension for more than ten working days, except as provided in clause (ii) of this subparagraph.

(ii) With respect to a request for which a written notice under clause (i) extends the time limits prescribed under clause (i) of subparagraph (A), the agency shall notify the person making the request if the request cannot be processed within the time limit specified in that clause and shall provide the person an opportunity to limit the scope of the request so that it may be processed within that time limit or an opportunity to arrange with the agency an alternative time frame for processing the request or a modified request. Refusal by the person to reasonably modify the request or arrange such an alternative time frame shall be considered as a factor in determining whether exceptional circumstances exist for purposes of subparagraph (C).

(iii) As used in this subparagraph, "unusual circumstances" means, but only to the extent reasonably neccessary to the proper processing of the particular requests—

(I) the need to search for and collect the requested records from field facilities or other establishments that are separate from the office processing the request;

(II) the need to search for, collect, and appropriately examine a voluminous amount of separate and distinct records which are demanded in a single request; or

(III) the need for consultation, which shall be conducted with all practicable speed, with another agency having a substantial interest in the determination of the request or among two or more components of the agency having substantial subject-matter interest therein.

(iv) Each agency may promulgate regulations, pursuant to notice and receipt of public comment, providing for the aggregation of certain requests by the same requestor, or by a group of requestors acting in concert, if the agency reasonably believes that such requests actually constitute a single request, which would otherwise satisfy the unusual circumstances specified in this subparagraph, and the requests involve clearly related matters. Multiple requests involving unrelated matters shall not be aggregated.

3. Under section 12(b) of the Electronic Freedom of Infomation Act Amendments of 1996 (Pub.L. 104–231; 110 Stat. 3054), the amendments made by section 7(c) of such Act inserting "(i)" after "(C)" and adding at the end new clauses (ii) and (iii), shall take effect on October 3, 1997. As a result of those amendments, upon that date clauses (ii) and (iii) will read as follows:

(ii) For purpose of this subparagraph, the term "exceptional circumstances" does not include a delay that results from a predictable agency workload of requests under this section, unless the agency demonstrates reasonable progress in reducing its backlog of pending requests.

(iii) Refusal by a person to reasonably modify the scope of a request or arrange an alternative time frame for processing a request (or a modified request) under clause (ii) after being given an opportunity to do so by the agency to whom the person made the request shall be considered as a factor in determining whether exceptional circumstances exist for purposes of this subparagraph.

Under section 12(b) of the Electronic Freedom of Information Act Amendments of 1996 (Pub.L. 104-231; 110 Stat. 3054), the amendments made by sections 7(a) and 8(a) and (c) of that Act adding at the end of this paragraph new subparagraphs (D) through (F), shall take effect on October 3, 1997. As a result of those amendments, upon that date subparagraphs (D) through (F) will read as follows:

(D)(i) Each agency may promulgate regulations, pursuant to notice and receipt of public comment, providing for multitrack processing of requests for records based on the amount of work or time (or both) involved in processing requests.

(ii) Regulations under this subparagraph may provide a person making a request that does not qualify for the fastest multitrack processing an opportunity to limit the scope of the request in order to qualify for faster processing.

(iii) This subparagraph shall not be interpreted to affect the requirement under subparagraph (C) to exercise due diligence.

(E)(i) Each agency shall promulgate regulations, pursuant to notice and receipt of public comment, providing for expedited processing of requests for records—

(I) in cases in which the person requesting the records demonstrates a compelling need; and

(II) in other cases determined by the agency.

(ii) Notwithstanding clause (i), regulations under this subparagraph must ensure—

(I) that a determination of whether to provide expedited processing shall be made, and notice of the determination shall be provided to the person making the request, within 10 days after the date of the request; and

(II) expeditious consideration of administrative appeals of such determinations of whether to provide expedited processing.

(iii) An agency shall process as soon as practicable any request for records to which the agency has granted expedited processing under this subparagraph. Agency action to deny or affirm denial of a request for expedited processing pursuant to this subparagraph, and failure by an agency to respond in a timely manner to such a request shall be subject to judicial review under paragraph (4), except that the judicial review shall be based on the record before the agency at the time of the determination.

(iv) A district court of the United States shall not have jurisdiction to review an agency denial of expedited processing of a request for records after the agency has provided a complete response to the request.

(v) For purposes of this subparagraph, the term "compelling need" means

(I) that a failure to obtain requested records on an expedited basis under this paragraph could reasonably be expected to pose an imminent threat to the life or physical safety of an individual; or

(II) with respect to a request made by a person primarily engaged in disseminating information, urgency to inform the public concerning actual or alleged Federal Government activity.

(vi) A demonstration of a compelling need by a person making a request for expedited processing shall be made by a statement certified by such person to be true and correct to the best of such person's knowledge and belief.

(F) In denying a request for records, in whole or in part, any agency shall make a reasonable effort to estimate the volume of any requested matter the provision of which is denied, and shall provide any such estimate to the person making the request, unless providing such estimate would harm an interest protected by the exemption in subsection (b) pursuant to which the denial is made.

APPENDIX 2

Selected FOIA Case List

Case titles are followed by relevant exemption or legal issue in **bold-face** type.

Abbotts v. NRC, 766 F.2d 604 (D.C.Cir. 1985), **(b)(1)**

Access Reports v. Department of Justice, 926 F.2d 1192 (D.C.Cir. 1991), **(b)(5), deliberative process**

Administrator, FAA v. Robertson, 422 U.S. 255 (1985), **(b)(3)**

Afshar v. Department of State, 702 F.2d 1125 (D.C.Cir. 1983), **(b)(1), deliberative process**

Allen v. CIA, 636 F.2d 1287 (D.C.Cir. 1980), **(b)(1)**

American Jewish Congress v. Kreps, 574 F.2d 624 (D.C.Cir. 1978), **(b)(3)**

Arleff v. Department of the Navy, 712 F.2d 1462 (D.C.Cir. 1983), **(b)(6)**

Association of Retired Railroad Workers v. U.S. Railroad Retirement Board, 830 F.2d 331 (D.C.Cir. 1987), **(b)(3)**

AT&T Information Systems v. GSA, 810 F.2d 1233 (D.C.Cir. 1987), **Reverse FOIA**

Beck v. DOJ, 997 F.2d 1489 (D.C.Cir. 1993), **(b)(7)C, "Glomar" denial**

Better Government Association v. Department of State, 780 F.2d 86 (D.C.Cir. 1986), **Fee waivers**

Black Hills Alliance v. U.S. Forest Service, 603 F.Supp. 117 (D.S.D. 1984), **(b)(9)**

Brant Construction Co. v. EPA, 778 F.2d 1258 (7th Cir. 1986), **(b)(7)**

Bureau of National Affairs, Inc. v. DOJ, 742 F.2d 1484 (D.C.Cir. 1984), **Personal records**

Chrysler Corporation v. Brown, 441 U.S. 281 (1979), **Reverse FOIA, (b)(3), (b)(4)**

Church of Scientology v. IRS, 792 F.2d 146 (D.C.Cir. 1986), **(b)(3)**

CIA v. Sims, 471 U.S. 159 (1985), **(b)(3)**

CNA Financial Corporation v. Donovan, 830 F.2d 1132 (D.C.Cir. 1987), cert. denied, 485 U.S. 977 (1988), **Reverse FOIA, (b)(3), (b)(4)**

Coastal States Gas Corporation v. DOE, 617 F.2d 854 (D.C.Cir. 1980), **(b)(5), attorney-client privilege, deliberative process**

Consumer Product Safety Commission v. GTE Sylvania, 447 U.S. 102 (1980), **(b)(3)**

Consumers Union v. Helmann, 589 F.2d 531 (D.C.Cir. 1978), **(b)(8)**

Core v. United States Postal Service, 730 F.2d 946 (4th Cir. 1984), **(b)(6)**

County of Madison v. Department of Justice, 641 F.2d 1036 (1st Cir. 1981), **(b)(5)**

Critical Mass Energy Project v. NRC, 975 F.2d 871 (D.C.Cir. 1992)(en banc), cert. denied, 507 U.S. 984 (1993), **(b)(4)**

Crooker v. Bureau of Alcohol, Tobacco and Firearms, 670 F.2d 1051 (D.C.Cir. 1981)(en banc), **(b)(2)**

Crooker v. Bureau of Alcohol, Tobacco and Firearms, 789 F.2d 64 (D.C.Cir. 1986), **(b)(7)(A)**

Cuneo v. Rumsfeld, 553 F.2d 1360 (D.C.Cir. 1977), **Attorney's fees**

Department of Defense v. FLRA, 510 U.S. 587 (1994), **(b)(6)**

Department of Justice v. Landano, 508 U.S. 165 (1993), **(b)(7)D, assurance of confidentiality**

Department of Justice v. Reporters Committee for Freedom of the Press, 489 U.S. 749 (1989), **(b)(6), (b)(7)C**

Department of Justice v. Tax Analysts, 492 U.S. 136 (1989), **Agency records**

Department of State v. Ray, 502 U.S. 164 (1991), **(b)(6)**

Department of State v. Washington Post Company, 456 U.S. 595 (1982), **(b)(6)**

Department of the Air Force v. Rose, 425 U.S. 352 (1976), **(b)(2), (b)(6)**

Dow Jones and Company v. Department of Justice, 917 F.2d 571 (D.C.Cir. 1990), **(b)(5), (b)(7), disclosure to Congress**

Ely v. FBI, 781 F.2d 1487 (11th Cir. 1986), **Procedural matters**

EPA v. Mink, 410 U.S. 73 (1973), **(b)(1), (b)(5)**

Eudey v. CIA, 478 F.Supp. 1175 (D.D.C. 1975), **Fee waivers**

FBI v. Abramson, 456 U.S. 615 (1982), **(b)(7), (b)(7)(C)**

Federal Open Market Commission v. Merrill, 443 U.S. 340 (1979), **(b)(5), commercial privilege**

Fitzgibbon v. CIA, 578 F.Supp 704 (D.D.C. 1983), **(b)(1)**

Formaldehyde Institute v. HHS, 889 F.2d 118 (D.C.Cir. 1989), **(b)(5), deliberative process**

Forsham v. Harris, 445 U.S. 169 (1980), **Agency records**

Founding Church of Scientology v. National Security Agency, 434 F.Supp. 632 (D.D.C. 1977), rev'd, 610 F.2d 824 (D.C.Cir. 1979), **Procedural matters**

Founding Church of Scientology v. Smith, 721 F.2d 828 (D.C.Cir. 1983), **(b)(2)**

FTC v. Grolier Inc., 462 U.S. 19 (1983), **(b)(5)**

Fund for Constitutional Government v. NARS, 656 F.2d 856 (D.C.Cir. 1981), **(b)(3), (b)(7)(C)**

Gardels v. CIA, 689 F.2d 1100 (D.C.Cir. 1982), **(b)(3),** *Glomar* **denial**

Getman v. NLRB, 450 F.2d 670 (D.C.Cir. 1971), **(b)(6)**

Goland v. CIA, 607 F.2d 339 (D.C.Cir. 1978), vacated in part and rehearing denied, 607 F.2d 367 (D.C.Cir. 1979), cert. denied, 445 U.S. 927 (1980), **(b)(1)**

Goldberg v. Department of State, 818 F.2d 71 (D.C.Cir. 1987), cert. denied, 485 U.S. 904 (1988), **(b)(1)**

Greentree v. U.S. Customs Service, 674 F.2d 74 (D.C.Cir. 1982), **(b)(3)**

Gregory v. Federal Deposit Insurance Corporation, 631 F.2d 896 (D.C.Cir. 1980), **(b)(8)**

GTE Sylvania, Inc. v. Consumers Union, 445 U.S. 375 (1980), **Improper withholding**

Halperin v. CIA, 629 F.2d 144 (D.C.Cir. 1980), **(b)(3), "mosaic," summary judgment**

Halperin v. Department of State, 565 F.2d 699 (D.C.Cir. 1977), cert. denied, 434 U.S. 1046 (1978), **Equitable discretion**

In Re Department of Defense, 848 F.2d 232 (D.C.Cir. 1988), **(b)(1)**

Ingle v. Department of Justice, 698 F.2d 259 (6th Cir. 1983), **In camera inspection**

Irons v. FBI, 851 F.2d 532 (1st Cir. 1988), **(b)(7)**

John Doe Agency v. John Doe Corporation, 493 U.S. 146 (1989), 110 S.Ct. 471 (1989), **(b)(7)**

Jordan v. Department of Justice, 591 F.2d 753 (D.C.Cir. 1978), **(b)(2)**

Keys v. Department of Justice, 830 F.2d 337 (D.C.Cir. 1987), **(b)(7)**

King v. Department of Justice, 830 F.2d 210 (D.C.Cir. 1987), **(b)(1), (b)(7)**

Kissinger v. Reporters Committee for Freedom of the Press, 445 U.S. 136 (1980), **Improper withholding, personal records**

Krikorian v. Department of State, 984 F.2d 461 (D.C.Cir. 1993), **Adequacy of search, reasonably segregable**

Kuzma v. U.S. Postal Service, 725 F.2d 16 (2d Cir. 1984), **Attorneys' fees**

Laborers' International Union v. Department of Justice, 578 F.Supp 52 (D.D.C. 1983), affirmed, 772 F.2d 919 (D.C.Cir. 1984), **Waiver of exemption**

LaSalle Extension University v. FTC, 627 F.2d 481 (D.C.Cir. 1980), **Attorneys' fees**

Lesar v. Department of Justice, 455 F.Supp 921 (D.D.C. 1978), affirmed, 636 F.2d 472 (D.C.Cir. 1980), **(b)(1), (b)(2), (b)(7), (b)(7)(C), (b)(7)(D)**

Long v. IRS, 596 F.2d 362 (9th Cir. 1979), **(b)(3)**

Lybarger v. Cardwell, 577 F.2d 764 (1st Cir. 1978), **Fee waivers**

Martin v. Office of Special Counsel, 819 F.2d 1181 (D.C.Cir. 1987), **(b)(5)**

Mayock v. INS, 714 F.Supp. 1558 (N.D.Cal. 1989), **Procedural matters**

McClellan Ecological Seepage Situation v. Carlucci, 835 F.2d 1282 (9th Cir. 1987), **Fee waiver**

McCutchen v. HHS, 30 F.3d 183 (D.C.Cir. 1994), **(b)(7)(C)**

McGehee v. CIA, 697 F.2d 1095 (D.C.Cir. 1983), **Procedural matters**

Mead Data Central v. Department of the Air Force, 566 F.2d 242 (D.C.Cir. 1977), **(b)(5)**

Mermelstein v. SEC, 629 F.Supp. 672 (D.D.C. 1986), **(b)(8)**

Mittleman v. OPE, 76 F.3d 1240 (D.C.Cir. 1996), **(b)(7), law enforcement purpose**

Mobil Oil Corporation v. EPA, 879 F.2d 698 (9th Cir. 1989), **(b)(5), waiver of exemption**

Montrose Chemical Corporation v. Train, 491 F.2d 63 (D.C.Cir. 1974), **(b)(5), deliberative process**

Nation Magazine v. U.S. Customs Service, 71 F.3d 885 (D.C.Cir. 1995), **Scope of request**

National Association of Retired Federal Employees v. Horner, 879 F.2d 873 (D.C.Cir. 1989), cert. denied, 494 U.S. 1078 (1990), **(b)(6)**

National Building Maintenance Inc. v. Sampson, 559 F.2d 704 (D.C.Cir. 1977), **Attorneys' fees**

National Parks and Conservation Association v. Kleppe, 547 F.2d 673 (D.C.Cir. 1976), **(b)(4)**

National Parks and Conservation Association v. Morton, 498 F.2d 765 (D.C.Cir. 1974), **(b)(4)**

National Security Archive v. Department of Defense, 881 F.2d 1381 (D.C.Cir. 1989), **Fee waiver**

National Treasury Employees Union v. Griffin, 811 F.2d 644 (D.C.Cir. 1987), **Fee waiver**

National Treasury Employees Union v. U.S. Customs Service, 802 F.2d 525 (1986), **(b)(2)**

National Wildlife Federation v. U.S. Forest Service, 861 F.2d 1114 (9th Cir. 1988), **(b)(5)**

9 to 5 Organization for Women Office Workers v. Board of Governors of the Federal Reserve System, 721 F.2d 1 (1st Cir. 1983), **(b)(4)**

NLRB v. Robbins Tire & Rubber Company, 437 U.S. 214 (1978), **(b)(7)(A)**

NLRB v. Sears, Roebuck and Company, 421 U.S. 132 (1975), **(a)(2)(A), (b)(5), deliberative process**

North v. Walsh, 881 F.2d 1088 (D.C.Cir. 1989), **(b)(7)(A), discovery tool**

NOW v. Social Security Administration, 736 F.2d 727 (D.C.Cir. 1984), **Reverse FOIA**

Occidental Petroleum Corporation v. SEC, 873 F.2d 325 (D.C.Cir. 1989), **Reverse FOIA**

Oglesby v. Department of the Army, 920 F.2d 57 (D.C.Cir. 1990), **Administrative remedies**

Open America v. Watergate Special Prosecution Force, 547 F.2d 805 (D.C.Cir. 1978), **Procedural matters**

Painting and Drywall Work Preservation Fund v. HUD, 936 F.2d 1300 (D.C.Cir. 1991), **(b)(6)**

Paisley v. CIA, 721 F.2d 686 (D.C.Cir. 1983), **(b)(5)**

Payne Enterprises v. United States, 837 F.2d 486 (D.C.Cir. 1988), **Procedural matters**

Pennzoil Company v. Federal Power Commission, 534 F.2d 627 (5th Cir. 1976), **(b)(9)**

Petroleum Information Corporation v. Department of the Interior, 976 F.2d 1429 (D.C.Cir. 1992), **Reasonably segregable**

PHE, Inc. v. Department of Justice, 983 F.2d 248 (D.C.Cir. 1993), **(b)(2), reasonably segregable**

Philippi v. CIA, 546 F.2d 1009 (D.C.Cir. 1976), **(b)(1)**

Pollack v. Department of Justice, 49 F.3d 115 (4th Cir. 1995), cert. denied, 116 S.Ct 130 (1995), **Administrative remedies**

Pratt v. Webster, 673 F.2d 408 (D.C.Cir. 1982), **(b)(7)**

Public Citizen Health Research Group v. FDA, 704 F.2d 1280 (D.C.Cir. 1983), **(b)(4)**

Public Citizen v. Department of State, 11 F.3d 198 (D.C.Cir. 1993), **(b)(1), waiver of exemption**

Quinon v. FBI, 86 F.3d 1222 (D.C.Cir 1996), **In camera inspection**

Ray v. Turner, 587 F.2d 1187 (D.C.Cir. 1978), **(b)(1)**

Renegotiation Board v. Grumman Aircraft Engineering Corporation, 421 U.S. 168 (1975), **(a)(2)(A), (b)(5)**

Rosenfeld v. United States, 859 F.2d 717 (9th Cir. 1988), **Attorneys' fees**

Russell v. Department of the Air Force, 682 F.2d 1045 (D.C.Cir. 1982), **(b)(5), deliberative process**

Ryan v. Department of Justice, 617 F.2d 781 (D.C.Cir. 1980), **(b)(5), waiver of exemption**

Schell v. HHS, 843 F.2d 993 (6th Cir. 1988), **(b)(5), deliberative process**

Selected Bibliography

Adler, Alan. *Litigation under the Federal Open Records Laws: The Freedom of Information Act, the Privacy Act, the Sunshine Act, the Federal Advisory Committee Act*. 18th ed. Washington, D.C.: American Civil Liberties Union Foundation, 1993.

Brown, Richard D. *The Strength of a People: The Idea of an Informed Citizenry in America, 1650–1870*. Chapel Hill: University of North Carolina Press, 1996.

Casey, William L., Jr., John E. Marthinsen, and Laurence S. Moss. *Entrepreneurship, Productivity, and the Freedom of Information Act: Protecting Circumstantially Relevant Business Information*. Lexington, Mass.: D. C. Heath, 1983.

Cooper, Kent. *The Right to Know: An Exposition of the Evils of News Suppression and Propaganda*. New York: Farrar, Strauss and Cudahy, 1956.

Cross, Harold L. *The Right to Know: Legal Access to Public Records and Proceedings*. New York: Columbia University Press, 1953.

Eldridge, Larry P. *A Distant Heritage: The Growth of Free Speech in Early America*. New York: New York University Press, 1994.

Halperin, Morton H. *Top Secret: National Security and the Right to Know*. Washington, D.C.: New Republic Books, 1977.

Hendricks, Evan. *Former Secrets: Government Records Made Public through the Freedom of Information Act*. Washington, D.C.: Campaign for Political Rights, 1988.

Hernon, Peter, Charles R. McClure, and Harold C. Relyea, eds. *Federal Information Policies in the 1990s: Views and Perspectives*. Norwood, N.J.: Ablex Publishing, 1996.

Houdek, Frank G. *The Freedom of Information Act: A Comprehensive Bibliog-

raphy of Law Related Materials. 3d ed. Austin: University of Texas at Austin School of Law, 1985.

Ingelhart, Louis Edward, comp. *Press and Speech Freedoms in America, 1619–1995: A Chronology*. Westport, Conn.: Greenwood Press, 1997.

MacKenzie, Angus. *Secrets: The CIA's War at Home*. Berkeley: University of California Press, 1997.

O'Brien, David M. *The Public's Right to Know: The Supreme Court and the First Amendment*. New York: Praeger, 1981.

Pell, Eve. *The Big Chill: How the Reagan Administration, Corporate America, and Religious Conservatives Are Subverting Free Speech and the Public's Right to Know*. Boston: Beacon Press, 1984.

Report of the Commission on Protecting and Reducing Government Secrecy. S-Doc. 105-2. Washington, D.C.: U.S. Government Printing Office, 1997.

Theoharis, Athan G., ed. *A Culture of Secrecy: The Government versus the People's Right to Know*. Lawrence: University Press of Kansas, 1998.

United States. Congress. House. Committee on Government Reform and Oversight. *A Citizen's Guide on Using the Freedom of Information Act and the Privacy Act of 1974 to Request Government Records*. Washington, D.C.: U.S. Government Printing Office, 1997.

United States. Congress. Senate. Committee on the Judiciary. Subcommittee on Administrative Practice and Procedure. *Freedom of Information Act Sourcebook: Legislative Materials, Cases, Articles*. Washington, D.C.: U.S. Government Printing Office, 1974.

Wiggins, James Russell. *Freedom or Secrecy*. Rev. ed. New York: Oxford University Press, 1964.

Williams, Frederick, and John B. Pavlik, eds. *The People's Right to Know: Media, Democracy, and the Information Highway*. Hillsdale, N.J.: L. Earlbaum Associates, 1994.

Index

About the Author

HERBERT N. FOERSTEL is the retired former head of Branch Libraries at the University of Maryland in College Park and is a current member of the board of directors of the National Security Archive at George Washington University. He is the author of *Surveillance in the Stacks* (Greenwood, 1991); *Secret Science* (Praeger, 1993); *Banned in the USA* (Greenwood, 1994); *Climbing the Hill* with his daughter Karen Foerstel (Praeger, 1996); *Free Expression and Censorship in America* (Greenwood, 1997); and *Banned in the Media* (Greenwood, 1998).

ISBN 0-313-28546-2

EAN

9 780313 285462

HARDCOVER BAR CODE

DATE DUE

DEC 18 2002			